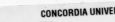

# THE REFERENCE SHELF

## Volume 25

No.
1. Immigration and the United States. Poyntz Tyler. $2.

2. Juvenile Delinquency. G. S. McClellan. $2.

4. Community Planning. H. L. Marx, Jr. $2.

No.
5. The Government and the Farmer. W. M. Daniels. $2.

6. The Middle East in the Cold War. G. S. McClellan. $2.

## Volume 26

No.
5. The Censorship of Books. 2d printing. W. M. Daniels. $2.

## Volume 24

No.
3. Representative American Speeches: 1951-1952. A. C. Baird. $1.75.

## Volume 23

No.
2. Representative American Speeches: 1950-1951. A. C. Baird. $1.75.

## Volume 22

No.
3. Representative American Speeches: 1949-1950. A. C. Baird. $1.75.

## Volume 20

No.
5. Federal World Government. J. E. Johnsen. $1.50.

# THE REFERENCE SHELF

Vol. 31                                                    No. 5

# ADVERTISING IN AMERICA

Edited by
POYNTZ TYLER

## THE H. W. WILSON COMPANY
NEW YORK                                    1959

# PREFACE

The earliest advertisements written in English are still with us. They are not signs nor cries nor the commercials of radio and television. They are people. People named Smith and Goldsmith. People named Wright and Wheelwright, Miller, Weaver, Fuller, Baker, and Lorimer. All such surnames denote the occupation of some long-forgotten ancestor, and their very adoption marked the birth of England's domestic trade. During the early Middle Ages men were known chiefly by their ancestry or residence or even their complexion—Tom Dick's son, Tom at the Wood, Tom the Black—and the names changed with each generation or each remove. With the rise of trade came the need for identification with the goods and services each man could provide, and as such trades and skills descended from father to son, so too did the names that advertised them. Thus trade and advertising were born together and they are inseparable to this day.

Not everyone believes they should be. "If a man write a better book . . . or make a better mousetrap than his neighbor," said Ralph Waldo Emerson, "tho' he build his house in the woods, the world will make a beaten path to his door." The world of advertising, holding with Adam Smith that "consumption is the sole end and purpose of all production," does not agree. "Build a better mousetrap," says Advertising, "and you will be free of mice. Advertise it and you will free the world." Emerson, never noted as an economist, has long been disproved, but whether advertising can free the world of mice or hunger or want or any of the ills that harass and beset it is still a subject of disputation. Millions of words (and ads) have been written to prove it can. Millions of words have been written to prove it cannot. This book, written by men of both persuasions, makes no claim or effort to settle an argument that has been waged in English ever since Tom at the Wood became Tom Smith. It is an introduction, and an introduction only, to an industry as pervasive in America as the weather and as little understood; an introduction to a force that nobody can measure and to an intangible that nobody knows—by the men who know it best.

To those men, to the writers and editors and practitioners and publishers whose works comprise this book the editor is indeed grateful.

POYNTZ TYLER

September 1959

# AND NOW, A WORD FROM—

*We are advertis'd by our loving friends.*—WILLIAM SHAKE-
SPEARE

*It is far easier to write ten passably effective Sonnets, good
enough to take in the not too inquiring critic, than one effective
advertisement that will take in a few thousand of the uncritical
buying public.*—ALDOUS HUXLEY

*You can tell the ideals of a nation by its advertisements.*—
NORMAN DOUGLAS

*Promise, large promise, is the soul of an advertisement.*—
SAMUEL JOHNSON

*Advertising is the supreme flowering of a sophisticated civili-
zation.*—EARNEST ELMO CALKINS

*Advertising is salesmanship in print.*—JOHN E. KENNEDY

*Advertising is hogwash.*—JOHN POINDEXTER

*He who says he doesn't read advertisements and can read is a
liar. . . . The woman who doesn't read advertisements isn't a
woman.*—NATHANIEL C. FOWLER, JR.

*Advertising is to business what steam is to industry—the sole
propelling power. Nothing except the Mint can make money
without advertising.*—THOMAS BABINGTON MACAULAY

*It pays to advertise.*—OLD AMERICAN SAYING

# CONTENTS

8                          CONTENTS

# I. MADISON AVENUE—
# THE AGENCY WORLD

## EDITOR'S INTRODUCTION

Given the cultural and commercial expansion of America following the Civil War, the rise of the advertising man from the early agents described by Ralph M. Hower in the opening article of this section to the tremendous, already legendary agencies examined by Daniel Seligman in the third was practically inevitable. Since Appomattox almost every generation has seen a new impetus and a new channel of communication for reaching the public. The conflict itself stimulated the first great medium, the newspapers, for their advertising columns were used extensively by the Federal Government to promote the sale of war bonds. Before 1861 most newspaper advertising had been local. War bond advertising opened the way for postwar commercial advertising on a national scale. It was needed. The huge industrial organization built to supply the armies converted quickly to peacetime production and a burgeoning national advertising sold its products in the keenest competitive era the nation had yet enjoyed. So keen was this competition, so relatively scarce the advertising space in newspapers, that a second great medium— almost against its will—was forced to become national in its distribution and in its editorial approach.

That medium, of course, was the magazine. The first to achieve any success in the United States had been the *Pennsylvania Gazette*—purchased by Benjamin Franklin in 1729 and ancestor, through a rather tenuous descent, of today's *Saturday Evening Post*—but until the appearance of *Harper's* and the *Atlantic Monthly* during the 1850's most magazines (with the notable exception of the *North American Review*) were either religious journals, temperance tracts, or such early excursions into feminine culture as *Peterson's Magazine* or *Godey's Lady's Book*. Few reached an audience the advertiser felt was worth reaching and the few that did were inclined to look down their noses at advertising on the grounds that it would impair their prestige. Only after the Civil War, when the demand for advertising space and the harsh economics of publishing forced them to, did they change from the provincial and parochial publications of the past into the organs of national circulation and national advertising that we know today.

National advertising, and the inauguration of second class postal rates in 1879, made national media of newspapers and magazines—and national media made the modern agency. There was really no alternative. The very size and complexity of national advertising made the services of an advertising specialist indispensable to both advertiser and publisher and, once the vexing problem of who represented whom and for how much was settled, the growth of this specialist from the confused and confusing agents of Dr. Hower's article into the amazing organizations of Mr. Seligman's was inexorable. Three slips of paper solved the problem of representation and payment, and solved it so effectively that the solution has carried over into the later national media of radio and television. First was the "open contract" introduced in 1875 by F. Wayland Ayer—the "son" of the still-prospering N. W. Ayer & Son—in which he stated that henceforth, in all his dealings with publishers, he would act exclusively *as the agent of the advertiser.* Second was the statement issued in 1893 by the American Newspaper Publishers' Association in which members formally announced that they would pay a commission to recognized independent advertising agencies and allow no discounts whatever to direct advertisers. Third was a 1901 letter from the Curtis Publishing Company to J. Walter Thompson establishing the same rule for magazine advertising in its *Saturday Evening Post* and *Ladies' Home Journal.* With their ethics thus clarified and their finances in order—albeit under an unorthodox arrangement wherein the agent of the party of the first part is paid his fee by the party of the second part— advertising men quickly attained the stature and the status they enjoy today and which F. Wayland Ayer was seeking for himself when he substituted his open contract for the hokery pokery of his contemporaries. In 1870 almost every building in New York with any pretension to decency had carried a sign in its lobby forbidding the premises to "peddlers, book agents, and advertising men." By 1896 there was only one.

Today there are over three thousand advertising agencies in the United States and they have for sale only talent, experience, ideas, business acumen, fact-finding resources, imagination, and creative skill. They offer no tangibles, and the fashion and the success with which each sells its intangibles are determined solely by the temperament and the intelligence of the men and women who compose the agency. The differences among advertising agencies are essentially differences in people, emphasis, and approach, but all of them—regardless of size—are prepared to render or secure the services represented by the eight basic departments of a modern agency:

*Contact.* Composed of "account executives," who maintain liaison between agency and client, advise the client on his advertising and marketing problems, and have general supervision of the account or accounts under their direction. As a group they oversee and coordinate the work of all departments.

*Research.* Gathers all facts pertaining to the client's business, his sales, his customers, his distribution, and his market and attempts to evaluate them for the guidance of the Copy, Art, Media, and Contact departments.

*Copy.* In conjunction with other departments it conceives the "theme" of projected campaigns—the basic sales appeal or approach to be used—and then writes the actual copy for advertisements in all media.

*Art.* Responsible for "visualizing" printed advertisements and for general oversight of TV commercials produced for the agency's client by outside firms. Concerned principally with newspaper and magazine advertisements it determines and conceives layouts, typography, and illustrations.

*Media.* Decides, in collaboration with Contact, Research, and Copy departments, which media (means, or forms) of communication will be used—newspapers, magazines, radio, TV, billboards, etc.—and purchases the required space, time, or facility.

*Production.* Supervises the mechanical and clerical work involved in getting plates and all other required physical material to the media.

*Traffic.* Responsible for seeing that all departments perform their allotted tasks on a prearranged schedule that will meet each and every deadline.

*Service.* The housekeeping department. Service runs the office, supervises agency correspondence, and takes care of the bookkeeping. Most important, after verifying the appearance and position of advertisements placed by the agency in all media, it bills each client at the list price (or "card rate") for his advertising in each medium and then pays the medium at its list price minus the agency's 15 per cent commission. This 15 per cent commission is generally looked upon as payment to the agency only for its professional services and skill in the preparation and placement of advertising. Additional charges are made for additional services. Photography for visual ads, the preparation of printing plates and stereotypes, and the production costs of programs for broadcasting are usually billed to the client at cost plus the familiar 15 per cent agency commission. For such other services as providing finished art work for ads, preparation of point-of-purchase displays, market research and analysis, publicity and public relations work for the client, it receives a flat fee determined by negotiation with the advertiser. The size of an agency is generally measured by its annual "billings"—that is, the total of all its charges to its clients.

Some agencies, as Mr. Seligman indicates below in "The Amazing Advertising Business," have additional departments designed either to aid or impress their clients. Others, such as the one founded and described by Gerard B. Lambert in "How I Sold Listerine," tend to lean the other way. But all of them, as the remaining articles of this section make abundantly clear, share a common determination to market their clients' merchandise and are equipped with a variety of tools and services with which to do it.

## THE FIRST AGENTS [1]

Until the nineteenth century there was no advertising agent either in Europe or in America. Anyone who wished to advertise dealt directly with the newspaper. So long as advertising was confined to small districts, so long as it originated with local advertisers and was intended for local readers, neither shopkeeper nor newspaper editor felt the need for outside assistance. Nor was there much opportunity for a middleman to force his way between them. To the editor a newspaper was primarily a political party organ; and advertisements, while as welcome as any other form of manna if they appeared without solicitation, were a matter of minor concern. So long as advertising technique was crude and advertisements did not have to compete with one another or with many other attractions in order to win attention, the businessman required no special skill to prepare an advertisement or see to its publication. All the details could be handled personally by the editor and the advertiser. The time required for this was of little importance, and, since the amount of money involved was never large, the savings which might be made by greater efficiency were probably not worth considering.

By 1800, however, difficulties and complexities were beginning to grow up around the simple, direct relation between merchant and newspaper. The expansion of markets which was then in progress entailed sales promotion over wider areas, and advertisers were reaching out beyond the local districts. This expansion might mean, for example, that an advertiser located in Boston had to make arrangements with newspapers in Gloucester, Concord, Plymouth, and even as far afield as Springfield, Hartford, and New London. He had to bargain about the amount to be paid for the advertising; he had to give directions for the printing of his announcements (not an easy matter for those unfamiliar with printer's jargon even in its early and unsophis-

[1] From *The History of an Advertising Agency* (N. W. Ayer & Son, Inc.), by Ralph M. Hower, professor of business administration in the Graduate School of Business Administration, Harvard University, and author of *The History of Macy's of New York*. This selection (from p7-19) is reprinted by permission of the publishers, Harvard University Press. Cambridge, Massachusetts. 1949. Copyright 1949 by the President and Fellows of Harvard University.

ticated days); he had to see that the advertising was inserted properly so that he got what he was charged for; and, finally, he had to send money in payment. In short, he had to manage for himself (or neglect) many of the tiresome details which have since become a part of the service performed by an agency. . . .

The newspaper publisher, too, was beginning to have his difficulties. It was clear by 1800 that no paper could long pay its expenses with the money received from the subscribers alone. As the Paris *Journal des Débats* confessed on abandoning (1799) its policy of refusing to print advertisements, *"Il faut bien vivre"* ["We have to live"]. And, in America, when the Massachusetts legislature placed a tax upon newspaper advertisements (1786-88), the *Massachusetts Spy* of Worcester was forced to suspend publication, and some of the other papers resorted to subterfuge in order to evade the tax. The income derived from advertising was absolutely essential to the newspapers' existence. As publishers began to realize this, they found it advisable, first, to facilitate the placing of advertisements by shopkeepers and manufacturers, and, later, to solicit business among those who might have occasion to advertise in newspapers.

About 1800, therefore, the new complexities of business had created a need for a specializing middleman. He would take as his province the purchase and sale of advertising space, leaving both advertiser and publisher free to devote full attention to their principal work. It was to meet this need for a redistribution of functions that the advertising agent came into existence. . . .

The work of the advertising specialist was to assist in the buying and selling of a commodity, namely, newspaper space. In other fields similar needs and forces have given rise to commission agents, brokers, and dealers who handle agricultural products; insurance underwriters, brokers, and agents; selling agencies in the textile industry; the various financial middlemen —bankers, underwriters of securities, investment counselors, bill brokers, and the like; and the vast army of specialists who assist in the intricate process of moving commodities from producer to consumer. Some of them buy and sell tangible goods; others buy and sell services; but this difference does not affect the value of their work. They win a place in our economic structure through their ability to perform a service more cheaply or more effectively than the non-specialized businessman can do it.

The exact line of evolution which leads to the modern advertising agent is not altogether clear, for at first we find the work which eventually became his being handled as a side line by men in several different callings. As early as 1786 English newspapers were appointing shopkeepers to collect and forward advertisements. The eighteenth-century American postmaster frequently accepted advertisements and forwarded them to newspapers; he probably received a commission for his services. It is evident that stationers and booksellers acted in the same way, for the early nineteenth-century directories for London and New York show that many of these were also "newspaper agents," "newsmen," and "news agents," and there is reason to believe that they forwarded advertisements, as well as subscriptions, to newspaper publishers.

The newspapers themselves, however, supplied the first advertising agents who attained any prominence in the United States. By the 1830's editors in large cities were finding it advisable to send out employees from time to time among the local merchants and manufacturers to solicit orders for advertising. Some of these employees soon perceived that they could solicit orders for several publications as readily as for one and that they could make a great deal more money by doing this on a commission basis than by working for a single paper. Such an arrangement had the additional advantage that it enabled the advertiser to buy space in a number of papers while dealing with only one person, thus saving time and trouble. That the number of publications might be important is apparent from the fact that the number of newspapers in the United States increased from about 75 in 1790 to over 360 in 1820, 1,000 in 1830, and 1,400 in 1840.

The two earliest advertising agents of whom we have definite record, Volney B. Palmer, of Philadelphia, and John Hooper, of New York, started their advertising careers by canvassing orders for newspapers. . . .

Volney B. Palmer (1799-1864) is said to have started his agency in Philadelphia in 1841. . . . Possibly the advertising business alone was not large enough to support him at the outset. American business had been severely depressed since the panic of 1837, and men were ready to try any sort of combination which seemed likely to yield profits. Advertising soon crowded out the other activities, however; and Palmer's stout, pompous figure, brass buttons, and gold-headed walking-stick became a familiar sight to publishers and merchants, not only in Philadelphia but in other cities as well. In 1845 he established a branch in Boston; about the same time he opened another in New York; and for a short time he maintained a third in Baltimore. Meanwhile, in 1842, another agency had been opened in New York by John Hooper, an honest, slow, and unpretentious man who had previously solicited advertisements for the New York *Tribune*. Little is known about Hooper's business.

Although it is often said that the advertising agent began as a space-broker, this is clearly disproved by Palmer's methods, which are a matter of record. On behalf of newspapers throughout the country, he solicited orders for advertising, forwarded the copy, and collected payment. One point is worthy of special note: Palmer stated explicitly that the publishers—usually they were editors and printers combined—were his principals and that, as their agent, he was authorized to make contracts with persons who wished to advertise in their papers. . . . It is true that Palmer pointed out the trouble and expense which he could save the advertiser. He also kept a large file of newspapers for inspection, assisted advertisers in selecting the particular papers to be used, and offered to help them with the writing of their advertisements. He made it plain, however, that he was working for the newspapers and stated that, if an advertiser dealt through his agency, the rates charged would be the same as those charged by the publishers.

Palmer frequently described himself as "newspaper agent" rather than as advertising agent. For his services he deducted a portion of the money paid by advertisers, usually 25 per cent, and the publishers quickly adopted this plan of compensation in dealing with other agents. Since many publishers named Palmer as their official agent, and since Palmer's competitors closely imitated his methods, the fact that the advertising agent was originally the agent of the newspaper (i.e., resembling the special representative of today rather than the modern agent) can hardly be questioned. . . .

## Early Changes in the Advertising Agency

The business of the advertising agent passed through four early stages of development: (1) *newspaper agency*, (2) *space-jobbing*, (3) *space-wholesaling*, and (4) *advertising concession agency*. . . .

The first or *newspaper agency* stage was the one inaugurated by V. B. Palmer, in which the agent represented the newspaper publisher. It lasted from 1841 to some time in the 1850's, and a vestige of it survives today in the so-called commission which publishers allow to advertising agencies.

In the second or *space-jobbing* stage the agent became an independent middleman. Instead of working for publishers for a commission, he became a jobber working for his own profit, who sold space to advertisers and then bought space from newspapers to fill his orders. Thus he bought and sold space on his own account, but piecemeal only, according to orders actually received. This new phase of the agency's development was not a sudden growth. It came about gradually, as a result of the lively competition which Palmer's success had attracted. In the 1850's newspaper publishers, going on the theory that the more numerous their agents the more space they would sell, were usually willing to deal with anyone who wished to imitate and rival Palmer. Before long, New York, Philadelphia, and Boston each had a number of advertising agents clamoring for business, and each agent claimed authority to represent every paper of any importance in the country. The advertiser found all these agents vying with each other for his business, and, since he could buy space in essentially the same papers from any of them, he quickly learned to seek the one who offered it at the lowest prices. Indeed, there was hardly any other basis for selection.

This state of affairs inevitably confused the relations and obligations of all parties concerned and encouraged the agent to butter his bread on both sides. To get business away from his competitors, an agent might offer space to advertisers at low prices, either by sacrificing a part of the commission which the publisher allowed him or by reducing the publisher's gross rate. In practice the agent kept the percentage of his commission intact. During the transition period he could do this because, as the authorized representative of the publisher, he was able to establish rates for space at what seemed to him a suitable figure, and his prices were understood to be binding upon the publisher. For a time many publishers permitted this demoralizing practice because (like most American businessmen until after the Civil War) they had never held to their stated prices. They tended to regard advertising revenue as so much extra income, and they preferred to accept almost any price for space rather than risk letting it go unused. In such circumstances it was inevitable that their rates, rather than the agent's commission, should bear the brunt of the price-cutting.

Owing to the abuses which naturally followed, publishers were sometimes compelled, for self-protection, to repudiate the rates established by advertising agents. Whenever this happened, the agent lost part or the whole of his commission from the publisher because he had already agreed upon a price with the advertiser and could not raise it. To guard against such contingencies the agent began to create a margin against loss by offering to each paper a lower gross price than the one which he set in contracting with advertisers. He hoped, not without reason, that enough publishers would accept the low figure to offset those who would repudiate his cuts in rates, thus enabling him to come out with his usual reward. In short, he began to deal in space. In this way, as a contemporary agent expressed it, "The principle of getting from the Advertiser all that he could be induced to pay, and offering to the Publisher as little as he would consent to accept, became established." In other words, the agent represented neither publisher nor advertiser but drove a sharp bargain with both. He had now ceased to be an agent in the proper sense of the term, and had become a space-jobber.

In this space-jobbing stage, however, the agent clung to his title of agent and to what he called his commission from the publishers (now really a discount), in spite of the fact that he was no longer an authorized representative of the newspapers. Publishers seemed to feel that they should continue the commission because the business which came to them from the agents involved less work and less credit risk than that which came directly from the advertisers. They believed, moreover, that the agent, in promoting the general cause of advertising for his own profit, advanced their interests and that the commission allowed gave him additional encouragement to push the sale of their advertising space.

This arrangement has been continued by the publishers and most agencies down to the present time, although it is a survival which changing conditions have, in the opinion of many observers, made irrational and uneconomical in certain respects. It explains, without excusing, the paradox which confronts many an advertiser: he employs an advertising agent to plan his advertising, supervise its execution, and guard his interests throughout; yet it is the publisher who provides the so-called commission by which the agent gains his pay; while the advertiser, at least in theory, has no voice in determining the amount of that payment.

In 1865 the third stage, a logical development of the second, was ushered in by George P. Rowell of Boston, who was soon to become the country's leading agent. This was the *space-wholesaling* phase in which the agent, anticipating the needs of advertisers, bought space in large quantities and resold it to them, as they wanted it, in smaller lots.

As advertising solicitor for the Boston *Post,* Rowell had discovered a chance for profits which earlier agents had apparently overlooked. The usual charge for a "square" (about one inch in a newspaper column) in country weeklies was one dollar for the first insertion and fifty cents for each of several subsequent insertions. Most publishers, however, were so glad to receive a large order for advertising that they would sell a whole column for a year for $100 or even less, and allow the agency a commission on this amount as well. Thus if Rowell could resell the space to advertisers at the comparatively low price of one dollar per square per month [i.e., four weekly insertions], he could make a handsome profit.

Rowell made several noteworthy changes in the business. His predecessors, in ceasing to be true agents and becoming independent middlemen, had made themselves into space-jobbers who assumed a certain degree of risk. Buying space only when they already held orders from advertisers, they staked their knowledge of the market and their bargaining power against the inferior knowledge and power of the publisher on the one hand and the advertiser on the other. But they were speculators only to a limited extent, for they did not buy space in anticipation of the advertiser's needs.

Rowell, however, speculated in a larger and more useful way. By purchasing large quantities of space in advance of actual orders, he took over some of the risk that the publishers had previously borne; and, while retaining a good profit for himself, he rendered a service to advertisers by parceling out the space to them at prices substantially lower than they could obtain elsewhere. He was, in short, a capitalistic middleman, like those who had intervened between producer and consumer in other lines of commerce—particularly in the handling of staple commodities—at a much earlier date. Rowell also introduced another financial change by agreeing to pay cash to any publisher who would allow an additional discount of 5 per cent. Country publishers are traditionally short of cash, and, since the prevailing commercial practice was to take three to six months' credit as a matter of course, Rowell's offer was particularly welcome.

Rowell's plan of buying space at wholesale and selling it at retail succeeded immediately. By concluding arrangements with a large number of papers he was able to announce to the advertising world such tempting offers as "One inch of space a month in one hundred papers for one hundred dollars." Other agents promptly imitated his scheme and turned the competition in this new direction.

The fourth stage began about 1867, when the idea of wholesaling space was carried one step further to what I have termed the *advertising concession agency*. Carlton & Smith (subsequently the J. Walter Thompson Company) and other agents began to contract annually with the publications they represented, to pay a lump sum and take over most of the risk and management of the *entire* advertising space in the papers. Thus they acquired, so to speak, the advertising concession in a publication. This arrangement revived the original close connection between the advertising agent and the publisher, but the so-called agent in fact continued to be an independent middleman, buying and selling space in the hope of obtaining a profit. When Rowell was asked in 1866, "Whom does the agent represent?" he replied frankly that he represented himself.

Thus arose both the practice of wholesaling space and the "list" system which dominated the agency business for many years. . . . Each agent owned space in a group of papers, and for advertising in this group—his list—he made a special price. Such a list, of course, would not be suitable for the advertising of all kinds of products, but the agent tried to convince the advertisers of its value, and, owing to the prevailing ignorance about effective sales promotion, he usually succeeded. To meet the demand for advertising in given geographical areas, agents usually made up a number of lists, one for New England, one for the Middle States, and so on.

It was impossible for the agents, however, to fit all advertisers into this bed of Procrustes, no matter how profitable for themselves. Different products went to different geographical areas, and some of them obviously could not be advertised so effectively in religious weeklies (for example) as in ordinary newspapers. Those advertisers, moreover, who had definite ideas about the media to be used insisted on the inclusion of papers not on an agent's list. To meet contingencies of this kind, every agent was obliged to send orders to many papers in which he owned no space. He demanded and received a commission from the publishers on such orders. If he could obtain the desired space only through another agent, he placed the order through that agent and received a commission from him rather than from the publisher. In other words, while an advertising agent operated primarily as an independent jobber or wholesaler of space, he continued to act as a broker in many transactions. And as a broker he received a commission on these transactions from the person on whose behalf he sold space. For these particular services the commission was a suitable remuneration. This arrangement undoubtedly helped to keep alive the idea that the advertising agent was an agent in the true sense of the word and was entitled to a commission on all transactions regardless of the part he played in them.

The agency business as it existed in [the late 1860's] was a confusing combination of all these arrangements. Contemporaries criticized the position of agents generally because it led to the abuses mentioned, but their shafts were aimed at evils which are inherent in most competitive commercial enterprises. Less obvious and usually overlooked by the critics was another bad feature of the arrangement, which was not the result of competition but came rather from the fact that the advertising industry quickly outgrew the machinery set up to carry it on. As a consequence the agent was forced into an attempt to serve two masters; he had to sell space for the publisher and, at the same time, to act as an expert and impartial counselor to the advertiser.

It was this duality of function which for years constituted the real evil of the agency business. Not one of the trading arrangements described above, taken by itself, can be challenged as unfair or unethical. The possibility of serious mischief appeared only when all were combined in the operation of one enterprise. Such a situation positively invited conflicts between the interests of the publisher, the agent, and the advertiser; and the continued use of the ambiguous terms "agent" and "commission" tended to conceal these conflicts.

In practice, no harm resulted unless the advertiser allowed the agent to influence him in the choice of advertising media. In that case the agent tended to recommend his own space, regardless of its merits. Both publisher and advertiser, unfortunately, encouraged the agent to act as a counselor in the use of advertising. At least, their separate interests thrust this role upon him. For, in order to sell the publisher's space, the agent had to show the merchant how to advertise, just as the early automobile salesman had to give driving lessons; and the prospective advertisers, in turn, wanted all the help that the agent was willing to give, because without advice they were only too likely to waste money on misdirected and ill-conceived advertising efforts. And yet the interests of advertiser and publisher did not always lie in the same direction; good advice for the advertiser was bad advice from the point of view of the publisher whose paper was left off the list of media to be used. Obviously the agent could not satisfy both. . . .

Such were the origins of the advertising agency. Apart from the interest which attaches to the inception of a spectacular modern phenomenon, it is evident from this sketch that the agency played a vital part in the development of American business. . . . The advertising agency came into existence because the ignorance of both publisher and advertiser, together with their genuine economic need for assistance, presented an opportunity for profit. The agent facilitated the purchase and sale of space. He made it easy for the publisher of the Podunk *Clarion* to fill his advertising columns with profitable advertisements from distant cities and for the merchant and manufacturer of Metropolis to advertise his wares in out-of-the-way markets. In a larger sense, however, the agency's chief service in this early period was to promote the general use of advertising, and thus to aid in discovering cheaper and more effective ways of marketing goods.

## HOW I SOLD LISTERINE [2]

The story of the growth of the Lambert Pharmacal Company between the years 1922 and 1928 has never been told with accuracy. For years I have had the fear that my tombstone will bear the inscription, "Here lies the body of the Father of Halitosis." Halitosis, as an advertising word, played a part, but it was far from the main reason for the company's rapid expansion. Here are the facts.

Before 1922 I had launched into a few grandiose ventures that had driven me $700,000 into debt. I came to the conclusion that the only chance I had of paying the debt was to go to work for the Lambert Pharmacal Company. I got on the train for St. Louis.

The morning I entered the office, I went to my cousin, Arthur Lambert, one of the trustees, and asked him how much they would pay me to work for them. He said that they would pay me a large sum of money to stay away. It was said in jest, but nevertheless I knew that he meant that my coming would not be welcome. I reminded him that we owned the business— it had been founded by my father, Jordan Wheat Lambert, in 1879—and that my four brothers were automatically vice presidents. My mind was made up. I was moving in.

After two months on the job I was made general manager. I asked for the name of the company that did our advertising. It was a Chicago firm, Williams & Cunningham. I requested that someone be sent down to see us.

The two men who arrived were to be among the best friends I ever had. One was Milton Fuessle and the other Gordon Seagrove. At that time I knew absolutely nothing of advertising. We went into my brother Marion's office and I closed the door. I announced that we would not leave that room until we had an advertising idea for Listerine. For a

[2] By Gerard B. Lambert, former president of the Lambert Pharmacal Company, the Gillette Safety Razor Company, and the Lambert & Feasley advertising agency, and author of *Murder in Newport*, a detective story. *Fortune*. 54:123+. September 1956. © 1956 by Gerard B. Lambert and reprinted by his permission. This article is a condensation of several episodes from Mr. Lambert's book, *All Out of Step*, published by Doubleday & Co., New York, in 1956.

long time we batted ideas around. Marion spoke up apologetically. "How about bad breath?" he asked. I glared, reminding him that this was a respectable meeting. Once more he brought it up. Impatiently, to get rid of the subject for good, I yelled over the low partition to Mr. Deacon and asked him to come in. He had been a close and dear friend of my father's and had been with the company from the start.

I asked him if Listerine was good for bad breath. He excused himself for a moment and came back with a big book of newspaper clippings. He thumbed through the book.

"Here it is, Gerard. It says in this clipping from the *British Lancet* that in cases of halitosis. . ."

"What's halitosis?" I interrupted.

"Oh!" he said, "that is the medical term for bad breath."

I bustled the dear old gentleman out of the room. "There," I said, "is something to hang our hat on."

We all agreed that we had found a way to refer to bad breath without quite so much offense. I asked Fuessle and Seagrove to have their agency prepare one of our current ads, merely a colored picture of the Listerine bottle, with a coupon for testing. Coupons, I thought, would give us a good notion of the relative pulling power of what we had been doing and what we intended to do.

It didn't take long to go downtown and buy a $2.50 picture of a girl. I took it back to the house and wrote the first halitosis ad. It told about a girl who had this one handicap. She had all the advantages in the world, but, poor lass, she was getting nowhere. The word "halitosis" had an asterisk by it, and at the bottom of the ad it explained that it meant unpleasant breath. Later, when, to my shame, this word appeared in the dictionary, everyone knew what it was.

We tested the two ads, and halitosis, even with the crude mechanism of coupons, outpulled our bottle ad by four to one. Fuessle told me later what happened in the office of Williams & Cunningham. It was a big agency, and they passed the halitosis ad around for comment. Eighty-two per cent of the staff said it would not succeed.

At that time we were spending about $100,000 a year on advertising Listerine. I made the board a proposition. If they would let me spend $5,000 more each month, *cumulatively*— that is, $5,000, then $10,000, and so on—I would resign if I couldn't show an additional net profit for each month of at least $5,000.

Some astute member of the board pointed out that they would be risking only one $5,000 on this gamble, and they agreed to take me up. I raised this wager to a much higher figure later, but we never failed to take in an additional profit in any one month that was greater than the increased advertising cost for that month. By 1928 our expenditures for advertising were above $5 million a year.

Things were now running very smoothly. I had hired a good factory manager, and it was clear to me that in a company of this kind the important thing was selling the products by successful advertising. It goes without saying that a product must be good, but even the best one gets nowhere unless the consumer is informed of its existence. With this belief, I felt sure that the factory could take care of itself and that I should return to my home in Princeton and concentrate on the merchandising.

Before leaving St. Louis, I asked my friend Fuessle to join me in a chat. I explained that I was going to set up my own advertising agency in New York and wanted him to come along. It was suggested that his name be used in the company title, but I saw a practical difficulty. The name Fuessle, I told him, was difficult to pronounce. Would he mind changing his name to something that sounded just the same but was spelled differently, such as Feasley? He had no objection at all, and the name of the new advertising agency became Lambert & Feasley, and it carries that name today.

## A Happy Ship

I insisted on one thing. I was to have all the common stock of the company and he was to have only a salary. This salary I started him with was, however, not so bad. It was four times

higher than he had ever received. There was a good reason
for this stock arrangement; advertising accounts and copy writers
are mercurial and uncertain. The Lambert account was controlled by our family, and I did not want it messed up with
some legal complication involving stock.

As soon as we got recognition, the money began to pour
in. Feasley and I did all the work ourselves. We would outline
an ad, sometimes on the back of an envelope, and get in a cab
and go to a professional photographer. There we supervised
the taking of the photos. When the proofs came back we would
go to work. There was one rule that I insisted on: no photographs were to be retouched. We had, of course, no art department, and consequently I had no battles with its director
on this point.

The sales of Listerine continued to skyrocket. It was during
this period that we were running some advertisements that attracted attention, to say the least, with captions such as "Even
Your Best Friend Won't Tell You," "Often a Bridesmaid But
Never a Bride," "If You Want the Truth, Go to a Child,"
and so on. Invariably these ads were full-page unretouched photographs, with the copy simple type below the picture or in a
band cutting across the photo.

In successful matters of this sort there is always the question of credit for the achievement. I give Milton Feasley full
credit for it all. He and I were great cronies, and I loved him
dearly. He had a pleasant little habit of keeping a glass of
straight gin back of the curtain in his office, which he sipped
from time to time during the day. Until his death he thought he
was fooling people about this. Sometimes, in the late afternoon,
we would gather in my office for a drink. There would be
Edith Whitlock, who was our bookkeeper, secretary, treasurer,
and space buyer, and Feasley and myself, half of the outfit.
Whit sometimes spread a large sheet of tin on the floor, and I
amused them by playing the harmonica and clog dancing. Miss
Whitlock was already getting elderly, and soon after this she
retired on a pension we had provided.

It was not long before the Lambert Pharmacal Company's earnings and the revenue from my wholly owned advertising agency rose to a point where I was able, in five years, to pay off, with full interest, my entire personal debt of $700,000.

Testing was the secret of the success of all the advertising I did. Since my day, of course, there has been a great deal of testing; most big agencies have their own research departments, and there are independent organizations that make a sole business of it. In many cases, this work is based on psychology. But much of this is not getting down to brass tacks. The acid test is not there. What does the ad do in practice?

There are times when an advertising agency finds it unwise to look too closely into this question. It is simpler to maintain a large new-business department and to obtain a new account while playing golf or drinking a cocktail. And the officers in the company that is spending the money are sometimes entirely content with this situation. They don't know a damn thing about it themselves, and couldn't earn a dollar on their own at the game. So why not just point out that one of the best agencies in the country has the account and if it fails it is the agency's responsibility?

In my case if the ads didn't work, I personally lost a lot of money. As early as 1922, I instructed our sales manager to set up a system in drugstores that would permit us to count the sales response to the appeals I wanted to test. He kept telling me it could not be done and was very stubborn about it. That sales manager is the only man in the company that I ever fired. I let him go and then went out and did the job myself.

In general, this is how our testing worked. We picked two groups of small towns with a population of about 10,000. One group was to be left alone as a control to show the results without advertising. In the other we could test the relative effectiveness of different appeals.

Before starting the test our men went into a town and saw every, and I mean *every*, retail outlet. They arranged to have an excessive shipment of the product sent to these retailers. In this way the retailer could not reorder from a wholesaler

*54319*

and so confuse the figures. The retailers accepted our big shipment because we guaranteed the sale of it.

Once a week our men would personally count the stock
at that time in each store. The difference between the amount
in stock on the previous week and the next count would show
*the sales over the counter.* This is quite different from psychological guessing. In those towns the sales manager was absolutely
forbidden to install any window displays, counter displays, or
to give any special discount. No good chemist would add several
ingredients while carrying on a single experiment.

With this setup we first let all towns run along as usual
for several weeks. In this way we got a norm or base from
which to start. When we had the norm established we broke
with advertising in all towns except the control towns. This
advertising was confined to local newspapers. In all cases the
amount of advertising in dollars was made four times higher
per capita than the amount that could be risked in a national
campaign. This exaggeration was to make it easier to read
results, and to save time.

Results show up very quickly in weekly checks. When
these early findings come in, it is wise to cross-check by setting
up a different set of towns in a different part of the country.
If this is done thoroughly, you will eliminate any chance for
accidental error. In my own case, at least, I have never known
the final national campaign to run counter to the results of
the tests.

During this period the manager is frothing at the mouth.
He sees this going on and he is not in on it. In many companies I consider an aggressive sales manager the greatest menace
the company possesses. His living depends upon a bigger sales
staff, more discounts, more free goods, and more deals. To hell
with the profits. The president of the outfit probably knows
nothing of merchandising. He is dominated by the philosophy
of the sales manager.

I am perfectly aware, of course, that some items must have
distribution, display, and competitive discounts above all else.

But there are many products where a dollar can best be spent on advertising and not on free goods, discounts, or deals. Listerine, a specialty, is one of these. I had only six salesmen for the entire country. Our advertising created a demand from the consumer so great that the dealer *had* to carry it, even if he did not like the terms of the sale.

### Testing Toothpaste

Earlier, I had convinced the company to come out with a Listerine toothpaste, and I found myself paying more attention to it as time went on. Most toothpastes then sold for 50 cents a package. I had set up some test towns in Ohio. In one group of towns we put a 50-cent paste on sale and in the other set a 25-cent paste. The 50-center made a profit from the beginning but arrived at a plateau and stayed there. The 25-center, although losing money at first, just kept on going. That told the story: our paste would be 25 cents.

Immediately we went to upper New York State and set up another group of test towns. From this test came one of the most interesting results I have ever encountered in advertising. It was obvious that our appeal on this 25-cent item should be economy. In some towns we ran the typical, unimaginative ads with girls showing shining white teeth, something that advertisers even today have not relinquished. These towns were to act as a control. In different towns we ran the economy appeal that we thought would pull best. It did. It far exceeded in financial results the more spectacular halitosis campaign, but it is seldom referred to.

The ads went somewhat as follows. If you save 25 cents a tube and if you buy twelve tubes a year in your family, you will save $3. There was almost no mention of the paste other than to say that it was a good paste put out by a reliable company. But the reason the ad succeeded was that at least half of the page was taken up by a *picture* of what you could buy with that $3 saving: a pair of stockings, a tennis racket, or something like that. It was a visualization of a specific reward for economy, instead of a generalization on the subject, and, like showing a colored picture of a red fire engine to a small boy, it meant much more than the mere promise of a reward.[3]

The minute I saw the results of these tests I acted quickly. I started a whale of a campaign all over the country. At the end of four years Listerine Tooth Paste was earning more than $1,500,000 a year.

Milton Feasley's death soon after he came to New York was a great personal blow to me and a real loss to the agency. I found myself trying to run the whole ball of wax by myself and I missed Feasley badly. But I had an inspiration. How about the second man that came to St. Louis that day back in 1922, Gordon Seagrove? I had seen something of Gordon since those days. He was an expert copy writer and he also was a lot of fun.

Gordon Seagrove came on to New York and we worked perfectly together. As I write he is still with Lambert & Feasley. Throughout most of the years since I left, Gordon produced practically all of the Listerine and Listerine Tooth Paste advertisements.

Early I reasoned that when we began to reach a point of saturation with any group of people, a new appeal for the same product would be like plowing virgin territory. We started advertising Listerine for sore throat and for dandruff. Then we used the appeal of after shaving. All of these things kept boosting sales.

It occurred to me one day that we might capitalize on the human memory. Surely, I reasoned, a man would be foolish to approach you in your office every day to sell pencils. This idea resulted in a peculiar "saw-tooth" campaign. We would start a three-month cycle with no ads, and then have the expenditure rise each month until it reached $600,000 on the third month. Then a drop to nothing again. The average per month was the same as before but we were letting memory carry the

[3] To a city official in an eastern state, indicted for misappropriation of civic funds, it meant a great deal more. Asked how he managed to bank $80,000 in four years on a $6,000 salary he replied amiably: "I saved it on my toothpaste money." An enchanted jury acquitted him.—Ed.

load for us.  The profits somehow went up another million
dollars that year.

It is my belief that when sales of a product and the advertising are both running along on a level, a company can wisely
spend an *additional* dollar on advertising even if that dollar
brings in net only an additional dollar and one cent.  This is
treason to the old-line businessman.  He will tell you that in
his business it is customary to spend, let's say, 13 per cent of the
sales on advertising.  That was good enough for his grandfather
and it is good enough for him.

### The Budget Menace

I shudder to think what would have happened if we had
run a stupid old-fashioned budget in the Lambert Pharmacal
Company.  A committee of stuffy men and accountants would
have sat around and said we will spend only the per cent of
Listerine sales that we spent last year or perhaps just a tiny bit
more.  And we would have probably still been earning $115,000
a year!

In our case, after checking our results carefully, we plowed
the money in, hoping for at least that one penny additional
profit.  Of course it didn't work out that way.  Every time we
spent the new money much more than a penny came in.  But
we always knew what the response to our advertising was.  This
was possible because we *never allowed the sales manager to put
on any deals, or sell carload shipments, or do anything to change
the sales arrangements with the trade.*  In these later years I
have watched with great amusement the frustration of the advertising boys who cannot find out the results of their advertising because of the crazy fluctuations in sales figures that come
from these practices of a zealous sales manager.

For some businesses I think an advertising budget is suicidal.
You stick to the planned figures when the truth is you may have
the thing on the run and a fortune in sight.  It is like a charge
of troops who are told to go to a certain line and stop there,
even if the enemy is running away in a panic.

In the late months of 1928 I decided to sell out all my hold-ings in the Lambert Company for cash. From time to time I have been credited by friends with uncanny wisdom in selling out before the big crash in 1929. Lambert stock went from $157 a share to a low of $8 a share after the break. But it was not primarily wisdom about the market that made me sell. There is a much simpler and more accurate explanation for my decision. Through sheer youthful recklessness and bad judgment I had acquired debts that had been on my mind night and day. When I found a way to pay them off I was content to quit, happy to be free again and with all the money I should ever need. I did not have the slightest desire to have more, and I didn't care how high the market went. Lambert stock went from $115 a share to $157 a share after I was out, but I have never had any re-grets that I did not hold on. Holding on, and seeking the last dollar, was what ruined thousands of people in this country, so perhaps my lack of greed was what saved me.

I can see now the room where we closed the deal. It was in Goldman Sachs's office. The room was full of lawyers and accountants and attorneys. They were gathered about a tremendous table, each with a batch of papers. I had told all those Wall Street people that the only thing I would accept for the stock was a certified check for cash. I was quite sure it was to be more than $25 million, all of which I had made in six years. I did not know the exact amount; I just wanted to retire with no more worry about debts, and the exact amount was unimportant. I was forty-two years old and there were so many things to do that did not involve business.

## THE AMAZING ADVERTISING BUSINESS [4]

The greatest boom in the history of the advertising industry is now entering its second decade, and is not yet running out of gas. The total volume of advertising in the United States, national and local, is running close to $10 billion—just about triple the 1946 level. Advertising expenditures have recently

[4] By Daniel Seligman, associate editor of *Fortune*. *Fortune*. 54:107-10+. Re-printed by special permission from the September 1956 issue of *Fortune* magazine. © 1956 by Time Inc.

been rising faster than gross national product, national income, disposable personal income, or almost any other relevant barometer.

But if it were possible to devise a new kind of barometer for the advertising business—one that somehow measured the tension and uncertainty suffered by agency men—then this barometer would probably be keeping pace with the swelling advertising appropriations. There are the jokes about account men whose hair turned charcoal gray overnight. Contrary to the dark suspicions of some corporate advertising directors, the great advertising boom has not led to any visible rise in agency profit margins. Meanwhile, the agencies are besieged, on many fronts, by a curious and formidable array of business problems.

• The Justice Department in 1955 issued a complaint against the American Association of Advertising Agencies and several media associations (representing many of the major newspapers and magazines of the United States), charging them with conspiracy to fix advertising commissions, and with other restrictive practices. The 4 A's, and then the other associations, signed consent decrees in which they agreed to shun certain practices.

• Picking up what looked like a cue, the Association of National Advertisers instituted a broad review of the way advertising agencies get paid. At the ANA convention in Hot Springs in March [1956] a number of advertisers suggested loudly that it might be time for a change.

• A number of agencies have been wrangling with CBS and NBC. The "network monopoly" has pushed some TV programs off the air and not allowed others on—even when the agency men had free-spending sponsors in their pockets. The indignities and revenue losses thus incurred led some agencies to support House and Senate investigations of the networks. Unhappily for the agencies, the investigations have not affected network control of programming. . . .

• For decades now, the basic services offered by advertising agencies have been expanding in so many directions that agency men have been obliged to do some serious thinking about the nature of their business. . . .

## The Happy Media

The agency problems ticked off above do not add up to a crisis in the advertising industry; the backdrop to these problems is, after all, the great advertising boom.  In the past several years, advertising expenditures have been rising at an average rate of about 10 per cent annually.  *Advertising Age*, which annually lists all agencies billing $10 million or more, reported thirty-one such in 1946; in 1955 sixty-six agencies were over the $10-million line.  The $9-billion grand total of advertising in 1955 reflected gains over the 1954 totals in every medium except radio.  The biggest gainer was television, on which $1.5 billion was spent in 1955, a gain of 25 per cent.

An important distinction is in order here.  A little more than 40 per cent of all advertising in the United States is accounted for by local retail stores.  This does not mean it is economically inconsequential; however, it does not importantly affect what is usually thought of as "the advertising business"— i.e., the agencies.  The bulk of newspaper retail advertising, and large pieces of local radio, television, and billboard copy, not to mention such ephemera as skywriting and handbills, come into this world unhallowed by any agency effort; the advertisers and media contrive to do the job themselves.  Some local and a lot of regional advertising is important to the big agencies; some of it even attracts national attention, e.g., Young & Rubicam's recent campaign for Piel's Beer.  In fact, such non-retail advertising is customarily included in the "national" figures. . . .

Why have advertising appropriations been rising faster than the economy as a whole?  The steam behind the boom has been provided by a variety of economic fuels.  Those that have been most commonly talked about are not necessarily the most important.

Taxes, for example.  Common sense would seem to suggest that a high corporate income-tax rate makes advertising (like other business expenditures that can be considered an investment in the future) an especially attractive buy, and that a tax cut might pull down the advertising totals.  But in fact things haven't worked out that way.  During the past decade, corporate tax rates have fluctuated wildly: they were 38 per cent from 1946 until 1950, later rose to 82 per cent (including excess-profits tax), and finally settled at 52 per cent when E.P.T. expired at the beginning of 1954. Yet all through these ups and downs in taxes, the rate of national advertising growth was remarkably stable. . . .

Other hypotheses for the boom abound. The rise of self-service, for example, is commonly cited—the argument being that packaged-goods manufacturers are increasingly obliged to pre-sell the consumer. The rise of television is another popular explanation of the advertising boom. This explanation assumes that a powerful new medium can be an addition to, rather than a replacement of, corporate spending in other media.

The merits of these hypotheses are uncertain, the evidence conflicting. But it is certainly true that advertising expenditures are still governed, basically, by sales levels. Indeed, some advertisers in the United States still determine their advertising appropriation by mechanical formula. It remains a fixed percentage of sales, year after year. In recent years most of the major advertisers have got away from this mechanical approach to the problem. They figure their sales *objectives* for the coming years, then calculate the size of the appropriation needed for the job. But the difference between the fixed-percentage technique and the sales-objective technique is partly a semantic matter. For the objective—"the sales job that has to be done," in the standard phrase—is itself largely an extension of current sales. In certain marketing situations, some advertisers—Procter & Gamble is perhaps the most conspicuous example—appear to throw percentages out the window, and to pour vast sums into advertising blitzkriegs. But the funds available for advertising are determined, in the long pull, by sales levels.

## A Better Buy

Whatever approach corporations have taken in determining their budgets, they have, in the aggregate, substantially raised advertising's share of United States business spending. Until about 1948, there was a close and consistent relation between total advertising expenditures and "gross national sales." But in the last few years, advertising has begun to pull away from sales—or, stated another way, the proportion of sales given to advertising has been rising. United States management plainly has a new attitude toward advertising. The notion that advertising was a sort of corporate luxury, to be indulged in when there were funds left over, now seems quaint and archaic. Businessmen may have difficulty determining the exact sales payoff from advertising; but they are increasingly inclined to view the appropriation as a true capital investment—as much so as new plant.

It is possible to speculate whether the advertising share may not be further increased in the future. For advertising has simply become a better buy in recent years. Part of the improvement stems from the vast research facilities that now backstop advertising (of which more below). Part of the improvement relates to media values. A recent *Printers' Ink* study of media costs indicated that for an expanding advertiser, represented in all the major media, the cost of bringing his message to a given number of consumers has gone up about 13 per cent since 1950. (Industrial prices have risen 16 per cent over the same period.) But Arno Johnson of J. Walter Thompson, the dean of the agency economists, makes the point that in the same period the consumers have come to be much more worth reaching. Since 1950 the number of consumer "spending units" with after-tax income over $4,000 has about doubled—there are now almost 26 million such units. Four thousand dollars is roughly the income line at which consumers begin to exert "discretionary" spending power; i.e., they can take care of their basic needs, and have money left over to shop around with. And precisely because they can and will "shop around," it is crucial for the national advertiser to reach this group. At recent rates of growth, there will be about 36 million spending units over the $4,000 line by 1960—and they will represent approximately 60 per cent of all the units.

The prospects opened up by such an era of abundance have moved a number of sociologists and economists to cast a fresh, inquisitive eye on the role of advertising. Professor David M. Potter of Yale has written, in his *People of Plenty,* that advertising is "an instrument comparable to the school and the church in the extent of its influence upon society." He expects this influence to increase, if anything. In the economics of abundance, writes Dr. Potter,

advertising begins to fulfill a really essential economic function. In this situation the producer knows that the limitation upon his operations and upon his growth no longer lies . . . in his productive capacity, for he can always produce as much as the market will absorb. . . . If this new capacity is to be used, the imperative must fall upon consumption, and the society must be adjusted to a new set of drives and values in which consumption is paramount. [See "Advertising: Institution of Abundance," by Dr. Potter, in Section III, below.]

The agencies that are creating these new values have somehow become the subject of a vast body of mythology. Budd Schulberg and Elia Kazan set out [in 1955] to make a movie (title: *A Face in the Crowd*) dealing in part with the advertising business. By way of soaking up atmosphere, they got permission to spend time, more or less anonymously, at several Manhattan agencies. After they had ogled and eavesdropped on a fair number of agency men, they confessed to President Sigurd Larmon of Young & Rubicam (one of their hosts) that they had been surprised at what they learned. What chiefly confounded them was the wide discrepancy between the advertising men of lore and those they met. They had met few three-martini men, at least at lunch. The language they heard was colorful but not outlandish; no one enriched business conferences with such sentences as "Let's just throw the idea up in the air and then climb after it." So far as Schulberg and Kazan could make out, the advertising business was eminently businesslike.

Madison Avenue, living by words, has been clobbered with words for years. Highbrows (or even middle-brows) could hardly be expected to admire the shrill old "four-way relief" school of advertising. Over the past generation, the general level of taste and informativeness in advertising has probably improved some; a beautiful ad is not a novelty today, and neither is a subtle or witty ad. But in TV commercials and elsewhere, there is still enough tedium and vulgarity to confirm the intellectual in his general distaste, freely expressed, for the esthetics of advertising. At the same time, the attack on advertising as "economic waste," a familiar theme in the thirties, has pretty much died down. As capitalism itself has grown more productive (and popular) in the United States, it has come to be more generally accepted that advertising has a good deal to do with the rising United States standard of living. But some intellectuals have made a plausible case for concern about the new social role of advertising. Professor Potter, for example, at the same time he is pointing to advertising's opportunities in an era of abundance, finds it noteworthy

that this new institution for shaping human standards should be directed, not, as are the school and the church, to the inculcation of beliefs or attitudes that are held to be of social value, but rather to the stimulation or even the exploitation of materialistic drives and emulative anxieties and then to the validation, the sanctioning, and the standardization of these drives and anxieties as accepted criteria of social value.

Then there is the direct, personal attack on the advertising man himself, conducted by a variety of imaginative writers. In *The Hucksters* (1946), by Frederic Wakeman, the industry was given the works, and saddled with a word that *Webster's New International* defines in part as "a hawker; a mean, mercenary person." . . . *The Exurbanites* (1955), by A. C. Spectorsky, supplied dismal details about the home life of the stereotype advertising man; and *The Man in the Gray Flannel Suit* (1955), by Sloan Wilson, somehow came to be rated a likely description of the agonies suffered by the junior adman—though in fact the book deals with a young man wavering between foundation work and public relations.

It is possible, of course, to find advertising men who seem to be living up to the stereotype . . . but, by and large, Madison Avenue's top executives no more resemble the huckster than do vice presidents in, say, steel or automobiles. Even the locale is wrong: of the sixty-six agencies that billed over $10 million in 1955, only twelve are actually located on Madison Avenue.

Twenty-eight of the agencies have their principal offices outside
New York City.

If it is true that advertising today is a businesslike operation, it is also true that the modern advertising agency is an
extraordinary business.  Its economics are bizarre, and mani-
festly unclear to some successful admen, to say nothing of
successful men in other businesses.  A reasonably sophisticated
executive in, say, the chemical industry might be startled to find
that successful advertising agencies can be losing money on half
their customers.  He might also be startled to learn what agencies do for their money.

Outsiders tend to think of agencies as creators of copy, but
the modern agency man aspires to—and attains—the loftier role
of sales strategist.  "Just before the war," says Robert F. Carney,
chairman of the board of Foote, Cone & Belding, "our employees were mostly copywriters, artists, and media buyers. Today, we have as many people in research, merchandising, and
marketing."  President Marion Harper Jr. of McCann-Erickson
remarked a while back, "We help [a client] select an advertising manager, often a marketing manager; we help him design
his new product; we help him plan it.  Often, we find ourselves
conducting his sales meeting, appraising his marketing . . .
helping him in areas that have little or nothing to do directly
with advertising."  This extension of agency services is continuing.  More than a score of the top agencies now offer public
relations to their clients.  Top Broadway producers and directors
now adorn the TV departments of big agencies.  Economists,
sociologists, statisticians are also on the payrolls.  The modern
"omnibus agency" is plainly a different animal from the "creative agency" of the early 1930's.

## So Big

There are in the United States today some 3,300 advertising
agencies, employing about 45,000 people.  It is apparent from
these figures that advertising is not exactly "big business"—
certainly not by the standards applied to industrial corporations.

The biggest agency in the United States, J. Walter Thompson, employs over 4,300 people. Its billings ran to $220 million in 1955, which suggests that gross income was in the neighborhood of $33 million (i.e., 15 per cent commission on billings). Its profit is estimated around $3.3 million. There are hundreds of U.S. industrials with higher profits and more employees.

Even within the confines of the advertising business, the big agencies do not loom as giants. Thompson's "share of the market" (i.e., of national-advertising expenditures) has been running around 4 per cent. The Big Four—Thompson, Young & Rubicam, McCann-Erickson, and Batten, Barton, Durstine & Osborn—have just 14 per cent of the market; and the top twenty-five agencies have only 36 per cent.

Nor have the big agencies gained disproportionately in the endless game of musical chairs that advertisers play with agencies; the smaller houses are holding their own, at least. Actually, there is a built-in brake operating against the big agencies: the principle that no agency will handle two competitive accounts. When an agency nears the $200-million line, the number of industries in which it has no accounts is small. Young & Rubicam, for example, which last year billed $182 million, could take on "less than a dozen" new accounts. Otherwise, its expansion must come from the growth of existing accounts—as, indeed, most of it has in recent years. Three-quarters of the agency's $90-million increase in billings since 1950 has come from accounts held in that year.

The relative advantages of big and small agencies is a topic endlessly, and nervously, debated on Madison Avenue. Generally speaking, the big agencies tend to stress their own research facilities—their market studies, huge technical staffs, experimental kitchens, consumer panels, etc. McCann-Erickson, with 1955 billings of $166 million, has 115 employees in its research department—a figure larger than the total payroll of some $10-million agencies.

But no agency in the top seventy or so is likely to concede that the very big houses really do better research work. David Ogilvy, whose firm [Ogilvy, Benson & Maher] now bills

$14 million, thinks that some of the big agencies are dreadfully bureaucratized. "It's easier to do good work if you don't have to submit everything you do to a Plans Board of elderly stuffed shirts." On research, Ogilvy's case is summarized in an episode that occurred [in 1954] when he won an account away from one of the biggest agencies. "With the account, we inherited about $30,000 worth of market research they'd done on it. It was a superb job—as good as anything I've ever seen. But their creative people had never used it; I suspect they never even saw it. Of course, we put it to work right away."

Bigness may bring bureaucracy, in research and elsewhere; it also has its uses. The big agencies have a tremendous edge, for instance, in their ability to move fast in television. The demand for TV network time between 8:00 and 10:00 P.M. is so great that open time is invariably snatched up in a matter of hours—even minutes. It is therefore crucial to an agency that wants a lot of television business to have good sources inside the networks. Inevitably, the agencies that give the networks the most business have the best pipelines.

One other competitive advantage enjoyed by the big agencies is peculiarly galling to the small agencies, though it apparently leads to only a few account shifts. This advantage is the business prestige and social distinction wielded by the top brass at the big agencies. There is sometimes a tendency for an *arriviste* company to pick one of the large houses, not so much for their copy or research facilities, but simply as a token of its own advancement in the world. Said an executive of an agency that lost a good account to B.B.D.O.: "All of a sudden they decided they were ashamed of us socially. They think they're big shots now—they want to be invited to Ben Duffy's place in Rye and they want to get a table up front at the Pavillon when they eat with an account supervisor, and all that. . . . The dirty dogs!"

### Where Is the Gravy?

What makes an agency profitable? Total billings being equal, an agency is more profitable if it has a few large accounts than if it has many small ones. (Though the more profitable agency is then living more dangerously.)   In general, an agency is more profitable if it is not obliged to maintain a lot of branch offices.   Another rough rule of thumb gauges an agency's profitability by the amount of its billings per employee.

But agencies of similar size show strikingly divergent profit margins—from one agency to another, and from one year to the next.   Among agencies billing over $40 million in 1954, after-tax profits ranged all the way from 3.85 per cent to 31.77 per cent of gross income (or .6 per cent to 4.8 per cent of billings).   The 4 A's [American Association of Advertising Agencies] divides its members into nine size classifications, of which the largest is the over-$40-million group.   In 1954 this top group showed the largest composite profit margin.   But in 1953, four other groups had higher average nets than the over-$40-million group.

Despite all these vagrant trends, there are some agency men convinced that there is an "optimum-size" agency.   Norman B. Norman, whose own agency, Norman, Craig & Kummel, is currently billing around $20 million, thinks that the optimum size would be in the $25-million to $30-million range, with perhaps three hundred employees.   Below that figure, he feels, an agency's staff people—research and merchandising men, especially—are not spread over enough billings, and constitute a heavy drain on an agency's resources.   (You cannot trim this staff much and remain competitive.)   But as an agency moves into the over-$40 million league, Norman suspects, there is a tendency to accumulate a certain amount of deadwood, i.e., employees operating at only half speed.

Utilizing employees efficiently is, in fact, a real management problem for the big agencies.   The problem arises from the normal turnover of accounts and from the high proportion of professional or creative people to total employment.   Foote, Cone & Belding (1955 billings: $76 million), for example, lost the Frigidaire account [in 1955].   All employees on the account were absorbed into other areas of the agency.   Meanwhile, the agency was acquiring an important new account—Ford's medium-price Car E [the Edsel] to be introduced late in 1957. To handle this account, it opened a Detroit office with fifty employees. At least five of the new men hired were brought in because of their automotive backgrounds.

On the other hand, the ability of big agencies to hang on to their employees has its advantages. Skilled manpower is, after all, hard to come by in the advertising business today. There are many agencies that wish they could afford this "luxury." When Norman, Craig & Kummel lost Revlon and Blatz within two months it had to lop off thirteen employees. Today, the agency has more than made up for these losses, and its staff is larger than ever. (But the men recently hired are not, of course, the same men who were fired last year. In the advertising world, the executives as well as the clients go in for musical chairs.)

The advertising business, then, is one whose economics hinge on manpower costs. For agencies of all sizes, personnel costs—salaries, pensions, profit sharing, etc.—average around three quarters of operating costs. Agencies have no plant or equipment to speak of, no inventories, no real assets at all outside of their cash and receivables. There are wheat farms in Montana with more net worth than some sizable, nationally prominent advertising agencies. From this wonderful state of affairs, two conclusions follow:

The first is that it is possible to get into the business on a shoestring. It helps ,of course, to have an account or two in your pocket. Dozens of new agencies are launched every year, and some of them catch fire spectacularly. One of the hottest postwar agencies has been Sullivan, Stauffer, Colwell & Bayles, which was started in 1946 on just $75,000 capital. In the beginning its only accounts were Noxzema and Smith Bros. cough drops; total billings the first year were $3.5 million. The agency held a tenth-anniversary celebration [in 1956] and announced that it was billing at a $36-million rate. David Ogilvy, of Hathaway Shirt and Schweppes renown, was in one room in 1948. His offices today would not disgrace Darryl Zanuck.

But if it is possible for bright, young newcomers to crash into the advertising business with little capital, it is also possible for established old agencies to go up in smoke. The Biow Agency in 1956, Cecil & Presbrey in 1954, Pedlar & Ryan in 1952, J. Sterling Getchell in 1942—all these collapsed, and in so doing, all illumined the economic moral that an agency's only real resource is its manpower. When the key men die, or retire, or lose the confidence of the big accounts, an agency may become a hollow shell; nothing is left but the furniture.

The emergence of the so-called "omnibus agency" in recent years has further fuzzled the already baffling economics of the agency business. The extension of agency functions and services has created a certain amount of confusion as to what business, actually, the agencies are in.

Agency research became important around the end of the 1920's. William Benton has a vivid memory of Benton & Bowles' first immersion in market research. In 1929, Benton and his wife, and Chester Bowles and his wife, set out ringing doorbells in Jersey City in an effort to measure the market for Certo (a fruit pectin, used in making jelly). "I'd hold up the local paper and say, 'I'm writing a story on jellymaking.' Then I'd ask the housewife if she used pectin, how often she made jelly, and so on. We actually developed a successful campaign from these studies." Another advertising veteran, Bruce Barton, now the chairman of B.B.D.O., has an equally sharp recollection of the revolution that took place in the advertising business when the clients began to get interested in research. Barton recently recalled that in 1926 the agency got an important account because its research man—it had just one—startled the president by showing him that there was a tremendous regional difference in the company's per capita sales. Today, B.B.D.O. has a ninety-man research department. "A while back," Barton reported, "I was leaving the office one afternoon, and I heard a shrill chorus of children's voices, as though a school were letting out. I asked what it was and they told me it was our children's television panel. Very few clients have any idea what we go through these days, trying to get the facts."

*Scientists for Sale*

A modern agency will tackle almost any kind of research that a client asks for, but there are four kinds of research principally in demand:

*Market research,* i.e., analysis of consumer demand and of distribution problems. Advertisers generally pay extra fees for this research.

*Copy research,* i.e., testing of advertisements before and after their appearance, became important after 1932, when Young & Rubicam hired Dr. George Gallup, then a Northwestern University professor of journalism. Most pre-testing at big agencies is done by the research staff, and its cost absorbed by the agency; but the "post-measurement" of ads (i.e., gauging the impact of ads that have appeared) is farmed out to independent testing houses. Some of the cost is absorbed by the agency; some is paid for by the advertiser.

*Media research,* i.e., determining whether the client's advertising campaign is best suited to television, magazines, newspapers, etc., always paid for by the agencies.

*Product research,* i.e., testing consumer acceptance of new products, is frequently farmed out by the agency. But whoever does it, the client is apt to pay for it separately. Similar arrangements are customary for research on package design.

It is not exactly true, as some copy men are wont to complain, that the scientists are taking over the advertising business; but it is certainly true that no agency of even moderate size can survive today unless it offers all of these research services. In the good old days the creative people hit on an idea, showed it to the client, got his approval, and then put through the advertisement with no further complications. Today, the copy writer does not even begin to work (in principle, anyway) until the research people have told him, for example, at which hour of the day Los Angeles beer drinkers are at their consumption peak. . . .

Some advertising men are skeptical of the value of all the research. An executive at one of the big agencies . . . says that there is often a tendency to turn the research job over to pedants who are not really interested in selling anything. "They turn in

a huge report that looks like the last word, and it tells you seven
out of ten say this and this, but on the other hand that and that,
and the upshot is that you can do anything you want to." Milton
Biow apparently regarded agency research as something of a
farce, though he felt obliged to go along with the game. "Don't
bother me with that stuff," he once told a subordinate who asked
him about a research problem. "Just give the client about three
feet of it."

The extension of research has led, imperceptibly but logically,
to the development of a broad role for agencies in the whole
marketing strategy of their clients. A good agency today expects
to work intimately with the top officers of a corporate advertiser
in formulating basic marketing plans. The marketing programs
devised by agencies today range over pricing policies, sales
promotion, publicity, and packaging, and would ordinarily include
a lot of opinion on market changes and the strategy of the client's
competitors.

The broadening of agency marketing functions has one
interesting implication. Agencies today are necessarily in possession of their client's most vital business secrets. What happens
to these secrets when the agency and the advertiser part company?
Or when an agency executive departs for another agency, one
which has a competitive account? Admen stoutly deny that any
business espionage problem has been created by their broadened
role, but it seems reasonable to question, at least, the future
effects of any greater intimacy with clients.

## TV Follies

Of all the changes that have shaken and reshaped the modern
advertising agency, few have been so pervasive as those involving
television. Television has thrust upon the agencies the need to
supply new kinds of research, new kinds of creative talent, new
merchandising techniques. A large agency today may derive over
half its billings from television; at McCann-Erickson, which is
the TV leader among agencies, billings from the new medium
are now [1956] running around $90 million annually.

But television has also been a fearful headache. Some agencies complain that they are treated like intrusive outsiders in TV.

Ideally, they would like to be in on the production of more shows; they would like to have something to say about which shows get on the air; they would like some firm assurances that shows would be allowed to stay on the air so long as the sponsor was happy with them. They would like, in short, to have as much influence in TV as they did in radio during the great days of that medium in the 1930's.

The reason they have less influence is the shortage of TV network time. Three hours a night, times seven nights, times two major networks, comes to only forty-two hours a week of prime time. The scramble for the time became furious; so did the competition between the networks. To exert control over both situations, NBC and CBS retained full charge of programming. At times, the networks have not hesitated to push around some large advertisers and agencies. Firestone was pushed from a top spot on NBC because the network wanted to replace the half-hour *Voice of Firestone* with an hour show that would get a larger audience. (A lesser spot was offered, but the company decided to move the show to ABC.) When it was trying to lure *The $64,000 Question* away from CBS, NBC appeared to be ready to move one of several big sponsors around, so that the new sensation would have a good time slot. However, it is probably safe to generalize that the big advertisers and agencies have fared better with the networks than their small brethren. B.B.D.O., for example, with television billings of $75 million, can generally get shows of its own in a fairly good spot. It can even produce its own shows with fair regularity. . . .

Some smaller and middle-sized agencies, however, are chronically unable to place their sponsors, and are often forced into the most elaborate strategems in order to get on the air. One possible gambit: persuading a disgusted sponsor with a sickly rating to give you half his show on an every-other-week basis. Then persuade the network to let you put on your own show in place of the weak production you have bought into. Finally, if your own show pulls, the network may let you push the other client off altogether; at least you can bargain effectively for a good opening.

*Normal Crisis*

From all of the foregoing, it is manifest that the advertising business regularly generates a lot of excitement. It is, all in all, an intensely stimulating business—in fact, a little bit too stimulating for some of its practitioners. A great many of them would like to see an era of "settling down" in the industry—an era in which the industry would not be tangled in so many conflicts. A lot of small and middle-sized agencies would especially like to find some way of doing business without the recurrent crises that client turnover has made normal to advertising.

Client turnover is still a conspicuous feature of the advertising business. So far as the larger agencies (those over $10 million) are concerned, the figures suggest that client turnover is actually speeding up. Part of this turnover is apparently related to the desire of some large advertisers to decentralize their advertising operations. . . . Some part of the heavy turnover is also related to the wave of diversification that has hit American industry in recent years. Since agencies cannot handle competitive accounts, a diversifying client will occasionally "bump" another client, and the agency must then give up one or the other. Thus B.B.D.O. had to give up Fedders-Quigan when American-Standard went into the air-conditioning business.

But many of the switches—probably most of them—simply represent "normal" client restlessness. . . . To this, no agency has a solution. Except, of course, the solution of competing harder than ever on its client services.

For all the competitive contusions suffered in this turnover, the total advertising business just gets steadily bigger. It grew substantially even in the two postwar recession years, 1949 and 1954, and the industry talks as though only an economic catastrophe could check further growth. Norman Strouse, the president of J. Walter Thompson, has estimated that by 1965 the advertising total will reach $15 billion a year—with over half that amount in national advertising.

When William Benton came out of Yale in 1921 and went into the advertising business, he got a letter from his mother expressing sorrow that he couldn't have picked something more respectable. This censorious view of advertising is by no means dead, but it is certainly dying. No one need apologize today for going into the business. (Total agency manpower has been increasing by over two thousand a year.) One of these days, an admirable advertising man may even get into a novel.

## THE DOG-FOOD ACCOUNT [5]

Morris L. Levinson, the new president of the Rival Packing Company of Chicago, faced the task of choosing a new advertising agency. Rival's principal product is canned dog food, and the company spends about $1 million a year advertising it. After some preliminary screening, five agencies were invited to make formal pitches to Levinson and his associates. It would be quite in order, the agencies were told, for them to make speculative presentations embodying advertising themes and copy specifically prepared for Rival. The five agencies included three big ones—Grey and McCann-Erickson of New York, and D'Arcy of St. Louis—and two smaller ones: Guild, Bascom & Bonfigli of San Francisco, and the Clinton E. Frank agency of Chicago. The presentations, which furnished Levinson with a number of challenging notions about the dog-food business, all took place in Chicago during the second week in October. This is how they went:

The Grey Advertising Agency was scheduled to make the first presentation, and at ten o'clock on Monday morning a team of four Grey executives was on hand in Levinson's office at the Rival plant in Chicago. The ranking vice president opened by saying that he and his colleagues had done some serious thinking about Rival's fundamental marketing strategy. He then turned the floor over to Richard Lessler, the agency's vice president in charge of research. Lessler got down to business by whisking aside a cover that had previously concealed a large flip chart, or presentation book, standing on a table at one side of the room.

[5] By Spencer Klaw, associate editor of *Fortune*. *Fortune*. 54:124+. Reprinted by special permission from the December 1956 issue of *Fortune* magazine. © 1956 by Time Inc.

The cover of the book bore the title "An Integrated Marketing Plan for the Complete American Family," and Lessler said his role in expounding this plan would be to discuss certain economic and social trends affecting the canned-dog-food market.

Turning the pages of the flip chart, Lessler proceeded to demonstrate, with the help of graphs and charts, that the number of potential dog owners in the United States has been rising because American families have been having more children, earning more money, and moving to the suburbs. "And while people have been doing these things," he said, flipping to a photograph of a litter of puppies being suckled by their mother, "the dogs have been busy too." He went on to point out that the dog population has been rising, that per capita consumption of canned dog food has been rising even faster (up 68 per cent since 1947), that three-quarters of the people who buy canned dog food live in cities or suburban areas, and that dog food is an item that is usually bought by the housewife. In bringing the food and the dog together, he said, "the woman is the primary stimulator."

Lessler's place at the flip chart was taken by a vice president named Hollender, who said he would talk about the proper media strategy for reaching this primary stimulator. He turned to a new page in the presentation book. "Within the target area," it read, "we seek—Reach, Frequency, Impact, Continuity." Hollender said of course some compromises would have to be made and pointed to another sentence on the page, which read: "Optimum compromise automatically assures relatively reasonable cost per target contact."

In the case of Rival, Hollender said, the optimum compromise in media selection was a judicious mixture of nighttime television and what he referred to, with a grin, as "Dametime broadcasting"—i.e., daytime radio and television. Hollender then analyzed rate structures in radio and television, and discussed the most economical use of these media in various markets where Rival is sold. He concluded by pointing out that Grey already handles advertising for Five Day Laboratories, which manufactures 5 Day Deodorant Pads and is owned by the same parent company—Associated Products, Inc.—that owns Rival. The agency, he said, could buy television time on a pooled basis for both companies, thereby enabling them to benefit from quantity discounts and to get more mileage out of their television dollars.

When Hollender sat down, Edward Meyer, the fourth member of the Grey team, got up to talk about consumer motivation, copy strategy, and related topics. He yielded briefly to Lessler, who said that while Grey hadn't done as much research in depth among users of dog food as it would like to do if it should get the Rival account, the agency had at least done enough to provide some psychological copy fodder for its creative people. Meyer nodded, and said that Grey's researches had led to the formulation of an important concept about the relationship between dogs and housewives. He said the relationship could be expressed in one sentence—"A dog is nothing more than a four-year-old child with fur."

To show how this insight might be exploited by Rival, Meyer exhibited three story boards outlining animated-cartoon commercials. Two of them made their points humorously with accounts of a dog named Hector. In one sequence Hector was shown at his doctor's:

*Video*

DOCTOR puts down stethoscope and shakes his head.

*Audio*

DOCTOR: Hector, my dog . . . you're doggone run down. Diet-wise, you're barking up the wrong tree.

HECTOR: I know, Doc . . . I'm at the end of my leash. It's those humans I'm boarding out with. The mother . . . thinks lean red meat is all a dog needs.

At the end of each commercial the mother-and-child motif was sounded by a friendly looking dog who was shown holding up a gigantic can of Rival and saying: "Right, mother, your dog needs a well-balanced diet just like your children.". . .

In winding up the Grey presentation, Meyer tossed out a number of ideas for increasing Rival sales through new packaging and promotional techniques. He displayed a new red-white-and-blue label worked up by the Grey art department; a cardboard container designed to hold three cans of Rival; and a twelve-can cardboard container, made to look like a real shipping case. Meyer said this last device was a variation of what he termed the old warehouse-sale gimmick, and was meant to give the housewife the illusion that she was getting a bargain by buying in quantity. Another thing that could be done, he said, would be to use Rival cans to create "color excitement" in the supermarkets. "The Rival shelf section," he said, waving his arms enthusiastically, "could be a veritable rainbow of color."

The second agency to make its pitch was Guild, Bascom & Bonfigli. Its spokesmen covered much of the same ground covered by the Grey team, but particularly emphasized what they had done in the way of nutritional research and straightforward creative thinking about dog food. The scene of their presentation, which took place on Tuesday morning, was the living room of a suite in the Ambassador East Hotel. Movie and slide projectors were already in place when Levinson arrived, and after Levinson had been seated, proceedings were opened by the agency's president, Walter Guild. Guild pointed out that Rival had a serious problem. Its sales, he said, had not been keeping pace with the rise in U.S. dog-food consumption. He went on to note that he and his associates were well qualified to help solve this problem because of their unusual know-how in the food business. As evidence of the agency's ability to sell food products, Guild presented a one-minute film starring one of the agency's clients, Jerome M. Rosefield, head of the Skippy Peanut Butter division of Best Foods. Mr. Rosefield delivered a testimonial for Guild, Bascom & Bonfigli, an agency that he said had the ability to come up with "unusual, different advertising" and possessed a "strong, stubborn streak of integrity."

After this commercial, Guild yielded the floor to David Bascom, chairman of the agency. Bascom, a small, slender, worried-looking man, said he would discuss a proposed copy platform for Rival, the essence of which was this: "Rival is the one and only dog food made especially for city dogs."

*More Smooch in the Pooch*

Bascom said farm dogs don't eat much canned dog food anyway, and Rival might as well write them off as consumers. He had the projectionist run off six Rival commercials filmed by the agency. Five of them took a strong city-dog line ("Dog nutrition authorities agree that your city dog needs a different diet than his country cousin . . ."), while one commercial emphasized that suburban dogs need Rival too. This film featured a commuter going home on the train with a briefcase full of Rival. "For people, the suburbs may seem like the wide-open spaces," the commuter explained. "But as far as your dog is concerned, he's still living a life pretty different from that of his country cousin. Maybe he has a little more room than a big-city pooch—but he doesn't get to roam all over the outdoors, chase rabbits, swim rivers, and forage for himself. . . Rival provides all the things the city and suburban dog needs to keep him in the best health."

Bascom wound up the presentation by displaying some sample newspaper, magazine, and car-card advertisements and by playing a one-minute Rival radio commercial. The commercial had two striking elements. One was a voice, rendered hollow and sepulchral by the use of an echo chamber, which proclaimed that "the city dog that eats Rival outlives his country cousin by two to three years." The other was a jingle that went as follows:

> *More spark in the bark—with Rival.*
> *More smooch in the pooch—with Rival.*
> *No sag in the wag—with Rival.*
> *It's a fact, in the city,*
> *A dog's best friend is his Rival.*

Of the five agencies competing for the Rival account, the only one that did not stage a speculative presentation was D'Arcy, which made its pitch on Wednesday morning at the Rival plant. The agency's lead-off man, Harry Chesley Jr., said he and his two colleagues were there not to present an advertising program for Rival, but to explain "how we would lend our organization, and our intellectual and mechanical tools, to your problem."

After speaking about some of D'Arcy's clients, and about the agency's basic philosophy ("We're selling a marketing concept now . . ."), Chesley introduced the head of D'Arcy's Chicago office, J. B. Wilson. While a series of colored slides were projected onto a small screen to illustrate his remarks, Wilson expounded D'Arcy's theories of marketing. These days, he said, the consumer is so beset by competing advertising claims that he doesn't respond to commonplace advertising that is tired and unimaginative.

To drive home this point, a slide was shown bearing the exhortation "Resist the tenacity of the commonplace." Wilson said this advice had been very helpful to D'Arcy in its attempts to "break through the barrier of indifference"—a statement illustrated by another slide showing colored arrows penetrating a brick wall (indifference) behind which a consumer had taken refuge. D'Arcy's task, Wilson said, is "creating a compelling product image and merchandising that image."

Wilson next turned to the sales problems of Rival Dog Food. With the help of a flip chart, he and a colleague named Edgar Clark discussed Rival's sales position in various markets, and the advisability of a "local-market approach" in laying out an advertising and sales-promotion campaign for Rival. Chesley broke in at this point and spoke in glowing terms of D'Arcy's field staff. "If there are soft areas in your sales picture," he said, "we can go in with these shock troops and pump up those percentages."

Chesley said in conclusion that a sound advertising campaign for Rival would have to be based on a good deal more information than the agency had been able to put together in a few weeks. "That's why we didn't write any speculative copy," he said. "We felt it would be presumptuous." Chesley went on to say, however, that they had fooled around with some new Rival label designs, and with an idea for a new Rival "Health-Pack" container. "It's just one little intangible," he said modestly, "but it might be the catalyst that would make housewives take Rival off the shelf."

*Dog-food Stew for the Anxious*

McCann-Erickson, which made its presentation later the same day, brought along plenty of speculative copy. Indeed, the agency had not only written copy for Rival's present product, but had thought up new varieties of Rival Dog Food and had written copy for these too.

The bulk of the presentation was handled by the head of McCann-Erickson's Chicago office, a young man named Peter Peterson who spoke with an easy authority suggesting years of study of the dog-food business. McCann-Erickson's own pilot study of dog owners, he said, had revealed a "lack of specificity in the brand image" of Rival and other dog foods. Many people, he added, seemed to feel that just because Rival was cheaper than some other dog foods it wasn't as good. Consequently, Peterson said, steps should be taken to improve Rival's quality image—possibly by raising its price—and to develop clear points of superiority or difference in the product itself.

In this connection, Peterson noted that a sizable group of dog owners seem to suffer from "gnawing nutritional anxiety" about the food they give their dogs. This anxiety, he suggested, might be allayed by new varieties of Rival Dog Food. He listed several possibilities, including special dog foods containing eggs, extra protein and what Peterson described as health additives; a low-fat dog food for summer promotion; a dog food consisting of meat patties; and a dog-food stew with vegetables.

Peterson introduced Chester L. Posey, chief of creative services in McCann-Erickson's Chicago office. Posey displayed a number of ads he and his associates had roughed out to show how some of these dog-food products might be presented. One ad was headed "New Red Rival packs more protein than any other leading brand." Others were headed "New dog food discovery has *twice* the protein of any other brand"; "Time to feed new summer Rival—*fat reduced* for hot-weather feeding"; "New Rival—the first twenty-four-hour dog food with Protein Reserve"; and "*Now* a dog food that strengthens teeth and fights decay—New Rival with Fluorides." Posey said the agency's creative people had even given some thought to changing the name of Rival's product, and he held up for inspection an advertisement for "New Rival Prime." Prime, he pointed out, is a natural as a brand name for a dog food because "it says meat, it says quality, it says health—and it says it in one syllable."

Levinson, who had been following Posey attentively, then asked Peterson: "How do you handle an account, structure-wise?" Levinson observed that all agencies promise clients the benefit of regular high-echelon consultations. "I've never yet known an agency who did what they said they would," he added, "but I might as well listen to what you have to say."

Peterson said he was glad Levinson had asked the question, and brought the presentation to a close by explaining, with the help of an organization-and-flow chart about twelve feet long, just how the best thinking of McCann-Erickson's top advisory board and plans group would be brought to bear on Rival's marketing problems.

## At Home with Clinton Frank

The fifth and final presentation, which took place the following afternoon, was an informal meet-the-boys-in-the-shop affair. It was held in the offices of Clinton E. Frank, Inc., on the top floor of the Merchandise Mart in Chicago, and was presided over by the agency's president, Clinton Frank. Frank, an All-American halfback at Yale in the 1930's, greeted the Rival contingent in his office and distributed sheets of paper listing the names of the agency's key employees. "Basically this business is people," he said. He then sketched in the background of his associates, and appraised their capabilities, characterizing one vice president simply as "a pistol."

When he had run through the list, Frank led the way into the agency's conference room, where some ten of the people he had described were gathered in the flesh. A large presentation book was propped up on the conference table, and the assembled executives took turns in raising questions about the agency's qualifications for handling the Rival account—e.g., "Do we have a sharp pencil in buying TV time?" and "Can we create fresh new advertising approaches?" To help answer this last question, a projectionist ran off a series of television commercials made for its clients by the Frank agency.

Frank and his associates then analyzed the dog-food market and dog-food advertising, and said that their own pilot study of dog owners had indicated that nutritional themes would probably work best for Rival. Frank Newton, the agency's copy chief, exhibited several proposed Rival ads. One of them featured color photographs of variety meats, wheat germ, cereals, liver and calcium—"Everything your dog likes and *needs* for good health." Newton said this particular theme could also be used on the Rival label and in store displays. As an example of the latter, he demonstrated a mobile whose principal elements were cut-outs depicting variety meats, wheat germ, etc. He also demonstrated a promotional folder for Rival salesmen constructed in such a way, he explained, that when the salesman opens it up, a dog leaps out and "bites" the chain-store buyer.

When Newton had finished, Frank summed up by saying that he felt the Frank agency resembled the New York Yankees in that it had plenty of hustle. He said that any agency would no doubt be delighted to land the Rival account, but that in the case of this particular agency "delighted" was much too mild a word. "If you call me up tomorrow and say we can have the business," he said to Levinson, "there will be an explosion, and you're likely to find the top of this building over in Lake Michigan."

---

Levinson and his associates had hoped to make an immediate choice among the competing agencies, but it actually took them three weeks to reach a decision. Levinson decided the account should go to an agency with a Chicago office, and this eliminated Grey and Guild, Bascom & Bonfigli. The Rival account was finally assigned to McCann-Erickson.

## A LITTLE SOMETHING EXTRA—A PREMIUM [6]

The premium, as we know it now, traces back to an epochal, pre-Civil War day in 1851 when B. T. Babbitt, a soap manufacturer, hit upon the idea of offering brilliantly colored lithographed panel pictures in exchange for soap wrappers.

[6] From *One Hundred Years of Premium Promotions—1851-1951*, booklet by Matthew A. Shannon, senior attorney of the General Foods Corporation. Premium Advertising Association of America, Inc. 527 Lexington Avenue. New York 17, New York. 1951. p 1-10. Reprinted by permission.

Babbitt's offer was the logical follow-up to the "trade cards," lavishly illustrated small cards used by professional men and American business since colonial days and handed out to the public as advertisements. George Washington, surveyor, and Paul Revere, silversmith, distributed trade cards, as did most other businessmen of the period, and the picture cards announcing ship sailings of those days were among the most interesting.

Before the Civil War, laundry soap was bought and sold by the pound. When Babbitt brought out the first soap in cake form (Babbitt's Best Soap), he found that the public, accustomed to buying by weight from long bars, and more or less irrespective of who made it, was unresponsive. Babbitt was sure that the principle of packaging was right, but the soap did not sell. To gain the interest of consumers, he conceived the idea of adding something extra—something desirable—something it was not possible to get elsewhere; he put a value on the wrappers. To any person sending in twenty-five wrappers, he offered a lithographed panel picture, and the idea took on quickly. Editions of some of the pictures ran into the hundreds of thousands. There was hardly an American home without them at the time. For the next fifty years, there was no more popular advertising device than panel pictures and cards.

As the years went by, manufacturers, as well as retailers, adopted the premium in a definite way, and gradually the public realized that they might become the possessors of sundry articles, conditioned upon their patronage of such manufacturers and retailers. From offering panel pictures and other items of merchandise, colored lithographed trade cards were inserted in the products themselves or on the product wrappers by manufacturers. It was a short and natural jump to the simple "premium lists," and the later more elaborate catalogs, offering an assortment of items for coupons or wrappers. Yet it was not until this transition had been made that premium merchandising began to assume important proportions. . . .

Like most new forces, premium use had to go through the refining stage. The earliest concept was that anything was good enough to give away. This led to the appearance of cheap, flashy, substandard merchandise, "premium goods" as they were known in the trade, and through their use this new sales force was nearly strangled. It took a long time for manufacturers to realize that, while the consumer desires something for nothing, he does not want a cheap, useless thing. Good will suffered from these tactics.

The error was rectified, however, when businessmen realized that premiums were given to induce patronage, which is the basis of all business, and that the inducement had to be worth the effort to secure it and the consumer be satisfied in its use. In later years, the inducement was effectually aided by the development of part cash premium plans, combination sales, purchase privilege offers, and other variations of premium use that brought within the reach of the consumer a wider range of quality merchandise.

By 1897, the premium idea had spread into a number of different fields. The chief users were the soap, coffee, canned milk, and tobacco manufacturers, who offered buttons, jewelry, glassware, pictures, and novelty items upon presentation of a certain number of coupons or wrappers. Several of the cigarette companies placed the premium in the package, which was a new application. At about this time, other manufacturers adopted the idea of soliciting housewives and children to sell goods for premium rewards, such goods as bluing, jewelry, and toilet preparations being offered. A number of firms dealing in coffee, spices, and soap asked their customers to solicit orders from their neighbors when ordering goods and thereby earn a premium. Most premium procedure, however, was based upon the collection of coupons, a form of premium promotion advertising which still continues strong.

The pattern of the premium-using business has changed . . . [since 1851]. From 1850 to 1900, the most popular premiums were the colorful panel pictures and trade cards (by that time called trading cards). They were collected, traded and swapped. The craze swept the country and many of the more ardent collectors jealously guarded and insured collections of thousands of different subjects. . . .

Use of trading stamps was introduced in 1896 by Thomas Sperry in New England and while there are many companies operating today in the field, the Sperry and Hutchison Company which he founded is most active. Large packaged food and tobacco companies offered trading stamps through the years, and recently S. & H. Green Stamp merchandise has been distributed in department stores and other places in three hundred cities throughout the country. Catalogs are issued by the millions, too, so stamp savers in areas not covered by redemption agencies can order their merchandise by mail. . . .

The premium coupon [not to be confused with the trading stamp] operates to insure continued patronage. This was the method adopted to win public attention and approval up to, and for the decade immediately following, the turn of the century. It continues strong today, although other adaptations of the premium device have grown in status.

Before the turn of the century, the American Cereal Company, which later became the Quaker Oats Company, inaugurated the practice of putting coupons in its packages of "Quaker," "Scotch," "Avenza," and its other brands of cereals. The scheme called for the collection of a stated number of coupons, plus a specified amount of money, in return for a variety of indicated premiums. The Cereta Plan was the term early applied to this adaptation of the premium, and a comprehensive catalog was published carrying illustrations of a wide choice of domestic and personal articles ranging from agateware and baby spoons to Turkish rockers and wringers. . . .

An advertising feature related to the premium coupon plan was the custom of depositing pieces of china and aluminum in packages. About the year 1900, the American Cereal Company adopted this practice, having obtained the idea from its successful use by a Rockford wholesale grocery firm. The company applied it first to its "Banner Oats" and then extended it to its other brands.

For a while, however, premium volume merely rode the business curve—up when general business went up, and down when general business went down—and not until about 1910 did premium advertising become a specialized tool with objectives fairly well defined.

Beginning around 1910, the premium came into more wide-spread use than ever. Now the offer was more directly coupled with the advertising. Originally, the value of the premium was believed to consist solely in keeping a customer buying the same brand in order to accumulate a requisite number of coupons or wrappers. In this new phase, it was adapted to definite sales promotional objectives, such as introducing a new product, removing price cutting temptation, improving sales in a "weak" territory, or minimizing substitution. When business conditions entered upon something of a decline in 1913, and as premium offers were now becoming recognized as a fairly infallible sales stimulant, the advertising of premium offers became more conspicuous. . . . In fact, the unparalleled use of premiums in the tobacco business during this period evoked the following comment: "So widespread has the use of the premium become that the tobacco business may fairly well be said to have become committed to that system of merchandising." It was estimated in 1915 that $125 million worth of goods were used annually for premiums. These goods represented over 3.5 per cent of gross sales. . . .

During World War I, the premium fell into relative obscurity. The war was directly responsible for this. The ensuing easy selling years offered no incentive to disinter the dormant premium. But many of the large companies like Swift, Colgate, and Procter & Gamble returned to the premium promotion in the fight to get business late in 1920 and 1921. "You can't get around the fact that people want something for nothing," is the way a member of Swift & Company's sales department sized it up. The emphasis was on useful articles instead of the traditional bric-a-brac, ship pictures, and ephemeral novelties. Staple, use-able household necessities—such as glass water sets, aluminum kitchen utensils, and crockery—were offered in exchange for premium coupons, and people began to weigh values in premiums as closely as if they were paying money for them.

In January 1928, the status of premium use was brought before the Advertising Commission of the International Advertising Association, as the Advertising Federation was known at that time, and the Commission, after an exhaustive hearing, unanimously recognized and declared that premium use was a form of advertising. Premiums thereupon became a specialty of the departments of the Association, and have functioned as such ever since. . . .

In the early 1930's, the premium . . . was applied in a way that had seldom been used before. Premiums had usually been confined to some sort of continuous selling. To get the premium the customer had to buy the product numerous times, saving coupons or labels and presenting them for redemption. Now, however, it was given a very wide employment on a single purchase basis, the buyer getting the premium on the spot from the dealer or sending in to the manufacturer for it. When the premium was of such a value that the manufacturer could not afford to give it with the purchase of one or two units, the purchase premium idea was resorted to, the buyer paying part of the cost of the premium in cash.

The stage was now set for the birth of the mail-in "self-liquidator" as we know it today [one in which the amount mailed in covers the *entire* cost of the premium] though similar deals had dotted the path for many years. The great age of the self-liquidator, the era of glitter, glamor, and soap operas began, and is today at a height undreamed-of a quarter century ago. But, unlike the first picture premiums and the catalog plans, the self-liquidator cannot trace its origin to a single promotion or even exactly to a single time in history.

The renewed interest in premiums, at this time, seemed to be due to two factors: the depression and the emergence of radio.

First was the depression of the thirties. Plants were idle; merchandise was dusty on the shelves; you could shoot a shotgun down the aisle of a grocery store at two o'clock of a Saturday afternoon and never touch a customer. Manufacturers were desperate. Sales—and not necessarily even profitable sales—were needed. The advertising blue chips of the day, who had never used coupons, gingerly tried giving premiums as a stimulant.

They got quite a shock, but it is doubted they would have gotten the reaction they did if it hadn't been for the second factor which many associate with the birth of our present-day big volume premium business. There had also appeared on the scene a fascinating, unknown, powerful, new advertising medium —radio. Radio turned out to be the percussion cap that exploded the premium dynamite.

In 1935, an official of the National Broadcasting Company reported that 129 of 213 sponsors on NBC had made premium offers during the previous year; that the deals totaled 256; that 59 of the 129 users required proof of purchase; and that 29 offers required cash with the evidence of purchase. About the same time, CBS said that 83 of its sponsors had made one or more premium offers.

The practice of asking for small cash amounts persisted and more and more advertisers adopted it. Most of the early offers kept the figure low—a dime was the commonest amount and anything above a quarter was a conversation piece. In 1936, Colgate-Palmolive-Peet Company was offering a complexion brush for 10 cents and three Palmolive wrapper bands; the same firm also offered a nail brush with Super Suds for 10 cents and a box top.

By 1938 and 1939, the self-liquidator had developed to a high level of performance, and, after a slackening during the World War II years, continued to rise steadily. Today its popularity is such that "self-liquidator" and "premium" are virtually synonymous terms in the thinking of many. . . .

The function of all advertising is to arouse the desire to possess the advertised product to the point of action. The "plus power" of premium advertising is the coupling of the desire to possess the product and the desire for something additional —the premium.

## MOTIVATION RESEARCH [7]

There was a time when U.S. businessmen took it for granted they knew what the consumer wanted and what would make him buy. The consumer would buy any good product

[7] By Perrin Stryker, of the Board of Editors of *Fortune. Fortune.* 54:144-7+. Reprinted by special permission from the June 1956 issue of *Fortune* magazine. © 1956 by Time Inc.

he really needed and could afford, and he could be persuaded by skillful advertising to buy a great many other items he didn't actually need but that satisfied well-known human cravings. And as advertising continued to sell more and more goods, the businessman assumed that advertising men were growing ever more expert in persuading the consumer. But recently a lot of businessmen, and advertising men, too, have begun to think otherwise. Specifically, they are convinced that the consumer's apparent reasons for buying (or not buying) are seldom his "real" reasons, and that the consumer himself (or herself) seldom knows those "real" reasons.

This increasingly fashionable concept of the consumer is neither an advertising man's brain child nor the discovery of a market researcher. A part of it is straight out of Freud, some of it draws on the social sciences, and it is out of these materials that a few shrewd men have fashioned "Motivation Research." Since this technique promises to reveal those real reasons why people buy, it has inevitably excited both marketing and advertising executives. To some advertising men, who see this technique as a threat to their "creative" functions, M.R. is now a fighting word. Others, adapting gracefully to M.R., have used its findings to dress up the same advertising strategy they would have recommended in the primitive old days before M.R. There are also those who have genuinely welcomed M.R. as a rich new source of selling ideas.

M.R. has been responsible for some major shifts in advertising appeals. Thus the Tea Bureau up to 1951 had rather unsuccessfully tried to popularize tea drinking in the United States by harping on such themes as "Nervous? Try Tea." After an M.R. analysis of tea consumers, the bureau's ad agency, Leo Burnett Company, Inc., switched to the slogan "Make mine hefty, hale and hearty." The aim was to erase the stigma of effeminacy that M.R. had found inhibiting tea drinking among American consumers. A more recent and even less subtle example of applied M.R. appears in Marlboro cigarettes, which for years were sold in a white package that seemed to be favored by women smokers. Last year Philip Morris, maker of Marl-

boros, decided to alter the sex of this brand, figuring that its
market would be greatly expanded if its package and advertising
could be given masculine overtones (men smokers outnumber
women smokers two to one). An analysis by Louis Cheskin's
Color Research Institute showed that a bold, red-topped package
would be the most eye-catching and the most appealing to men.
Meanwhile Marlboro's ad agency, Leo Burnett, has been crowd-
ing Marlboro ads with pictures of tattooed, muscular young
men pursuing male hobbies. Indeed, the tattooed, male hand
has become almost a Marlboro trademark. (Lady smokers probably outnumber tattooed men by seventeen to one, but that, of
course, is not the point.)

If Motivation Research is just a fad, it is a very potent
one, because once its claims are accepted as true insights into
one category of consumer purchases, it is very difficult to say
that any market is beyond its reach. In practice, M.R. has
probably been most influential in markets where the consumer
has a choice of products that are nearly the same in quality,
performance, and price—e.g., soap, gasoline, cigarettes, food
products, and beverages. But M.R. has also been used by public
utilities, charitable organizations, and medical associations, and
its practitioners are not prepared to admit that there is any
produce or service unaffected by the consumer's "hidden" motives. One M.R. expert conceded that water consumption would
not be a worth-while field for his studies. At any rate, of the
$260 billion spent on consumer products last year, a full half
probably went to industries in which one or more major manufacturers had tried M.R.

If the techniques of M.R. actually do reveal why the consumer buys, then a good many billion advertising dollars have
been squandered in the past. In recent years, however, more and
more of those dollars are being spent according to the dictates
of M.R. Of the close to $9 billion spent on advertising in 1955,
nearly a billion came from those big corporations—two-thirds
of the hundred biggest advertisers—that have used M.R. directly or through their advertising agencies. (Among them:
General Motors, General Electric, A.T.&T., Goodyear, Procter

& Gamble, General Foods, and Chrysler.) And in the future, the findings of M.R. may be still more extensively used by big corporations to meet the challenges of the fast-changing and increasingly complex and competitive American market. In that case, M.R. would certainly sharpen up some ethical questions, among them the question whether any manufacturer should exploit, as buying motives, the deepest human frailties that can be dug out by psychoanalytic method. . . .

The interest in M.R. continues to mount despite the fact that most advertisers and agencies using it are either unable (or unwilling) to reveal any concrete results that M.R. may have achieved. Such companies as Scott Paper and General Mills, which have used M.R. off and on for some time, speak well of it but use very cautious language. The common opinion now seems to run something like this: "M.R. has been valuable in helping us get new ideas about marketing; it gives us clues to consumer behavior and covers new advertising angles we previously overlooked. But we have not come to any conclusions as to its real value." Very few marketing executives are willing to give M.R. direct credit for any particular increase in sales; the entire marketing process is far too complex for that.

However, at least one big advertiser, G.M.'s Chevrolet division, recently paid tribute to the potency of one "hidden" motive. To be sure, this particular "hidden" motive is a somewhat open secret—that lots of people consider their cars a proclamation of their income and social status—but Chevrolet discussed this motive out loud, and then made a pitch to well-to-do consumers who sometimes consider it chic to buy a *low*-priced car. And a good many advertisers have been impressed with the insights that M.R. has contributed to perplexing sales problems. Corning Glass Works, for instance, was long concerned by the fact that engineers were reluctant to buy the company's Pyrex pipe, which tests had shown to be stronger than many other kinds of pipe. Corning's ad agency (Charles L. Rumrill & Company, Inc.) called in psychologist Charles Winick to perform an M.R. analysis, and Winick reported back that engineers were inhibited from using glass pipe because of disagreeable memories of all

the glass tubes they had broken as students in school laboratories. As a result of this and other findings, Corning's advertising, which had previously concentrated on the strength of
Pyrex pipe, now also openly refers to the fear of breakage.

## Depth Interviews and Eye-blink Meters

M.R. practitioners are by no means agreed on what their
art is or just what it can and cannot do. Definitions abound.
The technique has been described as "a simple process by which
the deep likes and dislikes of consumers can be determined."
But the process is far from simple. M.R. brings to bear on the
consumer's personality not only all the subtle interpretations
and assumptions of dynamic psychology; it also has subjected
that personality to the complex analysis of the social sciences,
notably those of anthropology, sociology, "socio-psychology,"
and "group dynamics."

What has confused many people about M.R. is that it
apparently includes the same kind of orthodox market research
that has been going on for years, i.e.., questionnaires and in-
tensive interviews, which have long been the profitable stock
in trade of the statistical market analysts—Alfred Politz, Elmo
Roper, Claude Robinson, and George Gallup. However, M.R.
has revised these tools to uncover responses that are then in-
terpreted psychologically. In addition, M.R. has introduced many
special psychological tools—e.g., "depth interviews," sentence
completion, word association, Thematic Apperception, and other
projective tests that purport to expose the consumer's suppressed
or unconscious ideas, motives, and feelings. With these clinical
probes, the practitioners of M.R. have dug up a fantastic assortment of reasons why consumers buy and don't buy.

Some M.R. practitioners have specialized in a few tools.
Thus James Vicary's New York firm has built a reputation in
word-association tests, which he offers as a help to companies
choosing new product names or renaming old products. One
of his clients, A.T.&T., used Vicary's services to find the name
that best communicated the idea of its long-distance dialing

service, and Vicary tested seven titles. All but one either failed to convey the idea clearly (e.g., "Nationwide Dialing" suggested to many customers that they could dial phone numbers all over the world), or evoked unfavorable reactions (e.g., "Customer Toll Dialing" was too heavily associated with money). A.T.&T. finally chose "Direct Distance Dialing," which aroused no unfavorable customer reactions and most clearly conveyed long-distance phoning without the help of an operator.

Vicary has also explored the mechanics of "impulse buying," which he found responsible for 38 per cent of what housewives buy in supermarkets. For this study he developed an "eye-blink" meter. He found that housewives' eyes blinked at a normal thirty-two times a minute before they entered the store and while they were looking at merchandise on the shelves. While the housewives were actually buying (i.e., picking up the goods) their blinking dropped to fourteen times a minute. This low blinking rate, Vicary holds, indicates a sense of gratification from release of the tension existing in the consumer while she was making her choice. He thinks a low blinking rate also reflects a condition of "semihypnosis," which many shoppers reach at the purchase point.[8] Vicary's own wife admitted she had to get into this state in order to shop in a supermarket. As soon as a purchase was made and the housewife reached the checkout counter, her eye-blink rate went up to twenty-five per minute; it soared to forty-five bpm while she was actually paying the bill. The blink test also indicated that buying impulses were inhibited by the tension produced when the consumer saw something she didn't believe; e.g., the blinking rate stayed low when a consumer saw merchandise bearing a seal of approval, but a guarantee on the label induced a swift rise in bpm.

The hottest arguments over M.R. have been waged between the ex-German statistician, Alfred Politz of New York, whose staff has probably done the most to refine "nose-counting" methods of market research, and the ex-Austrian psychologist, Dr. Ernest Dichter, who runs the Institute for Motivational

[8] The technique of hypnosis itself has been used by one ad agency, Ruthrauff & Ryan, to uncover consumer attitudes. Though the experiments seemed to offer possibilities, the agency, aware of the brainwashing connotations, has abandoned them.

Research, Inc., at Croton-on-Hudson, New York. Politz has repeatedly charged in speeches and articles that Dichter is practicing a "pseudo-science" when he attempts to explain consumers' motivations without the quantitative proofs of statistical research. In reply, Dichter contends that his methods represent "qualitative research" and often reveal consumer motives that statistical market surveys could never reach.

Those who, like Politz, put their faith in statistical surveys, consider M.R. nothing more than a useful producer of hunches about the consumer. And Politz' firm, which includes eighteen psychologists, in fact uses some M.R. techniques to hunt hunches that may be useful in developing questionnaires. These may be sent to anywhere from five hundred to twenty thousand consumers, carefully selected according to principles of "probability sampling." The summarized results, which may cost from $10,000 to over $100,000, give the client a detailed picture of the size, income levels, sex, social status, etc., of his consumer market, and also much information as to what consumers *say* they feel and think about his product.

Conversely, M.R. firms like Dichter's rely extensively on interviewing small groups of consumers—as few as a dozen, rarely more than a hundred. Interviewers, many of whom are students (or even housewives), probe and test respondents for answers and reactions that will furnish clues to common consumer attitudes and motives. The questions may be quite oblique: e.g., the question "What kind of person do you think would buy this product?" seeks to make the consumer reveal his true attitudes when he "projects" them onto another person. Later, more interviews and projective tests may be conducted to reinforce the hypotheses about consumer behavior that M.R. analysts may have drawn from the first sampling. Essentially, M.R. differs from orthodox market research in seeking the psychological and sociological reasons for consumer behavior, and in refusing to take at face value the conscious, often rationalized, replies of those interviewed. M.R. aims to predict the future reactions of consumers and not merely to report on their past behavior. The technique therefore makes no assumptions about consumer attitudes before studying them, whereas conventional market researchers usually develop a questionnaire intended to prove or disprove preliminary assumptions. . . .

## Three Brands of M.R.

There are three main schools of M.R. practitioners. One school, of which Dichter is the most prominent exponent, relies heavily on psychoanalytical interpretation of what has been drawn from consumers in "depth interviews" (a Dichter coinage) and projective tests. Freudian interpretations dominate the analyses, and are sometimes elaborated surprisingly. The effects of early toilet training, for example, are repeatedly emphasized in Dichter's explanations of consumers' responses to things as diverse as toothpaste and community-chest drives. Thus he says that the impulse of people to contribute to charity is not an effort to assuage guilt feelings (as often assumed) but an expression of the "sense of power" first experienced when a child finds he can please or displease his mother by obliging or refusing to oblige in the performance of his toilet functions. People therefore enjoy nongiving just as much as giving, and "generosity has nothing to do with it," according to Dichter. But a charity appeal featuring a kindly "mother figure" will be more effective in making people "oblige and give" than some abstract symbol or heavily sentimentalized picture aimed at their sense of duty or pity.

This may sound like tommyrot to many businessmen, yet most of those who have hired Dichter readily admit that his insights into marketing problems are frequently brilliant, and just one of his ideas (he tosses them off by the score) may make a client very happy.

A second school of M.R. experts includes psychologists and social scientists who place major reliance on the group behavior of consumers, and the impact of culture and environment on their opinions and reactions. In this school can be found both individual specialists, such as the eminent sociologist, Professor Lloyd Warner of the University of Chicago and commercial M.R. organizations, such as Psychological Corporation of New

York, and Social Research, Inc., and Science Research Associates of Chicago. There is, however, much overlapping between the psychosociological and the psychoanalytical schools of M.R., and to the untutored businessman the differences between them may seem imperceptible.

The third and apparently the most thorough M.R. approach has been developed at McCann-Erickson advertising agency under Dr. Herta Herzog, student—and a former wife—of another eminent M.R. authority, Dr. Paul Lazarsfeld, Viennese psychologist and onetime director of Columbia University's Sociological Research Bureau. Like Dichter (who also studied under Lazarsfeld in Vienna), Dr. Herzog has been applying M.R. techniques to U.S. marketing problems since the late thirties. Her method includes a series of four steps: (1) locating by conventional "nose-counting" methods of market research those consumer groups whose behavior importantly affects the client's market; (2) analyzing, through "depth interviews" and projective tests, between three hundred and four hundred consumers, tabulating the frequency of their reactions, and drawing tentative conclusions about their buying motives; (3) sending to a large sample (from twelve hundred to three thousand) a "structured" questionnaire—i.e., one designed to test out M.R. conclusions and establish how many consumers hold each particular attitude; (4) pretesting ads based on M.R. findings and predicting their relative drawing power by discussing them with selected consumers in various cities.

Dr. Herzog believes in using statistics to "quantify" M.R. findings, as Politz does. But unlike Politz, she uses M.R. techniques to explore the differences and discrepancies revealed by statistical market analysis. However, she is emphatic that "M.R. should never be substituted for conventional market research," and that M.R. is most useful where products are not distinguishable in quality, performance, or price. With such products, she considers that a major M.R. function is to locate and define those non-users who may be persuaded to switch brands.

M.R.'s prime aim, however, is to develop brand loyalty among consumers. But the consumer's capacity for loyalty varies greatly from product to product. In the case of a cigarette smoker, an original choice that was more or less random can harden into intense, rationalized loyalty to one brand. In the case of detergents, on the other hand, consumers are notoriously faithless. A study of detergents by Social Research, Inc., revealed a chaos of disloyalty; in one year, one representative housewife was found to have switched brands almost weekly, purchasing, all told, sixteen different brands. One M.R. explanation for such disloyalty: the housewife regards her washing and cleaning functions as basically distasteful and unproductive of praise from her family. One recommendation: switch the sales pitch and advertise the appreciation that the housewife's husband and children might bestow on her as the result of her cleaning chores.

The findings of M.R. have occasionally led to more realism in consumer advertising. Thus Pan American-Grace Airways, which once advertised its South American tours with conventional pictures of pretty models reveling in the pleasures of flying, shifted to illustrations featuring older couples who appeared to have enough in the bank to afford $1,650 per couple for a New York-Rio de Janeiro round trip by air. M.R. also changed another airline's image of its buying public. When American Airlines called on Dichter for help in handling the safety angle, his study showed that many businessmen were inhibited from flying by "posthumous guilt feelings." The man who is afraid to fly, said Dichter, "fears he would be embarrassed by what his wife might say after he had lost his life in a crash." He might imagine his wife saying, "The darn fool. He should have gone by train. Now see what he has done." Accordingly, Dichter recommended that American should start vigorously selling the wife on the virtues of swift business travel, but should be very careful not to follow the advertising line its competitors had adopted in urging the wife to urge the husband to fly because it "would get him where he wanted to go much sooner." Dichter pointed out that wives would reject this advice, because it only made them wonder what the husband would do when he got there. So, on Dichter's advice, American pointed out to the wife that by flying, the husband would get *home* sooner.

Dichter also persuaded American to promote its family-fare plan by featuring pictures of the whole family traveling by air. This was intended to motivate wives to fly with their husbands—thus resolving all uncertainties as to how the husband spends his time when he gets there, and also removing his "posthumous guilt feelings." Dichter thinks these feelings are still the major deterrent to air travel.

### Switching the Pitch

This example of M.R. is fairly typical, especially in its psychoanalytical overtones. And its recommendations for specific advertising copy are typical of Dichter's approach. In most M.R. studies, however, the findings are generalized and the development of the actual advertising copy is left to the agency. For example, a study of Chicago beer consumers by Social Research, Inc., showed that the great majority of middle-class consumers were unimpressed by ads that tried to put beer in a formal setting. Pictures of elegantly dressed people tippling beer in swank surroundings were repeatedly ridiculed by those interviewed, most of whom regarded beer simply as a low-cost, friendly, thirst-quenching drink to be enjoyed in shirt sleeves. This finding, made available to advertisers by the Chicago *Tribune,* is now widely recognized in beer advertising, which stresses friendly informality and easygoing, middle-class relaxation. . . .

No two M.R. studies, even of the same people buying the same product, are likely to arrive at identical conclusions, if only because the interpretation of social and psychoanalytical findings depends almost totally on the skill and insight of the M.R. practitioner. When a sociological M.R. expert and a psychoanalytical M.R. expert work on the same problem, they may disagree flatly in their findings and recommendations. Both Dichter and Gardner [social anthropologist Dr. Burleigh Gardner, head of Social Research, Inc.], for example, were hired to analyze consumer attitudes toward the advertising concepts used by Dial Soap. Dichter concluded that the emphasis on Dial's deodorant powers was all wrong, that it made people subconsciously uneasy about *losing* their own distinctve body odors, and "scared them away." He recommended less emphasis on the soap's deodorizing features. Gardner, on the other hand, found consumers well disposed to Dial's messages, and since Dial's deodorizing agent (hexachlorophene) was apparently winning the customers, Gardner advised the company to continue this sales pitch. Dial's ad agency, Foote, Cone & Belding, was not particularly impressed with either Dichter's or Gardner's analysis, but welcomed Gardner's findings as support for its own ideas about promoting Dial. . . .

## *The Future of M.R.*

The U.S. consumer is enjoying more and more "discretionary" spending power, as his rising income leaves him more money to spend on luxuries, hobbies, and all kinds of products not strictly essential to his well-being. As the consumer becomes better educated, his tastes and desires are changing, and, according to the advocates of M.R., his reasons for buying will continue to change right along with his standard of living. M.R.'s promise is to uncover these psychological, economic, and sociological changes in the tastes, attitudes, and behavior of consumers so that the sales efforts of American business can more and more profitably meet the consumer's needs and desires. M.R., in short, rejects the old marketing concept of economic man and loudly proclaims the concept of psychological man.

The modern consumer, according to Dichter, is "an entirely new type" who exhibits these five major characteristics: (1) desire to be treated as an individual, e.g. "she wants to add a red stripe to her refrigerator"; (2) desire for participation, e.g. he wants advertisers to recognize his personal interests by inviting his suggestions and criticisms, and not to ignore him by using high-priced testimonials of celebrities; (3) an increased maturity, e.g. he plans ahead further than he used to, and realistically accepts the fact that "many of his actions are guided by irrational motives"; (4) desire for recognition, e.g. he wants to take revenge on dealers and manufacturers who have treated him badly in the past, wants to "see them crawl, psychologically"; (5) desire for creativeness, e.g. the housewife who buys a cake mix wants to "keep on living under the delusion that she bakes the cake herself."

Dichter's newsletter [*Motivations*—subscription price $100 yearly] emphasizes "the changing American taste," citing Wayne Andrews, author of *Architecture, Ambition, and Americans,* who describes the conflict between the tastes of architects who are "Veblenites" and those who are "Jacobites." Veblenites are "cool, impersonal, dogmatic, worshipers of the machine and steel and glass building materials, etc.," while Jacobites are "warm, individualistic, casual, pragmatic, take the machine for granted, are interested in the texture of building materials, etc." The newsletter says M.R. shows that consumer taste is becoming more Jacobite with "overtones which are almost Victorian, even if in a quieter, simpler, more modern way"; and the consumer demands products with "greater elegance, graciousness, intimacy, and individualism which will combine the useful with the aesthetic and will be recognized by the public as both intelligent and refined. . . When physical differences among products are negligible, it will be the product which first catches up with the aesthetic demands of the public that will inevitably run away from the field."

Be that as it may, M.R. seems destined sooner or later to raise some disturbing questions. There is, for instance, the possibility that the widespread application of common M.R. findings might produce a dreary sameness in advertisements that would leave consumers cold. If competitive advertisers continue to demand at least as much uniformity as they have in the past, M.R. may only serve to give such uniformity a psychological *raison d'être.* However, up to now M.R. practitioners have advanced such a variety of explanations for consumer behavior that advertisers will be a long time exhausting these possibilities.

A far more serious question about M.R. has scarcely been mentioned even by its severest critics. It is this: will the use of such a technique reinforce consumer motives and attitudes that advertisers might better leave alone? Fears about nonconformity, anxiety over security, narcissism, reluctance to face up to some of the disagreeable but necessary chores of life, excessive emulation of the Joneses—these and other signs of immaturity M.R. has unquestionably revealed. M.R. is undoubtedly an invasion of the consumer's privacy, but the real trouble with M.R. is not that it exposes such weaknesses but that it often seems to recommend, openly or implicitly, that U.S. business nourish these weaknesses and pander to them.

It is possible, of course, that as more and more M.R. findings are translated into advertising symbols, more and more consumers will become aware of what the advertiser is trying to do to them, and will become inured to such symbols, which they will recognize and ignore as readily as they now recognize and ignore such old advertising stereotypes as the warning doctor. Beyond that, it rests with the good sense and ethical standards of businessmen and advertising men whether M.R. is to be a legitimate exploitation of healthy human desires.

## SUBLIMINAL PROJECTION—THE PHANTOM OF THE SOAP OPERA [9]

*Yesterday, upon the screen,*
*They flashed some ads that were not seen.*
*They were not seen again today—*
*Gee, I wish they'd go away.*

When subliminal projection darted from its launching pad in New York . . . [in September 1957] the resultant clamor made it appear to be the advertising shot heard 'round the world. Vociferous comment ranged from a Stanford Research Institute official's assertion that subliminal advertising is "a virtual social H-bomb" to a charge made by the WCTU president that breweries are eyeing "invisible" commercials as "a likely solution to their dropping sales."

[9] From "The Phantom of the Soap Opera," by William H. Kalis, head of the public relations firm of William Kalis Associates in Hempstead, Long Island, New York, and formerly a public relations man in New York City. *Public Relations Journal.* 14:6-8. March 1958. Copyright 1958 by the Public Relations Society of America, Inc. Reprinted by permission.

Dr. Ernest Dichter, the motivation man [president of Institute for Motivational Research, Inc.], perhaps happy to be on the offensive side of the critical fence, declared that subliminal projection could be classed as hypnosis and would "give the whole field of motivation research a bad name." To this James M. Vicary, the subliminal man, retorted that Dichter's criticism was "like saying a whiff of martini is worse than a swallow," and he added that subliminal projection is "a new band in human perception, like FM."

As the controversy continues to boil, one significant fact stands out: as yet, there is no independent, objective evidence which proves that subliminal advertising "works"—that it meets an advertiser's one stiff requirement that a technique, to be successful, must persuade the consumer to buy his merchandise.

The one consumer test on record was reported by Vicary and his associates . . . [in 1957] when they demonstrated the subliminal technique in a film studio before some fifty reporters. In a "scientific" test in a motion picture theatre, Vicary said, 45,699 persons unknowingly were exposed to two advertising messages projected subliminally on alternate nights. One message advised the movie-goers to "Eat Popcorn," while the other said, "Drink Coca-Cola."

Sales figures over the six-week test period were compared with previous sales records to check for any fluctuation in the sales of the products subliminally advertised, Vicary said. The invisible advertising increased popcorn sales on the average of 57.5 per cent, and increased sales of Coca-Cola on the average of 18.1 per cent, he added.

No details were offered as to exactly how and under what circumstances the tests were made. Vicary stated that this information formed part of his patent application for the projection device and must remain secret, but he said that "sound statistical controls" were employed.

Later, the findings of the test were questioned by *Motion Picture Daily,* which disclosed that the Fort Lee Theatre in Fort Lee, N.J., was the site of the experiment. The trade paper said that the theatre manager reported no effect on refreshment stand patronage during the test period.

Following publication of this story, Vicary unfolded his test data before Charles Moss, head of the circuit operating the Fort Lee Theatre. Moss then issued a statement which said that as a result of the "confidential" figures put before him, he believes that "this type of subconscious advertising could help increase sales." But "additional testing" is needed, he said.

Vicary, nettled by *Motion Picture Daily's* refusal to run a retraction along with the Moss statement, reiterated that the New Jersey test was made only to collect information for the patent application and that he expected advertisers and networks to test the subliminal technique thoroughly before using it commercially.

Subliminal projection's most vocal critics are those who believe that if the technique can sell the king-sized package it can also "sell" a political candidate or an ideology. Long before the first cry that "1984 is here . . . Big Brother is watching you," Vicary had anticipated these criticisms by suggesting that commercial use of the subliminal process may require a built-in assurance of proper usage, due to the fact that the message cannot be seen. One practical safeguard, he said, might be a prior disclosure of the message and a report that it is being projected subliminally, similar to radio and television announcements when transcriptions and films are broadcast.

"We recognize the responsibility that grows out of our discovery and development of this process," Vicary said. "We feel its commercial use eventually may have to be regulated, either by the industries which use it or by the government.". . .

Vicary believes that subliminal advertising will have its biggest initial impact in televison, with benefits for viewers as well as for sponsors. For the viewing public, he sees two substantial gains: fewer interruptions for sponsor messages and added entertainment time.

To describe sponsor benefits, Vicary uses a favorite definition of his brainchild. "This innocent little technique," he says, "is going to sell a hell of a lot of goods."

What is this "innocent little technique" which is causing all the commotion?

Vicary's group apparently has two devices—a projector for theatres and an "apparatus" for television. Because of pending patent applications, Vicary is secretive about the exact nature of the devices.

Subliminal is defined by Webster's as "below the threshold of consciousness or beyond the reach of personal awareness." (An interesting secondary definition is "too small or weak to be perceived, felt, etc."). . .

The subliminal impressions, or advertising messages, projected by the theatre device are flashed onto the screen at a speed of 1/3000th of a second every five seconds. (TV projections appear to be flashed at lower rates such as 1/20th of a second.) These messages are not consciously visible to viewers because they are flashed at a lower light intensity than that of the film or TV show on which they are superimposed.

Because subliminal impressions are rapid and brief, many critics of the technique have pointed out that a weak stimulus can provoke only a weak response. Vicary candidly agrees that subliminal projection lends itself best to "reminder" advertising, but he points out that the effect of much current advertising— such as the highway billboard messages caught out of the corner of a driver's eye—is subliminal.

The subliminal technique gives us a weak message which we can put on the screen quickly and to the viewer painlessly at a time when we are assured of having the greatest number of persons in the audience [Vicary says]. No hypnosis is involved. Since the stimulus must be weak and the message very simple, so far as we know it will not be so effective person for person as other forms of advertising. Therefore, we call it reminder advertising.

### 100 Years Ago

Historically, experiments in subconscious perception go back almost one hundred years, with a number of investigations reported in professional literature, starting around 1900. The word "subliminal" was first used in 1938 in a paper in the *Journal of Psychology* titled "Perception of Subliminal Visual Stimuli." The author, A. C. Williams, Jr., noted in connection with extrasensory perception tests that the subjects showed higher scores when the tests were made in a strongly-lighted room, indicating the impact of light intensity and time of exposure on an individual's threshold of awareness.

Since World War II, laboratory research into subconscious perception has increased. At about the same time that Vicary announced his invention Drs. Sheldon Bach and George S. Klein, of New York University's Research Center for Mental Health, conducted an experiment on a group of twenty young women. The subjects were shown a projection of a line drawing of a man's face and were led to believe that it was changing expression from "happy" to "angry." Actually, the experimenters flashed the word "happy" on the screen for a few thousandths of a second, followed by the word "angry," and the subjects believed that they saw a change of expression.

The British Broadcasting Corporation conducted a mass audience test of sub-threshold awareness during a ballet performance televised in mid-1956. During the show, a four-word message was flashed on the screen at 1/25th of a second. The text read: "Pirie Breaks World Record." At the end of the program, viewers were told that a news item had been projected subliminally, and anyone who had seen anything was asked to write in. Of 430 replies, 20 gave the correct text and 130 were close to being accurate.

Scientists did not consider the BBC tests conclusive proof that sub-threshold messages could be conveyed to a TV audience, but the British association of advertisers—the IPA—banned subliminal techniques and warned members that any use of subliminal advertising would be regarded as a grave breach of the code of ethics.

In the United States . . . the National Association of Radio and Television Broadcasters, with three major U.S. networks and three hundred independent stations as members, issued a six-page memorandum regarding the implications of subliminal advertising.

The statement said that while it was not then technically possible to transmit projections of 1/3000th of a second over existing TV facilities, it could be done in the future. The

NARTB called for research to determine the visual and aural efficacy of subliminal techniques, and expressed grave concern over public reaction to advertising which affects people "so that they are not able to exercise conscious control over their acceptance or rejection of the messages."

It suggested further that the code of ethical practices be amended to cover the new development. On the following day the NARTB Code Review Board announced recommendations to members that any proposals made to use the TV medium for subliminal techniques immediately be referred to the Board. . . . ABC, CBS, NBC and the Canadian Broadcasting System offered assurances that they would not expose set owners to hidden commercials.

During this period, a number of congressmen were importuning the Federal Communications Commission to take action to protect the public from phantom advertising. FCC Chairman John C. Doerfer said that his agency had appointed a "task force" to investigate the matter, and he pointed out that the law states that advertisers must be identified.

Representative William A. Dawson (Republican, Utah), asserted that the FCC should insist that stations desist from using a "secret pitch" until the investigation had been completed. Doerfer replied that there were "some indications that this technique may have been used on TV, but the three major networks and Vicary denied that subliminal techniques had been used through their facilities. Later, Station WTWO in Bangor, Maine, reported to the FCC that it had experimented with on-air tests of subliminal projection and had failed to produce noticeable results. The Subliminal Projection Company conducted a closed-circuit television test of its technique in Washington for FCC members, congressmen and the press. The "Eat Popcorn" message was flashed at five-second intervals, but the only hunger reaction noted in the audience was from Senator Charles E. Potter (Republican, Michigan), who said, "I think I want a hot dog."

Inventor Vicary, unabashed by the results, said: "Those who have needs in relation to the message will be those who respond." He told newsmen that subliminal techniques would not force a Republican to vote Democratic or vice versa, but that he believes the technique could aid in getting out the vote.

He described subliminal advertising as a "mild form of advertising" and a "very weak persuader," a method designed to augment rather than supplant visual advertising. In contracts with television stations, Vicary said, his company would insist that all subliminal messages be shown visually in advance to viewers. . . .

And in Scotland, a subliminal researcher named Peter Randall claimed to have developed a method of projection which boosts the receptivity of the viewer so that each sub-threshold message is absorbed by at least 75 per cent of the audience. Randall calls his method "Strobonic Psycho-Injection." At this writing no one yet has suggested that "Out, Damned Spot" may be a twentieth-century rallying cry of Scots against the little ads that aren't there.

## TRADEMARKS [10]

From TV screen, billboard, and printed page, Americans are bombarded daily with thousands of trademarked signs, symbols, and trick words, each with something to sell and each with a heavy load of the selling job to carry. In an era of hot competition, proliferating products, and mass communication, the 350,000 trademarks registered with the United States Patent Office have become more than simple marks of identity—since simple identification is not enough to reach the benumbed eyes and ears of the U.S. consumer. As the public forms opinions faster, says New York industrial designer Norman Schoelles, "it is essential that the corporation say who it is, what it does, and how it differs from competitors, quickly and efficiently. Call it what you will, it's an indispensable part of marketing today."

Just how indispensable was pointed up . . . in a [1959] suit filed by the Jay S. Conley Company, a California manufacturer of chemical cleaning products, which claimed that its

[10] From "The Male Animus." *Newsweek.* 54:61-2. August 3, 1959. Reprinted by permission.

very existence hung on two words. Word 1: "Jeenie," the brand name that Conley claims it has been using for four years. Word 2: "Genie," the brand name for a new liquid detergent just introduced by giant Colgate-Palmolive Company. Suing for infringement of its trademark patent, Conley claimed that the confusion had already cut into its sales and led many customers to believe it had sold out to Colgate. Colgate, with a $1.8 million advertising campaign for Genie at stake, filed a counterclaim, asserting that Conley's trademark applied only to chemicals, not detergents. [The Federal District Court in San Francisco held in September 1959 that the name "Genie" conflicts with the trademark rights of Conley in the fourteen western states in which "Jeenie" is distributed.—Ed.] . . . Even the Russians are involved in a capitalistic trademark squabble. Chicago's Admiral Corporation filed an official protest when it learned that a Russian-made TV set displayed at the [1959] Soviet exhibition in New York was labeled "Admiral."

With some 20,000 new trademark applications flowing into Washington each year, this kind of confusion is being steadily compounded. In the brand-happy consumer industries, batteries of company lawyers keep watch on rival companies for infringement of trademarks. Coca-Cola, possibly the most infringed-upon company in the world, has fought and won literally hundreds of suits to protect both "Coca-Cola" and "Coke" (although it can't claim exclusive use of the "Cola" part of its name, since this is a generic term for a type of bean).

Fame can be a trademark's worst enemy, since common usage may make it a part of the language. Recalling what happened to "aspirin," "cellophane," celluloid," "nylon," "escalator" and "zipper" (all good trademarks until the courts ruled them in the public domain), firms like Minnesota Mining & Manufacturing (Scotch Brand tape), Chesebrough Manufacturing (Vaseline), and Johnson & Johnson (Band-Aid) are constantly watching for (and protesting) generic use of their brand names.

Along with the batteries of lawyers come the industrial designers, motivational researchers, and other Madison Avenue

denizens who have swarmed into the field. Time was when a
trademark might spring full-blown from a company president's
brow; three underwear makers named Bradley, Voorhis, and Day
merely combined their initials to create a brand name that swept
the world, and Harley T. Procter found a name for his new
floating soap in church when he heard a phrase from the 45th
Psalm (". . . out of the ivory palaces whereby they have made
thee glad").

Today, however, teams of specialists may pore over every
line and letter of a company's trademark in search of merchandising innuendoes, or to tie it in with the "corporate image" (a
compote of all a company's public impressions, which may
range from its price structure to the uniforms of its elevator
operators).

To touch up its "image," Singer Sewing Machines gave its
"sewing lady" a modern hair-do, changed her silhouette to make
it more fashionable. Socony-Mobil revised its shield trademark
the better to catch the eye of fast-traveling motorists. Worthing-
ton Pump discarded the "Pump" from its title in deference to
its growing diversification. Union Carbide, for all the size and
diversity of its operations (chemicals, plastics, alloys, "Prestone,"
and "Eveready" products), felt a lack of corporate "identity"
and has been brushing up its trademark accordingly. "We went
to an industrial designer," says a Union Carbide man, "and told
him to put us in something like du Pont's oval. He put us in
a hexagon."

There is a general trend to more "masculine" (i.e., more
forceful, boldly colored) company symbols, which are apparently
preferred by both sexes and have greater "impact." Yet the
volume of new trademarks competing for attention is apt to
soften the impact through sheer repetition. Example: There
are no less than 9,000 registered trademarks which use a dia-
mond shape ("signifies wealth, prestige" in motivationese).

For these and other good reasons, some companies refuse
to monkey with trademarks that already have familiarity and an
established reputation like du Pont and Esso (with their ovals
symbolic of security, according to designers), and General

Motors with its square (denoting strength and integrity).
General Electric intends to keep right on using the old-fashioned
curleycued GE it has displayed since the turn of the century.
Reason: A nation-wide survey showed the monogram was the
best-recognized of all American industrial trademarks. . . .

## ELSA MAXWELL LOVES MAZOLA [11]

Jules Alberti is president and owner of Endorsements, Inc.
He produces absolutely nothing. As was said of Willy Loman
[the unhappy protagonist of Arthur Miller's play *Death of a
Salesman*], "He don't put a bolt to a nut, he don't tell you the
law or give you medicines." The difference between Willy
Loman and Jules Alberti, however, is that Jules is unable to
carry his samples in a valise . . . and seems to be in excellent
spirits. Also, he is very well liked.

And yet Jules—slight, bespectacled and so polite ("It'll be
my pleasure, my *honor* to talk to you")—is a salesman, too, in
his unlikely way. He sells people—"the people you want"—to
advertisers. For Jules is king of The Testimonial, an institution on which the men of Madison Avenue have spent an
estimated $500 million over the past ten years. Jules, who
claims the distinction of being the only fellow in America engaged exclusively in this line of work, figures that he had his
finger in about half that enormous pie.

A former saxaphone player, band leader and manager of
vocalist Benay Venuta, Jules began to hit his stride as a manipulator of Names in the forties when the Treasury Department
titled him Coordinator of Celebrities and Talent for its War
Finance Division. His wartime connections with the great inspired him and a lady named Hazel McCabe to set up Endorsements, Inc. in 1945. Ends never quite met during the first year,
but in 1946 Batten, Barton, Durstine and Osborn came through
with a request to Jules to round up some Schaefer beer enthusiasts. The name-procurers made $6,500 that year; in 1947 bill-

[11] From an article by Walter Goodman, senior editor of *Redbook* magazine,
author of *The Clowns of Commerce*, and a frequent contributor to periodicals.
*The Nation.* 182:295-7. April 14, 1956. Reprinted by permission.

ings came to $11,800; in 1948, $67,000. Since 1949, Endorsements, Inc. has been in the six-figure bracket.

Jules woos customers by promising to "get the people you want, speedily, through our exclusive, intimate contacts with the great." He is, in fact, a dual middleman—first between the advertiser and the endorser, and then between the endorser and the consumer. In his daily operations, he is a parody of [the] "other-directed man." He gets people to like him so that they will say publicly that they like a certain product so that people who like them will maybe develop a liking for the product too.

For all his prominence in his profession, however, Jules lays no claim to having invented anything. He is the expediter and the reformer, not the innovator.

A hundred years ago or so, common gravestones were providing endorsers in abundance who never objected to having themselves quoted in praise of some life-giving nostrum. In 1889, the Reverend Henry Ward Beecher made common cause with Lillie Langtry and three other maidens in hailing the happy properties of Pears' Soap. A possibly apocryphal story has it that early in this century, one stage beauty wrote the following open letter: "Dear Mrs. Pinkham, I have taken three bottles of your Lydia Pinkham compound and feel like a new man." As advertising boomed in the twenties and thirties, so did testimonial-giving. Silent-film star Constance Talmadge established a record for the course when, in the interests of her latest movie, she juxtaposed her charms to some four hundred products, ranging from an aspirin tablet to a grand piano, in one brief day. As she was in a hurry to go to Europe, she didn't find out exactly what she had plugged until a rash of ads appeared in *Liberty* several weeks later.

Constance may just have been an energetic consumer, but every now and then one of her fellow testifiers, by a burst of candor or slip of tongue, has given skeptics grist for their nasty mills. Lady Diana Manners, for instance, after having joined the highly placed ranks of Pond's face-cream endorsers (two Queens, a battalion of Princesses and several regiments of society women), told newspaper reporters that her beauty was attributable to "fresh air, exercise and plenty of soap and water."

Then there was Princess Maryanna Mayorskaya ("Mindful of the inherent responsibilities of royalty in shaping the ideas of bourgeoisie, I am careful never to be seen in public without a Borzoi book") who turned out to be a small, non-titled man. And how can one forget C. K. "Red" Cagle, the celebrated West Point football player of a generation or so back, who always used a Royal portable typewriter? "It is the greatest aid I ever knew in keeping up my grades," swore Red. Upon investigation, it was discovered that in a class of 266, the Royal portable user was 232nd in math, 207th in English and 239th in history.

It was into a compromised world, then, that Jules Alberti leaped after the war, determined to bring *believability* back onto the billboards. "It cannot be emphasized too much or too often," expounds the slick-paper *Revised Primer of Testimonial Advertising*, put out by Endorsements, Inc., "that testimonials are *only effective when believable and only believable when*: 1. The testimonial is true. 2. The personality and product are logically connected. 3. The testimonial copy is simple, sincere and honest."

How does Jules meet these requirements? Well, he has a "research" staff which keeps tabs on the doings of celebrities; dossiers on some seven thousand more or less famous persons are now held at Endorsement, Inc.'s offices. When an advertising agency calls on Jules, he immediately sends samples of the product to be plugged to potential and *believable* pluggers. A month or so later, he asks the recipient notables if they can "sincerely endorse the products" they've been asked to try out. One or more is likely to respond in the affirmative, their sincerity having presumably been whetted by the offer of $1,000, a large quantity of whatever they are prepared to enthuse over (Elsa Maxwell, Cobina Wright and Gracie Allen got a year's supply of Mazola oil) and gobs of free publicity.

Of course Jules is very careful about selecting his notables. He's been quoted as advising a group of advertising executives to "examine yourself and explore your soul." He elucidated: "I'm critical of the endorsement that has obviously been bought and paid for without any attempt to disguise the fact." What does this mean exactly? It means: "Don't show Marilyn Monroe waxing her own car. People won't believe it."

Guided by such high principles, Jules has given Joe DiMaggio an opportunity to tell America which breakfast cereal, aftershave lotion, cigarette lighter and other manly items he goes for. Jules also amassed a bushel of actresses who sigh over a shampoo, athletes who exult in a chewing gum and—after a long, hot search—ten Southern farmers who live on a laxative. . . .

In all his labors, one is continually reminded, Jules seeks *believability*. Marlene Dietrich's picture appears in a magazine spread for Amm-i-dent ammoniated toothpaste. But her name isn't mentioned. No quote as to Amm-i-dent's efficacy and tastiness comes from her sealed lips. (Not a single glistening tooth is visible.) *Believability?* Why, what is there for the reader to believe or disbelieve? There's Marlene and there's a tube of Amm-i-dent. Jules bears no responsibility for what the reader adduces.

The campaign of which Jules is most proud is the one he pulled off for Cyma watches. A series of ads for this relatively minor-brand timepiece featured General MacArthur, Mrs. Roosevelt, J. Edgar Hoover, Robert Oppenheimer, Warren Austin, Carlos P. Romulo, Leopold Stokowski, Cecil B. DeMille, Helen Keller and good old testifying Joe DiMaggio. Does every one of these eminent folk keep their momentous appointments by a Cyma? Sorry, no way of telling, since all any of them did was to accept an award from the company. Under the headlines, "World Famous for Distinguished Service," each layout puts forth a picture of the given personage, then—a little ways down the column—suggests: "For those you would honor with pride there is nothing finer than a Cyma watch." *Believability?* One may believe in General MacArthur or not, but any connection between the General and Cyma watches is purely the doing of Jules and Cyma's ad man. Jules reports that the series "paid off handsomely."

Why do testimonials pay off—"skeptics and cynics to the contrary" as Jules puts it? The identification of acned teen-agers and frustrated matrons with Grace Kelly? Young America's adulation for Joe DiMaggio? Mature America's regard for Helen Keller? Are these feelings somehow being distorted when they are put to the service of soaps, watches and breakfast cereals? But this again is not within the ethical purview of Jules Alberti. His one solid axiom is the need to sell, and all his major propositions follow.

What exactly is one to believe from the Cyma campaign? Is there some difference between the original concept of an endorsement and the endorsement paid for in advance? And what of the coincidence of a movie star publicly declaring her affection for a cigarette just as her latest hit reaches town? But Jules's ethical system, which starts with the need to sell, stops at these nice questions. . . .

The days of the patently phoney testimonial, of "the endorsement that has been bought and paid for without any attempt to disguise the fact," are over, thanks to the codes of the Federal Trade Commission, the Better Business Bureau, Jules Alberti and common sense. As the world becomes a more sophisticated place, the techniques of advertising are continually being refined by sophisticated men like Jules, but somehow, despite the very latest appurtenances of sincere public relations, like charcoal-gray suits and narrow brims and large sentiments, the good old huckster spirit lingers.

Twenty-five years ago, when Constance Talmadge was smiling indiscriminately on all free enterprise, Alva Johnston wrote:

It has become an unwritten law with the better testimonial houses to avoid obvious mendacity, when artfully arranged truth works just as well. . . . The ideal endorsement technique today is to make no false statements. The golden rule is never to fool the public; let it fool itself.

So the new *believable* look in testimonials is not so very new after all, and the reforming proclivities of Endorsements, Inc. notwithstanding, it still looks like a case of *caveat emptor*.

# II. MEDIA

## AN INTRODUCTION [1]

"Markets make media," writes [professor of advertising at Harvard Business School] Neil Borden; a bald but complete, apparently simple but unquestionably true statement. The problem is: there are too many markets, and they overlap. There are male and female markets. There is an upper-class market, a middle-class market, a lower-class market. There are urban, rural and (definitely, now; painstaking research has proved the visible fact) suburban markets. There are old-folks markets, middle-aged markets, young-married markets, teen-age markets, children's markets. And, of course, there are the markets segregated by common interests: the home-furnishings-and-decorations market, the sports-car market, the high-fidelity market, the baby-products market, the gourmet market, the fashion market. To reach these many markets there are many media: some 1,750 daily newspapers, 450 television and 3,300 radio broadcasting stations, 600 consumer magazines, 325,000 billboards, and several million car cards in vehicles of public transportation. Only the blind and deaf or utterly comatose (who rarely spend much money anyway, or some method would be found to reach them) can avoid daily contact not with just one but with dozens of advertising media. No company—not even General Motors, with some 4 per cent of the entire national output rolling through its factories—can hope to make a splash in all of them. The advertiser's problem is one of selection; and standing in serried ranks, waiting to help him make that selection, are thousands upon thousands of media salesmen, carrying literally millions of facts and figures, real and alleged.

In no other area of his work does the advertising man find so much information, so much apparently logical basis for his

[1] From *Madison Avenue, U.S.A.,* by Martin Mayer, author of *Wall Street: Men and Money,* writer for magazines. This selection is from Chapter IX ("Oysters and Pearls: Media Selections," p137-42). Harper & Bros. New York. 1958. Copyright © 1958 by Martin Prager Mayer. Reprinted by permission of the author.

decisions. Circulation and audience figures, combined with rate cards, give a "cost per thousand" figure, which tells the advertiser how much he must spend to put his message before a thousand people by the use of this particular medium. Breakdowns of the circulation number enable the advertiser to compare his sales in a market to the circulation delivered in that market by each advertising medium. Often a medium will even deliver an analysis of the brand preferences, economic status, personal habits and psychological quirks of its audience, which the manufacturer can then compare with the characteristics of the people who buy his product, as developed by the consumer research companies. And yet, media buying remains as personal a matter as anything else in advertising—a business of hunches and intuitions, of favors done and favors received, of calculated threats, denunciations and punishments. "Anybody who tells you that media buying is entirely scientific," says senior vice-president Jim McCaffrey of . . . [Ogilvy, Benson & Maher], "is either a liar or a coward."

The problem is that all media purchases represent a choice of alternatives, and only rarely are the alternatives really comparable. No advertiser can know for sure that a $3 million network television program will do more or less for him than the same amount of money put into local television, or radio, or newspapers, or magazines, or billboards, or a combination of all of them—or even a different network program. He can, it is true, get relative cost-per-thousand figures if he insists: he can discover that his $65,000-a-week television program went into 9 million homes, at a cost of $7.22 per thousand homes; that his $22,242 full-page black-and-white weekly ad in *Life* went to a paid circulation of 6 million, at a cost of $3.71 per thousand primary readers; that his one-minute announcements on radio station KWK St. Louis, running thirty times a week for $21 each, cost about $1.27 per thousand households listening; that his 1,000-line ad in the Louisville *Courier-Journal* cost $830, or $2.08 per thousand homes receiving the paper; that his 20-second spot announcement on WRCA-TV, New York, appearing Monday through Friday at 7:29 P.M., all year long, cost $880 every night, or about $2.80 for every thousand viewing households; that his

46 billboards in Portland, Oregon, cost him roughly $48 each every month, or 25 cents per thousand for the 192,000 pairs of eyes which will pass by during the month.

Unfortunately, when the advertiser knows all this (and he can find out most of it easily enough, by checking survey data against the figures in the Standard Rate and Data Service monthly books), he still knows nothing   Even as a matter of statistics pure and simple, the figures are meaningless.   The audience for the network television show is extrapolated from a study of the viewing habits of some 930 families which happen to have Nielsen Audimeters in working order attached to their television sets, and this procedure does not give an exact measurement. (Measurements of audiences for local stations are even more inexact; they might be described as sound guesses.)   Moreover, the sponsor of a half-hour network show gets three one-minute commercial cracks at his audience, reducing the cost per thousand *per commercial minute* to $2.42 a home.   This figure for a minute compares favorably with $2.80 per thousand for a 20-second spot announcement on WRCA-TV, a local station.   And, finally, two and one half people are watching every television set (it says here; perhaps the half is a nitwit), so the cost per thousand *people,* per commercial minute is only $1. Demonstrably, though it costs $3 million a year, the television show is really very cheap; on the bandwagon, everybody, please.

*Life's* circulation, as compared with the TV audience, is very directly measured, the final figures sworn, certified and examined by the Audit Bureau of Circulations.   (How the circulation was obtained, of course, is another matter; people turn on their television sets more or less voluntarily, while somebody sells them magazines subscriptions, often forcibly.)   But the paid circulation is obviously not the full measure of *Life's* audience; several people live in the home which subscribes.   Uncle Joe comes visiting and riffles through, the copy is thrown in the dustbin and picked up by the garbage man, who carries it home for the baby to cut up.   Studies by Alfred Politz Research tell *Life,* which tells the world, that no fewer than 28,033,000 Americans over ten years old see any given issue of *Life* magazine. On this basis, the cost per thousand readers of the magazine is only about 86 cents—and a magazine ad doesn't flash right off the screen and go for good, it stays around the house for a while. Truly, a bargain.

Then there are the intangibles. Billboards may be very cheap, but how much of a selling message can you put on a billboard? Most American families do a good part of their shopping browsing through the newspaper, looking at the grocery store and department store ads: what is the value to a manufacturer of being there on the page with the retailers while the lady shops? Radio time is so cheap that you may be able to hit the lady on the head with your jingle over and over again, until you get it so firmly implanted in her noggin that she will remember it until the day she dies; what is the commercial (ignoring the moral) significance of making your brand name part of a customer's mental climate? Sponsorship of a network television show associates your product with an entertainment feature and perhaps a well-beloved personality, and there must be some money in this "gratitude factor." Appearance in a magazine associates a product, however dimly, with that magazine's editorial prestige, and people tend to believe what they read. But who are people? And what does any manufacturer care about how many *people* he reaches with his ad? He needs prospects, customers; and to separate the active, extravagant, upper-middle-income younger wheat from the tired, thrifty, low-income older chaff, all bound up together in the one mass-audience statistic, is a task beyond even the panjandrums of the research business (though they try; God knows, they try). Lots of women watch the championship prize fights and World Series baseball games sponsored by Gillette Blue Blades; what use are they to Gillette?

Even when the *type* of medium is clearly dictated by the nature of the product—a women's magazine for a baby food, for example—the advertiser has some hard choices ahead of him. He can aim directly at his market with a page in, say, *Baby Talk,* at slightly more than $6 a thousand, going to half a million recent mothers but going to them in a peculiar way, arriving free of charge, wrapped up in a package of diapers from the diaper service.   Or he can hit at the lower-class young women's market, buying a page in, for example, *Modern Romances* at a cost of $2.55 a thousand, reaching a circulation of more than a million (82.4 per cent of them married, runs the litany; 72.5 per cent with children; 22.4 per cent with children under two years old), presenting more editorial matter on baby care than any other nonbaby magazine except *Parents'*.   Or perhaps he should buy *Parents'* at $4.85 a thousand.   Or hook his wagon onto one of the three big general women's magazines, with their high prestige value: *Ladies' Home Journal* ($3.65 a thousand), *McCall's* ($3.60 a thousand), *Good Housekeeping* ($3.40 a thousand).

Each magazine offers more or less different readers, though there is obviously some overlapping (try to find accurate statistics about overlapping, someday; it isn't easy).   And each offers something more than readers—an editorial approach, an atmosphere, a position in the community.   Different agencies take different attitudes toward these immeasurable factors.   Ogilvy, Benson & Maher would not wish to put money into *Modern Romances* because it feels, in Jim McCaffrey's words, "that a product is judged by the company it keeps."   Grey Advertising, on the other hand, sees no reason not to spend clients' money in the "romance books," because they offer prospects at a low cost per thousand.   "If a lady's reading *True Story* magazine," says Grey's Larry Deckinger, "does she think she's reading junk? No.   She reads it because she believes in it."   The final decision may boil down to a choice between the *Ladies' Home Journal* and *Good Housekeeping*, "LHJ" with its big page, high-quality coated paper, superior printing job; "Good House" with its small page and lesser printing job—but with the "Good Housekeeping Seal of Approval" to offer any advertiser who buys at least two pages a year.   "What's the Good House Seal worth?" asks president Bill Kearns of Ted Bates & Company.   "I don't know.   I think it's worth something—I *know* it's worth a good deal to *Good Housekeeping*.   But I can't measure it."

And yet, somehow, after much anguish and analysis, the allocations are made, the client's money is spent.   In 1957 the allocations among types of media, in terms of money spent by national advertisers, were approximately as follows:

$150 million on billboards and car cards;

$300 million on radio commercials and programs;

$1 billion on television commercials and programs;

$1.2 billion on newspaper advertisements, including ads placed by local retailers under "co-operative" arrangements whereby the manufacturer paid the bills (this figure is most inexact because of the difficulty of estimating co-op money spent);

$1.35 billion on advertisements in the three main categories of magazines: consumer, farm and business.

The largest single advertising medium was the CBS Television Network, with sales estimated at $210 million; the NBC Television Network trailed about $40 million behind. In third position, with $130 million of advertising sales, came *Life*. No other single medium took in more than $100 million from advertisers; and the great majority of media, of course, took in less than $10 million.

### THE BIG THREE [2]

#### 1. *Newspapers*

The local advertising medium is, of course, the newspaper. Newspapers are the oldest advertising media, and they are still, in grand total, by far the biggest. Though they receive only 27 cents out of the manufacturer's media dollar, they take nearly 78 cents of every dollar spent by retailers and grocery stores to advertise themselves and the wares they sell. (Some of this money comes from manufacturers, too, via "co-operative advertising programs," by which the retailer advertises that the manufacturer's products are for sale in his store and the manufacturer pays part or all of the advertising bill—usually all, whether he planned it that way or not.)

[2] From *Madison Avenue, U.S.A.*, by Martin Mayer. This selection is from Chapter X ("Hitting Them Where They Live," p 153-69) and Chapter XI ("All Across the Country: Magazines," p 172-81). Harper & Bros. New York. 1958. Copyright © 1958 by Martin Prager Mayer. Reprinted by permission of the author.

Advertising space in newspapers is sold at so much per agate line per column (there are fourteen agate lines to an inch, roughly twenty-two inches of type, usually eight columns wide, on a standard-size newspaper page; a full page runs 2,400 to 2,500 agate lines). Sometimes the line rate is "flat," and will not change however much space an advertiser buys; sometimes it is subject to quantity discounts, which may range up to 25 per cent for the advertiser who takes the equivalent of forty or so pages a year (a considerable requirement: forty pages of national advertising in the Chicago *Tribune,* for example, costs $162,489.60 at full discount).

The basic line rate applies to an ad placed "r-o-p," for run-of-paper, meaning that it can appear anywhere at all, on any page, at the top or the bottom of a column, buried in among other ads or next to reading matter, as the luck falls. A good agency space buyer ought to be able to protect his client against a really evil fate, but if the advertiser wishes a complete guarantee, he may order specific pages or positions, at an extra charge. Thus, the basic national rate of the daily New York *Times* is $2.05 per agate line ($4,920 a page) before discounts; an advertiser who wants to guarantee a position at the top of a column and next to reading matter must, however, pay an additional 85 cents per line; an advertiser who insists that he must be on the society page pays an extra 25 cents a line; an advertiser who demands a specified position on page 2 or page 3 pays an extra $1.50 a line. In practice, these charges are at "publisher's option," and apply only if the advertiser insists on his position. If his agency merely asks for it nicely, and he is a regular customer, he will likely get what he wants at no extra charge.

Many national advertisers feel that they are already paying an extra charge—indeed, that they are being held up on the highway—because the newspaper's line rate is always far lower for the local retail store than it is for the manufacturer. On the average, the retailer pays less than half what the newspaper will charge a national advertiser for the same space. This argument is quite old now, and to all practical purposes it was settled in St. Louis in the 1930's, when the newspapers cut their national rate to bring it level with their retail rate and gained virtually no additional national advertising for their pains (which were considerable: the first reaction was a howl of rage from retailers, who wanted corresponding cuts in *their* rates).

The national advertiser's complaint was never entirely legitimate anyway, since a considerable rate differential is clearly justified by the facts. The newspaper keeps every penny of the retail rate, while 15 per cent of the national rate must go to an advertising agency. Newspapers do not need to maintain large sales staffs to convince the local retailer that he needs them, while the national advertiser and his agency must usually be wheedled and wangled, wined and dined, and sold. Local ads are a positive asset to the paper in the eyes of its readers, who look for retailers' announcements of sales, bargains and specials, while the national ad is just something on the page. Finally, the local merchant advertises week in, week out, at all seasons, while the national advertiser usually schedules his appearance only in the heavy buying seasons of spring and fall. "The retailer signs up for a year," says Herbert Moloney of Moloney, Regan & Schmitt [New York] which represents such papers as the Denver *Post,* the Cincinnati *Enquirer,* the Portland *Oregonian,* the Houston *Post* and the Toledo *Blade.* "If the copy for his ad doesn't arrive on time, the paper simply puts a box around his space and writes, 'Compliments of John Smith's Store.' A national advertiser who comes in and goes out can't expect the same rate." . . .

Media representatives like Moloney, Regan & Schmitt sell the great bulk of newspaper space which is bought by national advertisers, and are ordinarily the advertiser's and the agency's only regular contact with the newspaper. (Somebody from the paper will usually come to town once a year, and the rep sets up a cocktail party for him; and he may sell too.) New York newspapers handle their own national advertising sales to Madison Avenue agencies, and a few out-of-town papers maintain their own national sales offices in New York. Usually, however, a salesman representing a number of papers can do a better job for less (the newspaper rep's commission customarily though not always runs around 10 per cent), and the paper relies on its rep. Though reps solicit each other's papers once in a while, the relationship between newspaper and national representative is a highly stable one, and shifts occur very rarely.

The rep's job is threefold: to sell newspapers as a medium, to sell the markets in which his papers are published, and to sell his specific newspaper against competing journals in the same market. Even in big cities, the second part of the job may be the whole battle, because there is only one paper in the market—in three of the nation's twenty-five largest cities, Kansas City, Atlanta and Providence, the newspaper business is a monopoly. "But sometimes it's more difficult to sell a single-paper market," says Leonard Marshall of Cresmer & Woodward [New York], the firm handling, among others, the Los Angeles *Times*, which carries more advertising linage than any other newspaper in America. "You're the only one shouting, 'Tucson! Tucson!' When there are two of you shouting, you seem more important."

Selling a market to an advertiser whose sales in the market are low is usually a hopeless task, but the reps will try it if their papers give them sufficient statistical material to make a good case. Some markets, for example, are expanding rapidly by the stimulus of new industry; the rep offers the advertiser a chance to win a dominant position "in the fastest-growing market in North Carolina." Often a brand which is important nationally sells poorly in a given city; the rep for a newspaper in that city (arriving with a study of brand sales in the market, ordered by the newspaper) urges the advertiser not to let his competition run away with this "A" market, but to push forward via newspapers to his rightful place. At the same time, the rep is selling the competition on the need to advertise more heavily, to hold a leading brand position. Some newspapers have gone to considerable trouble to organize their medium-sized cities as good "test markets" for new products or new packages, arranging with retailers for inexpensive store audits and supplying certain research services at low fees or without charge. The Springfield (Massachusetts) *Union-News-Republican* advertises the slogan, "Test Effectively, Test Efficiently, Test Springfield." For the convenience of manufacturers who want to try something out in several medium-sized cities scattered through the country, there is a special organization, the Burgoyne Test-City Group, which advises on proper balancing and on technical aspects of the test.

Competitive selling in a market often involves a good deal of infighting. Paper A may have a larger circulation than paper B, or a lower cost-per-thousand; or it may reach a section of the community which is more desirable from the advertiser's point of view. "Suppose we're running a grocery ad, and the budget gives us only one paper in Cleveland," says J. Walter Thompson's Art Porter. "The Cleveland *Press* has the big, family circulation. But if we have an ad for the New York Central or for F. I. du Pont [a stock-brokerage house], we want to reach men readers, we'll put it in the morning *Plain Dealer,* get the commuters." Often, two newspapers make completely conflicting claims: page 607 of a recent issue of *Newspaper Rates and Data* contains a full-page ad announcing that "Dallas *News* readers have MORE . . . spend MORE . . . and there are MORE of them!"; on page 608 the Dallas *Times Herald* claims that it "Reaches More People with More Money to Spend!" The explanation is that the *Times Herald* has a larger circulation in the Dallas metropolitan area ("Where 57.9 per cent of the families have 68.8 per cent of the buying power in the whole Dallas Retail Trading Zone"), while the Dallas *News* has a large circulation in the surrounding countryside ("Out-of-town customers are responsible for 35.2 per cent of Dallas' retail sales volume!").

Newspapers, capitalizing on their important position in the community, sell an advertiser more than just space; they also sell "merchandising help," offering to broaden a manufacturer's distribution in local stores and convince local retailers that they should put their best efforts behind a brand advertised in the local paper. Representatives from the newspaper will work with the manufacturer's sales staff in analyzing the local market, and may even go along with the salesmen to pep up a presentation to local buyers. The case is stated most simply by Jim Gediman, a lean, traditionally cynical, dedicated newspaperman who is executive vice-president of the Hearst Advertising Service, which acts as a national rep for nearly all the Hearst papers: "Nobody

will ever know a market like a newspaperman; it's a relationship like a parish. Even if he's a dope he can't help being an
expert, better than an Einstein if Einstein's perspective is the
Biltmore bar and the Westchester route. A rabbit, to put the
matter crudely, knows more about warrens than an eagle."

Newspapers love to publish case histories of what their merchandising staffs have done for advertisers, without charge. One
big booklet, called *The Big Plus* in honor of what newspapers
give advertisers, described half a dozen such cases—among them
a set of seven mailings sent to all salesmen at local appliance
stores by the Indianapolis *Star* and *News,* to back up a Frigidaire
campaign; a free carton of cigarettes and a free silent butler
(somewhat gaudy, this) sent to the *wives* of executives and
buyers at major local tobacco outlets, distributed by the Toledo
*Blade* in honor of a Philip Morris campaign announcing a new
package; a set of Squibb "Open House Specials" displays physi-
cally set up in drugstore windows by members of the Seattle
*Times* advertising department. (The displays, of course, were
provided by Squibb, and bold as brass on each of them appears
the common box, "as advertised in *Life.*")

It is general practice among newspapers in medium-sized
and smaller cities to send a weekly newsletter to all drugstores
and grocery stores, notifying proprietors that certain brands will
be advertised by their makers in the newspaper during the coming week. Often, for a larger campaign, special mailings will
be sent, including some gimmick to remind the retailer that he
ought to stock up now, to be ready for the big demand that will
follow the newspaper ads. (If the retailer stocks up, the manufacturer has already won the battle: "inventory pressure" always moves merchandise.) And, of course, the newspaper's retail advertising staff will suggest "tie-in" ads to the retail stores,
to accompany the big national campaign; this activity, while useful to the manufacturer, cannot be counted as a favor to him by
the paper.

In their efforts to help the manufacturer while helping themselves, some newspapers make great expenditures on market and
consumer research. The Chicago *Tribune* runs a Consumer Pur-

chase Panel. . . . The Los Angeles *Times* and the Cleveland *Press* conduct home inventories, sending members of their staff to a selected sample of households to check personally on the contents of the pantry shelves; they also look around to see if a newspaper is in the house. Other papers, among them the New York *World Telegram,* the Cincinnati *Post,* the Boston *Herald-Traveler* and the St. Louis *Globe-Democrat,* conduct regular store audits in a carefully selected sample of local stores, to determine the effective distribution of nationally advertised products in the local market.

The most elaborate such program, by far, is run by the Hearst Advertising Service, which supplies national advertisers with "an operating sales control" for each of the twelve markets in which there is a Hearst newspaper. These "control" plans include complete detail maps of each city and its suburbs, subdivided into sales districts according to traffic flow, with the different kinds of stores clearly marked on the maps. Pittsburgh, for example, has twenty sales divisions; Baltimore has twenty-seven. Experience has taught the Hearst people that by keeping an eye on a few of these districts a manufacturer can predict what will happen throughout the entire city; if desired (for a small fee), the Hearst merchandising staff will watch these districts for him. When a Hearst merchandising man, checking through a retail store, finds that an advertiser's product is out of stock, he will kindly call the distributor; if he finds the advertiser's point-of-sale posters and display cartons reposing quietly in their shipping box, he will (bullying the retailer if required) put them up himself. Little things like that can make a great difference.

Not every newspaper likes the idea of merchandising support to advertisers. . . . And not every advertiser is sold on the value of the newspaper's merchandising support: as some clients would rather dispense with fancy agency services and pay less than 15 per cent commission, agencies would often like to eliminate the merchandising help and pay a lower line rate. "These guys," says one media buyer, "put more money into preparing the reports of what they've done than they put into actual work on the job." Others feel that a distinction must be made between work done by the newspaper on its own initiative, in a disorganized way, and work carefully planned by the paper, the agency and the advertiser in conference to determine what this brand really wants in this locality and what this newspaper merchandising staff can really do to help it.

There is another problem about newspaper merchandising support, too, which most people in the business would rather not discuss—the question of when the nice offer to help the advertiser becomes a nasty threat to hurt the company which does not advertise or (worst of all) withdraws its advertising from the paper. In *National Advertising in Newspapers,* a book published in 1946, Neil Borden reported on the pressure which newspaper publishers have brought to bear on reluctant advertisers and their agencies—floods of inspired mail from local retailers and distributors, queries from local bankers, planted questions at board of directors meetings, even letters from congressmen. Borden's book was too pessimistic about the future of newspapers as national media. He did his research in wartime, and used as his reference figure the newspapers' 28-cent share of the national advertiser's dollar in 1941, the last prewar year. With television on the horizon and magazines showing spectacular circulation gains over 1941, Borden clearly felt that the newspapers would be unlikely to hold on to their 28 per cent share; in fact, however, despite the emergence of television, newspapers in 1957 had held even, at 27 per cent. But Borden's contention that many advertisers are reluctant to buy into newspapers, for fear that they will have terrible trouble buying out, still held true eleven years after his book was published.

## 2. *Radio and TV*

Advertisers who put their local budgets into radio and television stations, buying "spot announcements" on local programs, receive neither the rewards nor the punishments that may come from close association with so powerful a member of the community as the newspaper publisher. Most broadcasting stations do offer merchandising services (some of them swap free announcements for chain stores against a guarantee by the stores to favor advertisers on the local station in putting up point-of-sale material), but the broadcaster cannot pretend to the expertise of the publisher. Considerably less of a broadcasting station's revenue comes from local advertisers, and the station staff is not nearly so closely in touch with the retailing community as a newspaper staff will be. What the local broadcaster sells is, essentially, his audience—plus the special selling values, if any, of locally originated programs.

Though both must sell their local markets, the newspaper and the broadcasting station have essentially different selling problems. Newspapers, as the Sunday New York *Times* and Chicago *Tribune* prove every week, are almost infinitely expansible: a newspaper can make space for all the ads it sells. The broadcasting day, however, has specified limits, and it is considered bad business as well as bad public relations to sell more than seven minutes an hour for advertising messages. There is some disagreement as to the values of forward placement in a newspaper, but even those who believe that there is a diffierence between an ad on page 7 and an ad on page 15 will agree that the difference is slight. The difference between being on a television station at 9:30 P.M. and being there at 9:30 A.M. is on the order of five women to one—ten to one if you are aiming at both the male and the female audience. Moreover, a newspaper's circulation is known to the last integer, verified by the Audit Bureau of Circulations on sworn statements; and a newspaper's audience is loyal, taking the same paper day after day, so an advertiser can be told with some exactness what he is buying. The audience for a local station flows in and out by twists of the dial, with loyalty to programs rather than to stations, so the composition of the station audience changes from half hour to half hour. (Though people do appear to have some loyalty to *radio* stations.) And the number of people in that audience at any minute is, simply, undiscoverable. Four research services try to measure these matters, and they come up with four different answers.

Many television stations have very little time of their own to sell. Of the nation's five hundred stations, one hundred (all

of them among the 150 largest) are members of the "basic"
CBS or NBC network, which means that any advertiser buying
a CBS or NBC network show automatically buys time on these
stations. (Another 50 are on the "must-buy" list of the ABC
network.) Of the eighteen possibly valuable broadcast hours,
the two big networks "option" nine hours from their basic
affiliates, which means that these stations cannot without damned
good reason (and not too often, even then) carry anything in
these nine hours except sponsored network programs. For giving the network the use of its facilities during these hours, a
station receives from the network roughly 28 per cent of its
charges for time, plus the right to sell some sixty seconds an
hour, thirty each during the on-the-hour and on-the-half-hour
breaks for station identification (most stations charge about 60
per cent of their full hour rate for these two spots). In addition,
of course, the local station receives the immensely popular network programs which draw the big audiences.

Though the networks can (by Federal Communications Commission rule) compel their affiliated stations to accept no more
than nine hours of network programming during the eighteen-
hour broadcast day, both NBC and CBS offer another five to
seven hours a day of network television shows. Provided the
network shows are sponsored and produce revenue, most affiliated stations will accept them, taking the sure 28 per cent
(plus 60 per cent for the spots, which are easier to sell when
the station offers "adjacencies" to network programming) rather
than going after the full-time rate and assuming the costs of independent programming. On these key network affiliates, which
have the biggest audiences and cover areas accounting for two-
thirds of the nation's total retail sales, the national advertiser
looking to buy local markets finds only a limited list of "avail-
abilities." Still, there are the "chain breaks" (the twenty-second
spots and ten-second "ID's," so called because they appear with
the station identification), the occasional local programs, the
"syndicated" non-network half-hour film show (*Zorro, Whirly-
birds*), and the late movie, a few remaining bits of merchandise
for sale.

All but a handful of the nation's five hundred television stations are affiliated with one network or another, and during the peak viewing hours (7:30-10:30, more or less, depending on time zones) more than four hundred of them will be broadcasting network shows. Nevertheless—despite the limited amount of time for sale on the best stations—advertisers in 1957 paid some $400 million for television spot announcements, local programs, half-hour films and "participations" on local movie shows.

The sale of local television time is handled mostly by the same sort of organization—the national representative—which handles newspaper space. (The NBC and CBS networks both maintain "spot sales" organizations for the five stations that each of them owns and operates, and these organizations also handle spot sales for a handful of key affiliated but independently owned stations. The national reps feel—and feel strongly—that the networks have pressured their key affiliates into giving the spot representation business to the network's own office; as one of them puts it, "There's no question that some stations which wanted network affiliation badly were told that affiliation and representation went hand in hand." ABC does not maintain a sales office for the stations it owns; ABC's spot business is handled mostly by Blair-TV [New York] partly by the Katz Agency.) In one respect, the station rep's assignment differs from that of the newspaper rep: an advertiser who wants to reach the entire newspaper-reading public will have to buy space in every paper in town, while the flowing nature of the broadcast audience gives him the chance to reach just about everybody with several TV spots on a single station. "When we hear that an agency has money for one of our markets," says Wells Barnett of Blair-TV, "we want it all." Possibly for this reason the station rep receives a higher commission—a customary 15 per cent instead of the newspaper rep's customary 10 per cent.

Stations divide their broadcast day into periods which carry different price tags, according to the estimated differences in the size of the audience. In some smaller towns there may be

only two categories—"A," for 7 P.M. to 11 P.M., and "B," for
6 A.M. to 7 P.M. and 11 P.M. to midnight. In the bigger cities
some of the most prosperous stations have managed to make
five and even six divisions of the broadcast day, to soak the
last few hundred dollars out of the very peak listening hours.
Thus, WCAU-TV, Philadelphia, charges $750 for a twenty-
second announcement between 8 P.M. and 10:30 P.M., $500 for
the same announcement just before or just after this choice
period, $350 after 11 or before 7:30 P.M., $225 during weekday
daylight hours, and only $150 before 8 A.M.

These neat pricing divisions are obscured, however, by a
bewildering overlay of quantity discounts, frequency discounts,
special plans, and the like. Thus, on WCAU, an advertiser
who buys an announcement for twenty-six consecutive weeks
receives 5 per cent off the rate; 10 per cent if he buys it for
a whole year. Or he can buy a "six-plan," which gives him
six announcements in a week, before 6:45 P.M. or after
11:30 P.M., at 25 per cent off the usual rate; or a "twelve-
plan," on the same terms, at 45 per cent off. Few stations have
so simple a system as this one; at most, spots per week, spots
per year, dollar volume, "anchored" spots (where the time slot
is guaranteed), "floating" spots (where the station merely
guarantees to put the announcement on the air at some time
during the broadcast day), combinations of programs and spots
all give different discounts. A few smaller stations offer advertisers a pure gamble: all the spots not sold today for, say,
$1,000, which may buy a minimum number or ten or twenty
more than the minimum, as the ball bounces. Scientific media
buyers do not like this sort of thing.

Almost every station also has some time to sell in larger
than twenty-second pieces. "The cross we bear in this business,"
says Daniel Denenholz of the Katz Agency [New York], an
unusual representation firm which handles newspapers as well
as broadcasting stations, "is that people think of spot announcements only. We can offer film shows, live local shows,
too." About three fifths of station revenues from non-network
sales to national advertisers comes from spot announcements;

the rest comes from sponsorship of local programs or film shows
bought individually from film producers, or of segments of
Hollywood movies which the stations broadcast more or less
full length. Many stations try to give their movie presentations
a local flavor—"at least," says Wells Barnett, "the best of them
do. They take an announcer and make him a kind of film
jockey, 'Your host for Bacchanalian movies, every day at this
hour.' "

Until 1956 only a limited amount of modern feature movie
material was available to local stations; then the Hollywood
studios suddenly opened the floodgates, selling off great quantities of former box-office triumphs. Television rights to the
films were bought by syndicates organized for this purpose,
and the syndicates peddled packages to the local stations. For
the stations feature films have been an audience bonanza, and
occasionally a business headache, because a promising film
package will often cost more money than a station has on hand.
There has been a good deal of bartering, the station giving
the syndicate a certain number of spot announcements in return for a showing of the feature film. (The syndicate then
sells the spot to advertisers at bargain prices.) In a few cases
advertisers have bought the film rights themselves, supplied
films to the stations, and taken big spot campaigns in trade.
Station reps watch such shenanigans with mingled emotions
—but their arrangements with the stations give them some
commission, usually at a reduced figure, on the bartered spots;
and, as Dan Denenholz says, living with the situation while
not accepting it, "the stations have got to have a product."

Feature films also have promoted a little jiggery-pokery in
the measurement of station audiences. Several of the most
widely used "rating" services make their audience surveys during the first week of each month, so the stations make sure
they put on their most attractive feature films, the Clark Gable
and Humphrey Bogart pictures, for that week. Some media
buyers, estimating the size of the local audience for a feature
film program in the three unserviced weeks, deduct 25 per
cent from the rating numbers, "to give a more reasonable fig-

ure." Station reps try to avoid opinions on ratings as much as they can. They discover which of the rating services each advertising agency prefers, and use only that survey when talking to the media buyers from that agency. But, says Wells Barnett, "we don't sell ratings. We can't do it. Some of our stations have good ratings and some don't; if we talk ratings, how are we going to sell the stations that don't have good ones?" Most station reps regard Barnett's attitude as wishful rather than real; a station has nothing to sell but its audience, so there is no way of escaping audience ratings, even though nobody really believes that local ratings are accurate. "Hell," says George Castleman of Peters, Griffin, Woodward, "we *have* to sell ratings. They won't listen to us otherwise."

One of the reasons why station reps must pay so much attention to admittedly inaccurate ratings of local audiences is the fact that many advertisers are currently using spot television for full-scale national campaigns and not merely for local purposes. Expensive as spot announcements are, they still cost less than network shows. "It's contrary to all history," says Clifford Parsells of Ted Bates [ad agency], which puts something more than half its total billings into spot announcements and is the largest spot buyer in the country. "It always used to be true that syndicate buying was cheaper, a page in the *American Weekly* cost you less than a page in all the newspapers that carried *American Weekly*, a radio network show cost you less than spots on all the radio stations. Today, television spots give you a big price advantage over a network buy." Network salesmen would quarrel with Parsells' analysis, arguing that a half-hour network show gives the advertiser *three* one-minute commercials, and that the cost-per-thousand for the three together is slightly lower than the cost-per-thousand of *three* spot announcements on the same line-up of stations. But Parsells and many other media directors feel that there is far more value in three spots reaching different audiences at different times than in three one-minute commercials during a single program. "If your story is good," Parsells says, "you can do a lot more than one third of your sales pitch in the first minute."

If spot television is reasonably priced, however, spot radio is the discount house of the media business. Six one-minute announcements a week at 12:00 noon will cost an advertiser $903, after all discounts, on Philadelphia's WCAU-TV; for the same money he can buy 25 minute spots on WCAU radio. A four-to-one ratio is common in the television/radio comparison (it cuts down to about three-to-one for those television spot advertisers big enough to take advantage of "twelve-plans" instead of "six-plans"). The realization of this big numerical difference—plus the realization, which dawned suddenly on many advertisers, that people still listen to radio—has produced a continuing boom in radio time, which will probably last until the demand for radio spots has raised radio rates to a level where the medium no longer commands so considerable a competitive advantage.

The word is "saturation": radio spot campaigns are saturation campaigns. Exactly how many radio spots must be thrown into a market to saturate it is a question nobody can answer. Daniel Denenholz of the Katz Agency, speaking very conservatively, mentions a minimum of 24 spots per week per station, or 120 every week in a five-station market. BBDO, introducing Hit Parade cigarettes, bought 96 announcements plus 24 news broadcasts a week on each station—600 performances of the Hit Parade jingle going over the airwaves every week in a single five-station city. Ogilvy, Benson & Maher's Jim McCaffrey thinks that 600 a week *must* be too many spots to throw into a single market. "There must be a point of diminishing returns somewhere," he says. "People get fed up, and they're no longer interested in what you have to say." Nevertheless, McCaffrey feels that 200 spots a week is the minimum size for a saturation campaign in a larger market. As Thompson's Art Porter sees it, the question is one of what the competition is doing rather than one of diminishing returns: "If I reach you once, and he reaches you three times, he seems more important than I do."

Perhaps the greater contributor to the present prosperity of spot radio is Henry I. Christal, a cheerful, nervous, broad-

shouldered older man with a fringe of gray hair and big black
eyebrows, who in 1952 retired from Edward Petry & Company, a station rep which handles both radio and television
stations, "and looked around for what I ought to do next.
Radio seemed the most exciting field." Christal was virtually
alone in that opinion in 1952, when radio was cringing away
from the very sight of television's monstrous growth, and published rate cards were being undercut by 70 per cent and more
to try to get some business. Setting up his own office as a rep,
to handle radio alone, Christal took some radio stations from
Petry and lured others to his side by the sheer confidence of
his manner. By the end of 1952 he was selling time for eleven
major stations in eleven major markets.

Christal felt that radio's first need was to establish the fact
that it still had an audience, and there was only one way to
do it: a research study, preferably by the most respected and
incorruptible research organization in the business. That meant
Alfred Politz, whose audience studies for *Life* were agitating
the media world. Christal took his proposal for such a study
to the board of what is now called the Radio Advertising Bureau,
and its members turned him down flat. Among the opinions
expressed was one that radio could not afford to have its
weaknesses exposed by impartial research. So Christal himself,
with his eleven stations, put up all the money for the Politz
study; as he likes to point out, three thousand AM radio stations have benefited from the expensive initiative of these eleven.

Briefly, Politz took a sample of some five thousand people
in twenty-six areas where television was already strong in 1952;
of his sample, 72 per cent owned a television set. He asked
them whether they had listened to radio yesterday, and found
that nearly 70 per cent of them had; he asked them to break
their listening into seven periods—before breakfast, during the
three meals, between meals, and after dinner. He asked them
where they listened (kitchen, dining room, bedroom, living
room, car, etc.) and why. He asked people what they liked
about radio (42 per cent said music, 32 per cent said news),
and what they didn't like (24.6 per cent said too many com-

mercials). And then he asked them a question with truly spectacular publicity value: "Suppose you were at home and heard a sudden rumor that war had broken out. What would you do to find out if the rumor was true?" Sure enough, more than half the people interviewed said they would turn on the radio. This question and answer, though irrelevant to an advertiser's needs, helped bring the Politz study to the attention of almost everybody in the advertising business, and radio was suddenly on its way up again.

What the Politz study proved was that radio had listeners all day long. Politz found that about 15 per cent of all American women listened to radio in the kitchen while preparing dinner, and that about 15 per cent of all men listened to the radio in their cars while driving home from work. The almost immediate result of the study was to sell out the 4 to 7 P.M. period, a circumstance that Christal views with grim humor. "Five years ago," he says, "you couldn't *give away* time between four and six—everybody was supposed to be watching television with the kids." These days the station reps are having a little trouble selling the 9:30 A.M. to 3:30 P.M. stretch (and the evening stretch, when everybody really is watching television), but they're working on it. So is Politz. What troubles advertisers is not fear of a small audience but concern that their commercials are appearing too close in time to other commercials; Pall Mall, for example, has asked all radio stations to be extra careful not to put Pall Mall spots too close to spots for competing cigarettes, or for "objectionable" products, like mouth washes.

Radio stations sell more than audience: they also sell the personalities of their disk jockeys and announcers. "We tell advertisers," says Wells Barnett, stepping out from under his Blair-TV hat and donning his John Blair, Inc. (radio representatives) hat, "that this man on the radio station is your local salesman. He's on from seven to nine in the morning, every day, and he's a known quantity in town. He goes to teen-age proms, runs his show sometimes from a glass-enclosed trailer in the heart of town, everybody knows him." The Radio

Advertising Bureau (now revivified and capable of some spectacular promotions, such as the broadcast of a hundred spots for the Brooklyn-Staten Island ferry over radio stations in Omaha, Nebraska, deliberately driving listeners crazy to prove to advertisers that radio spots are heard) makes the claim in an even stronger fashion. "There are maybe three or four hundred guys in this country today," a spokesman says, "who may not be as good as Arthur Godfrey, but they're doing the same thing, and you can buy them for peanuts.". . .

### 3.  Magazines

More manufacturers advertise in magazines than in all other media put together. Most products are not, after all, of interest to everybody. Only gardeners and exotic cooks want grass seeds, only adolescent girls want slave bracelets, only sportsmen, soldiers and criminals want rifle bullets. To the manufacturers of such products, magazines can offer what no other medium can supply: a selected audience, every member of which may be assumed to have some interest in the manufacturer's product. Magazines thus make it possible for companies with very small advertising budgets to cause a considerable splash in the limited markets at which, by the nature of their product, they must aim. The costs of full-page advertisements in specialized magazines are often under $1,000, and the cost-per-thousand can be (though it usually is not) low. *Popular Gardening, Seventeen* and *The American Rifleman* (necessaries, respectively, to the grass seed maker, the slave bracelet confectioner and the bullet manufacturer) all come in for less than $3.90 per thousand of circulation; if the advertiser can make do with a quarter page, as most advertisers to specialty markets can, his cost-per-thousand drops below a dollar. No other medium can reach certified prospects anywhere near so cheaply.

On the other hand, people who read specialized magazines are often themselves specialists, opinionated, cussed, somewhat unamenable to advertising. Though the manufacturer usually must go after them, if only to keep his name before the most articulate group of people in his market, he may find better sales results with an audience less belligerently interested in his product but still within his market potential (*Living for Young Homemakers* for grass seed; *Field & Stream* for rifle bullets). Some of the circulation of these magazines will be wasted—on apartment dwellers, for example, who read . . . *Living,* on fishermen in the *Field & Stream* audience—but by and large the bulk of the readership is in the advertiser's market. Or the manufacturer may wish to reach out to a market segregated only by sex, the grass-seed man advertising in *Ladies' Home Journal* or *McCall's* to interest women in new ways to achieve a beautiful lawn, the rifle-bullet company advertising in *True* or *Esquire.* Here the waste circulation will begin to run to more than half the total audience—but there is a chance of making new customers for this kind of product. Or the manufacturer may decide to go after everybody who uses grass seed and everybody who buys rifle bullets by advertising in the three mass-circulation "general editorial" magazines, *Life, Saturday Evening Post* and *Look.* Any one of these will probably give him more product users than any of the specialized books—but since the bulk of the vast circulation will be wasted, he will have to pay much higher cost-per-thousand for his customers. On the other hand, his retailers will be impressed with his prosperity and his importance and may give special prominence in the store to a brand which appears "as advertised in *Life.*"

Again, a manufacturer may have a product which appeals to a market segregated by attitude: a man selling a high-quality liqueur or an imported sports car wants people who consider themselves sophisticates, and advertises in *The New Yorker;* a man selling a home ice-cream maker wants people who do *not* consider themselves sophisticates, and advertises in *The American Legion Magazine,* in *Grit,* in *Farm Journal,* all of which go primarily to rural and semirural America. Here, too, *Life* or the *Saturday Evening Post* may reach a greater absolute number of prospects; as always, at much higher cost.

To the media buyer, therefore, the magazine market appears as a great set of eccentric and overlapping circles. The three great circles of *Life,* the *Post,* and *Look* fill nearly all the mar-

ket, reaching nearly two thirds of the households in America—
five sixths of the households with more than $7,000 annual in-
come—during any given month. Partly inside each of these
circles, and covering small sections of the market which the
mass-circulation magazines do not reach, are the magazines
aimed at major categories of the population—men or women,
urban or rural, upper income or lower income. And dotted
mostly inside, a little outside, and all around the bigger circles
are the specialist magazines, for hobbyists, limited age groups,
limited interest categories. New advertisers with new products
usually start in the little circles and work out eventually, if they
are successful, to the mass media. Big advertisers with widely
consumed products like to spend their money to reach the great
audiences.

In selling their space only the small specialized magazines
have a market to themselves, among advertisers whose budgets
are too small to attract salesmen for major media. Otherwise,
every magazine sells in competition with other magazines that
have roughly the same sort of audience (*Newsweek* must sell
against *Time* and *U.S. News and World Report*), in competition with smaller publications covering a product market more
directly (*Newsweek* must fight for a piece of the liquor advertiser's magazine dollar against class magazines like *The New
Yorker,* men's magazines like *Esquire,* leisure-time magazines
like *Sports Illustrated* and *Holiday;* for a piece of the "corporate" advertiser's dollar against business magazines like *Fortune* and *Business Week*), and in competition with the three
giants (any of which can offer an advertiser a big chunk of
*Newsweek's* circulation among their own readership, plus much,
much more). Hence the roughhousing which so disturbs the
leaders of the magazine industry; each magazine salesman, knowing that other magazines are constantly in the advertiser's mind
as alternatives to his own, feels positively obliged to denigrate
his rivals.

Magazine space is sold in theory on a per-line basis, but
actually on a basis of pages, half pages, quarter pages, and so
on. Three sets of rates are quoted: for black and white, black

and one color, or four colors. Thus, the *Saturday Evening Post* charges $23,475 for a black-and-white page, $29,340 for a two-color page, $35,000 for a four-color page (all these prices are subject to quantity discounts ranging from 3 per cent for the advertiser who spends roughly $150,000 a year in the *Post* to 16 per cent for the advertiser who spends about $2 million). Fancy special effects—a fifth color for the manufacturer's package, or a "bleed" effect, with the ad running out to the end of the page instead of maintaining the usual margin—cost extra. Except for the back cover (which in the *Post* costs $12,600 more than an inside four-color page; it is much in demand, because people reading the magazine usually display the back cover to everyone around them), position is not sold in magazines: the advertiser buys his page and takes his chance on where it will appear. But any position can be earned by the regular advertiser. The most prized position is one of the two inside covers, which advertisers earn by steady appearance in the magazine. Once an advertiser has been given an inside cover, he will keep it for that issue every year, provided he maintains his advertising schedule. Among the few selling advantages which a new magazine has is the fact that it can promise inside covers to every advertiser its salesmen approach.

Most magazines sell their circulation figures, the sort of people who make up that circulation, the individual editorial "feel" of the magazine (which must rub off to some extent on its advertisers), and some variety of national merchandising support. The circulation figures are absolutely accurate and audited, and the magazines break them down for advertisers into states, cities and even counties to enable the media departments to keep their statistical tallies. The sort of people included in the circulation is something which the magazine has to prove to the media buyer's satisfaction; among the factors which led to the downfall of *Collier's* was its inability to prove that it held a particularly strong position with any one desirable segment of the community.

Every media buyer uses a copy of the "CMR" *(Consumer Magazine Report)*, issued semiannually by Daniel Starch and

Staff and containing a breakdown of the paid circulation of each
major magazine into age groups, occupations, income categories,
ownership of hard goods from automobiles to iceboxes, and so
forth. The CMR is the result of interviews at some 26,000
households scattered throughout the country ("probably," says
Daniel Starch, "the largest probability sample in the country").
But only a relatively small proportion of the sample buys any one
magazine; data on any magazine with less than a million paid
circulation will be drawn, by statistical likelihood, from less than
500 purchasers. So a salesman who does not like the Starch
results can present to the media buyer a study made by his
publication, which has sent out a mailing (asking age, occupation,
income, etc.) to every twentieth name on the circulation list,
and has received back some 8,500 completed questionnaires. On
the basis of this study, involving many more subscribers than the
Starch sample could turn up (but conducted, perhaps, with
somewhat less impartiality), the salesman supplies the buyer with
a new and more comprehensive analysis of the market he will
buy when he buys this magazine. . . .

The editorial "feel" of a magazine is more difficult to pin
down and thus more difficult to sell; and this question brings
the salesman up against the advertiser's or the buyer's tastes in
national media. Media buyers on Madison Avenue do not as an
ordinary matter read the Fresno *Bee* or listen to station WCCO,
Minneapolis: all they know about the contents of local media is
what somebody has told them. Like everyone else, however, they
are consumers of national media, and they have opinions about
editorial content and television programming which must in some
way color their attitudes. . . . There is one objective measurement
in this area: the *Lloyd Hall Editorial Reports,* a service which
measures the editorial linage devoted by each magazine to each of
some forty-odd topics. In theory, a magazine prints pieces on
subjects that interest its readers, and if some kind of product
has been receiving "support" in a magazine's editorial section
(beauty care, music, furniture, fishing), this magazine should
be a good medium for that product's advertising. In fact, of
course, a magazine is quite capable of running articles on a

subject simply because it would like to get some advertising money out of manufacturers in this area. . . .

Often an advertiser will develop an irrational loyalty to one magazine and will refuse even to listen to sales talks from its competitors. *Life* had great difficulty cracking the automotive market because most automobile people were intensely loyal to the *Saturday Evening Post.* One *Life* salesman remembers a trip to Chrysler headquarters in Detroit, and the senior executive who broke into his spiel by taking his arm and leading him over to the window. "See that factory?" the executive said. "Know what built that factory? *Saturday Evening Post* built that factory." Another salesman wooed Chevrolet into *Life* for the first time, after much elaborate presentation had failed, by noting that Chevvy was advertising itself as the nation's number-one car in the same newspapers that *Life* used to advertise itself as the nation's number-one magazine. He tore out the two ads, roughened the edges convincingly, and pinned them together with a hand-written note: "Why isn't the nation's number-one car in the nation's number-one magazine?" The last great support of *Collier's* in its final, fading year was the alcoholic beverage industry, still grateful for *Collier's* uncompromisingly wet stand throughout the prohibition years. . . .

The most remarkable job of building an editorial "feel" has been done by *McCall's* magazine, using the slogan "Togetherness." It is strongly denied at *McCall's* that the slogan was coined with advertising sales in mind.

You may get confused on this thing [says Gilbert, *McCall's* vigorous, good-looking and very young advertising manager], a lot of people do. You'll understand it if you will buy the concept that the criterion of a successful publishing venture like this one is to keep at least abreast and probably ahead of the trends of the time. Now, our editor and publisher, Otis Wiese, has four kids, and he likes to spend time with them. He found out everybody else was doing it, too. He took his family with him on vacation, ran into similar family groups on vacation in Bermuda, Yellowstone, everywhere he went.

Around 1900, it was not unusual for a woman to refer to her husband as The Governor. Somebody said that if you put men and women together around the turn of the century all you got was children. Today, there's a 90 per cent overlap, a man and his wife share the same life. Otis gave it the word "Togetherness," didn't expect the word to stick. He announced it first as an editorial philosophy, began editing the magazine for a woman with a family instead of for a woman as an individual. In fact, we didn't realize the marketing overtones, ourselves.

Without casting doubt on Lea's exposition, it would be well to note that Togetherness solved a number of selling problems for *McCall's*. Of all the women's magazines, *McCall's* offers the oldest audience: the median age of the women who buy it is 40.7 years, according to the Starch CMR. Politz studies of the *McCall's* audience indicate that the magazine is in its field the most heavily read by teen-agers (who do not buy it; they live in the homes of women around forty years old). Every successful mass-media sales story, for reasons psychological as well as economic, was youth—which *McCall's* subscribers did not have. The Togetherness theme, implying the existence of children old enough to participate in family decisions (including buying decisions) gave the sales staff a "feel" to sell, a "feel" which matched exactly with the known audience characteristics of the magazine and had an attractiveness all its own.

Merchandising services by magazines are a fairly new development, pioneered by *Life* in the years shortly after the war when it appeared possible that newspaper merchandising helps would persuade manufacturers to shift some of their budget from magazines to newspapers. *Life* sales trainees were sent around to stores all over the country on missionary duty, to tell them about *Life* and how much *Life* valued the retailer, and to push the idea of featuring products which bore the tag "as advertised in *Life*.". . . The promotion was immensely successful, revealing again to advertisers the blind faith which people tend to place in a magazine they read. Although most analysts believe that the bloom is now off the rose . . . a survey performed for *Life* in November, 1956, indicated that 26 per cent of the nation's grocery stores, 30 per cent of its drugstores and 14 per cent of its appliance stores were using display material tied in to advertisements in *Life*. "In calendar 1956," says *Life's* Richard Wilson, "retailers bought 37 million lines of newspaper advertising to announce that they carried products 'as advertised in *Life*.'"

Magazines have for some time capitalized specifically on public willingness to trust print media. "People do not expect an advertiser to lie," Claude Hopkins [then president of Lord & Thomas agency] wrote in *Scientific Advertising* in 1923. "They know that he can't lie in the best mediums." And it is, of course, true that no magazine ever wants people to be unhappy about purchases they have made as the result of an ad in the magazine. Three magazines particularly have accentuated this possibly naïve public faith by granting advertisers a specific recommendation in return for a certain minimum advertising schedule: the *Good Housekeeing* Seal of Approval, the *Parents' Magazine* Commendation Seal, and the *American Medical Association Journal* Seal of Acceptance. In all three cases some testing of the product is performed by a special section of the magazine staff to determine that it will not actually harm people who buy it (there is a possible legal liability in these situations if the new blood-iron remedy, for example, turns out to be poisonous). Other magazines simply give away a kind of recommendation as one of the benefits an advertiser buys for his money: the *Saturday Evening Post* will supply tags announcing "A *Post* Recognized Value," which means that there doesn't seem to be anything much wrong with the product so far as a space salesman can tell by looking at it.

## THE GREAT OUTDOORS [3]

The early history of the outdoor advertising medium is in reality the history of mass communication. Until the fifteenth century, public posting was the only means—other than a public address—of disseminating information on a wide basis. . . Then in 1450 Johannes Gutenberg, a German, invented printing from movable type and the dream of duplicated messages became a reality. The whole concept of mass communication changed. Wide commercial application became economically practical, and advertising, in the modern sense, was launched in the form of

[3] From *Essentials of Outdoor Advertising,* a book prepared by the Outdoor Advertising Committee of the Association of National Advertisers, Inc. Copyright 1952 by the Association of National Advertisers, Inc. Distributed by Outdoor Advertising, Inc. 360 Lexington Avenue. New York 17. p 15-45. Reprinted by permission.

the handbill. About 1480 William Caxton introduced the new art of printing to England, and the first poster printed from type in the English language was made. It measured five by seven inches and was posted on church doors to advertise a religious law book, "The Pyes of Salisbury Use."

The printing press made possible the development of two media where only one had existed throughout history. The handbill, because it could be distributed in quantity, became a "circulating" medium as contrasted with the "posted" bill. The circulated bill was the progenitor of our newspapers and magazines, while the posted bill was the forerunner of modern outdoor advertising.

During the seventeenth and eighteenth centuries, another form of outdoor advertising appeared which was to have a direct effect on bill posting. This was the outdoor sign. As one historian described it: "London was literally darkened with great swinging sign boards of every description during this period." Some of these were outstanding works of art and provided the means for famous artists to exist between patrons. Taverns, bootmakers and apothecaries identified their place of business with signs symbolic of both trade and firm. When in 1796, Alois Senefelder, a German inventor, perfected the lithographic process, he provided the means for merging these rapidly developing art forms with the all-type handbill, and the illustrated poster became a reality.

Billposting methods were rather primitive at this stage of outdoor advertising's development. An urchin was given a fistful of bills and a few pence to stick them on the walls and fences of London. As the medium became more popular and good locations scarce, the piecework billposter had no scruples about following his competitor around and slapping bills on top of those newly applied.

Gradually, measures were taken to insure exposure of a message for a fixed period of time. This required exclusive permission to post on a given fence or wall. Having purchased this permission, the billposter than sought to retain his right by painting his name on the posting area. In order to offer more desirable locations where traffic was heavy, billposters began to erect their own structures. Because of the prevalence of the fence as a posting surface, these new structures became known as "fences," a term which persisted for many years.

The technique of posting spread rapidly to the colonies, and America picked it up with enthusiasm. The special structure which gradually evolved for use by the billposter in giving a listed and protected service for bills was called a "billboard" or merely a "board." The British equivalent is to this day, "hoarding," deriving its name from the rough board enclosure surrounding construction work and commonly used for posting. "Billboard" embedded itself so firmly in the vernacular of the trade that it has been hard to replace it, even though the steel-sectioned poster panels of today are a far cry from the fence.

At first, "fences" or "billboards" were erected cheaply from rough lumber. By 1896, these had been pretty well replaced with structures made of matched lumber with tongue-and-groove construction. Since the majority of posters compared in size with today's 3-sheet, several different advertisements would be posted on each billboard.

With the development of larger lithographic presses, advertisers gradually increased the size of their posters, until the "24-sheet poster" of today became standard. It was realized that posters of this size were, in reality, pictures, requiring a mat and a frame to set them off individually. This need was met with the individual poster panel so familiar today. To facilitate pasting, the board facing of the panel was gradually replaced with galvanized sheet metal.

Another important form of modern outdoor advertising—the painted bulletin—had an equally humble beginning. The itinerant sign painter is to the big individualized bulletins of today what the London urchin is to the modern poster panel. He worked his way through cities or wandered over the countryside practicing his art on fences, walls, barns, and rocks. He left behind him a colorful swath of reminders for chewing tobacco, patent medicines, and fertilizers. Like the billposter, he gradually developed this art form into an organized advertising medium. . . .

## *Outdoor Advertising Today*

Broadly speaking, outdoor advertising includes all forms of advertising which are exposed to people out-of-doors. [For a discussion of the ethics and esthetics of outdoor advertising, see "Outdoor Advertising: A Debate," in Section III, below.] These forms may be written, pictured or spoken. Most familiar of these forms are the 24-sheet poster panel and the painted bulletin which have become reasonably standardized throughout the country and can readily be employed by advertisers on a national scale. Together they account for the bulk of national outdoor advertising volume.

Other forms of outdoor advertising, which may be equally as familiar, are the "spectacular"—most readily recognized as the large, individualized, electric signs in the Times Square area of New York—exterior store signs or displays, posters or placards on the outside of vehicles, skywriting, and blimp advertising, miscellaneous small highway signs of various shapes and sizes, painted walls, and street vending by voice. Transportation advertising which reaches people in railway stations or bus terminals, and in public conveyances could also be considered outdoor advertising. While national advertisers make frequent use of these other forms of the medium, they are strictly local in nature and are individual rather than standard in appearance.

The 24-sheet poster accounts for approximately 80 per cent of the national outdoor sales volume. Its name, "24-sheet poster" is derived from the old method of assembling the paper sheets on the outdoor panels. At the time this poster came into prevalent use, it was the custom to print each design on twenty-four separate sheets of paper. These sheets would then be pasted on the panel in an overlapping manner, using register marks on the selvedge to assure the proper positioning of each sheet. Later on, as lithographic presses were made larger, the number of sheets required to fill the area of the 24-sheet panel was reduced to about ten, the number most widely used today. However, the old name of "24-sheet poster" has remained to describe this form.

The standard posting period of the 24-sheet poster is thirty days, so that the advertiser achieves twelve changes of copy a year where he utilizes a twelve-month showing. Most 24-sheet posters are produced by lithography since the large runs required for national posting make the lithographic method most practical and economical. Much research has gone into the types of inks most suitable for outdoor conditions, with the result that the modern lithographic colors afford a high degree of fastness in the face of sun and rain. Where smaller quantities of posters are desired, they can be reproduced by the silk screen process, although the use of illustrative effects is more limited with this process than with lithography. . . .

Poster frames are 12 feet high by 25 feet wide, outside dimensions. The size of the poster when assembled on the panel is 8 feet 8 inches high by 19 feet 6 inches wide. The area between the outside dimensions of the poster and the inside edge of the molding is called the "blanking area" and is covered with plain white paper which acts as a mat for the poster design. The name is derived from the blank sheets used to post this area.

Individual poster panels are located throughout a market in high traffic areas so the advertiser's message may receive maximum exposure in all sections of the market. When the advertiser purchases outdoor coverage of a market, he buys what is known as a "showing." If he purchases a No. 100 showing, he will receive sufficient panels to give him what is considered complete coverage of the particular market. Because the panels are carefully placed to intercept the traffic flow in the market, the assumption is that this designated number of panels will expose his message to almost everyone who is moving about in the market in a thirty-day period.

The advertiser may also purchase a No. 50 showing for which he will receive approximately half the number of panels designated in the No. 100 showing. He will pay proportionately less for the No. 50 showing, and will get proportionately less total exposure or impression opportunities for his message. According to authenticated studies in terms of *coverage*—the per cent of persons in the market exposed some time during thirty days—he will get proportionately more with a No. 50 showing than with a No. 100 showing, but the *frequency* with which each person is exposed during thirty days will be only about half as great as with a No. 100 showing.

In certain markets a No. 25 showing is available and consists of roughly one quarter the number of panels in a No. 100 showing. "Fractional" showings—less than a No. 25—are available in certain areas, notably the Pacific Coast. Likewise, a No. 75 showing is available in certain markets.

If the advertiser should wish to saturate a market, he may buy a No. 150 showing which would give him about one and one half times the number of panels in the No. 100 showing. For practical purposes, the No. 150 showing approaches maximum intensity.

The 24-sheet poster panel can be either "regular" (non-illuminated) or "illuminated." The ratio of regular to illuminated panels in a showing will be governed by the type of market. Cities with heavy after-dark traffic flow will normally have a higher ratio of illuminated panels in a showing. This ratio is determined by the local outdoor advertising company in view of the coverage requirements of the market. Illuminated panels are usually located in downtown areas or within the urban limits of a market at points where night traffic is heavy.

The 3-sheet poster usually is printed in three sections and assembled on a galvanized sheet metal panel surrounded by a narrow wooden molding, the outside dimensions of which are 8 feet 7 inches high by 4 feet 10 inches wide. Because of their smaller size, 3-sheet posters can be more readily located in congested areas primarily to reach pedestrian traffic. They are effectively used on walls of buildings near retail outlets, where they serve as reminders to shoppers on their way to buy. They also have wide use in railroad, subway, or bus stations where pedestrian traffic is at a premium. Like the 24-sheet giant, the 3-sheet poster is usually reproduced by lithography although again in the case of small runs, the silk screen process will prove more economical.

Three-sheet posters usually are sold in groups or "packages" which are tailored within a market to meet the advertiser's need. An exception to this is the use of 3-sheets in subway and railroad stations. This falls under the classification of transit advertising which is sold on a market coverage basis. There are no "illuminated" 3-sheet posters.

Advertisers can make effective use of the 3-sheet poster to supplement 24-sheet poster programs since this form offers an opportunity for repeating the same message carried on the 24-sheet poster panel often closer to the point of sale. Painted bulletins and walls, or "paint"—as this form is termed in the trade—account for slightly less than 20 per cent of the volume of all national outdoor advertising. Just as the name implies, the message is painted on the face of the structure, rather than posted. This painting may be done right on the face of the bulletin, working from what is known as a "painter's guide"—which is a grid of the design together with a color key. Some bulletins have a face which is composed of removable sheet-steel sections which can be transported to the paint shop for painting and later assembled on the bulletin. . . .

Painted bulletins are not purchased by showing. They are bought as individual units. There are, however, both illuminated and non-illuminated bulletins.

The number of copy changes—or repaints—which the advertiser is entitled to per year varies depending upon his contract. Usually he gets an original and two additional repaints per year on illuminated bulletins, and an original and one additional repaint on non-illuminated. . . .

Painted walls are usually located in high traffic arteries or in neighborhood shopping areas. They vary widely in size due to the nature of the wall available for painting. Painted walls are often used to supplement poster or painted bulletin programs, and as in the case of the 3-sheet poster, enable the advertiser to place reminder messages on or near his retail outlet.

Painted walls can also be illuminated if the area is suitable since walls are purchased on an individual basis and locations can be carefully selected with a view to the needs of the advertiser.

The chief difference between spectaculars and semi-spectaculars is one of degree. A spectacular is usually considered to be a large permanent sign individualized with special lighting and action effects. . . . The semi-spectacular is basically a painted bulletin to which can be added in varying degrees, neon lights within the panel area or on top thereof, three-dimensional effects, animation, reflector material, and more recently a combination of fluorescent paints and special lighting which combine to give an effect known as "black light."

The use which an advertiser makes of these various forms of outdoor advertising will depend to a great degree on his sales and advertising objectives. . . . Simplicity of idea and brevity of message are essential. An automobile moving at a normal speed down a street gives its occupants little more than five seconds to assimilate the message. Because the audience is an audience in motion, the advertiser must talk fast, and must talk clearly.

## DIRECT MAIL [4]

Those "swift couriers" hyperbolized on the façade of the New York Post Office would not, in their own wildest flights of fancy, consider themselves salesmen. Yet, plodding from door to door, the postmen deliver more sales pitches to more customers than all other salesmen put together. Many of their messages are in the magazines they deliver, to be sure, but a prodigious number are the brochures, pamphlets, and other printed appeals that arrive in personal envelopes. For direct-mail advertising ranks second among all advertising media in total dollar volume. It is bigger than magazines, radio, or television; only newspapers absorb a larger share of the advertising dollar. . . . But despite its size and ubiquity, the direct-mail effort is so diffuse and fragmented that it escapes continued attention. Indeed, of all the elements in the distribution system, direct mail is probably the least understood and most underrated.

Businessmen tend to react to it ambiguously. They use it themselves but generally deplore the way it is used by others. They criticize its prodigality and the fact that it is so often re-

[4] From "The Postman Rings For Sales." *Fortune.* 47:134-7+. Reprinted by special permission from the February 1953 issue of *Fortune* magazine. © 1953 by Time Inc.

ceived by the wrong people. They justifiably resent sucker lists, mail-order rackets, and phony philanthropic solicitations. They criticize the pedestrian quality of most mail copy. Those who are more familiar with the medium lament the lack of research, reliable statistics, and operating standards.

On past performance, much of this criticism is warranted, but there are hopeful stirrings of change. A direct-mail campaign can produce highly gratifying results, and reports of these experiences are causing both advertisers and agencies to reconsider their previous attitudes of passive tolerance. A number of firms are conducting research on readership, response, audience composition, list use, and the like. Hundreds of new small businesses are being built by mail; more and more retailers are experimenting with the medium. Within the direct-mail trade there is new evidence of a desire for improvement. The practitioners are castigating their own deficiencies in print and forum with almost morbid zeal. Even the list brokers have appropriated money to study the thorny problems of list selection. It is too early to suggest that the weedlike growth of direct mail is at an end, but as a result of cultivation its form, odor, and economic value may eventually be greatly enhanced.

Right now there is uncertainty even as to what the term "direct mail" embraces. Since there is no such thing as *indirect* mail, the modifying adjective is not particularly descriptive. In general, however, it can be said that direct mail is any printed matter, other than periodicals, that attempts to sell or promote sales by mail.

The most familiar form is mail-order selling. The enticing letter that urges the reader to order, donate, or subscribe using the enclosed convenient reply form (no postage necessary) is a clear and direct kind of selling and is often mistakenly considered to be the whole of direct mail. Actually mail order accounts for a relatively small part of the total promotional effort conducted by mail—at most a fourth. There are only about eight thousand mail-order firms according to industry estimates, while there are hundreds of thousands of individuals and companies that send letters, brochures, pamphlets, broadsides, postcards, manuals, and gadgets that may enhance their sales only indirectly.

The major oil and motor companies spend millions of dollars on cooperative direct-mail advertising designed to boost their dealers' service business; insurance companies flood the mails with letters to help their salesmen make and maintain contacts; nearly every industrial firm sends out annual reports and other informative material to its stockholders and customers. The immediate objective, the approach, and the quality of these efforts may vary; it may be called advertising, promotion, publicity, or something else; but all of it has the underlying purpose of creating a favorable seller-buyer relationship and hence is a form of selling.

While it is difficult to generalize about such a heterogeneous process, a few of the basic characteristics can be noted:

• Direct mail is both the cheapest and most expensive form of selling. It can be undertaken by the corner grocer with a dozen postcards or involve a mailing to several million persons. On any large scale it is almost always the most costly advertising medium per person reached.

• It is a rifle medium, most effectively and economically employed when the audience can be precisely identified and isolated. The apocryphal story is told of the tycoon who wanted to sell his million-dollar yacht and authorized his agent to spend $30,000 on the job. With an unlikely disdain for personal gain, the agent accepted only 30 cents—enough to cover the cost of mailing ten letters to the only ten men who might conceivably be interested and able to buy such a yacht.

• It is a medium that most large ad agencies shun, and that too often lacks the touch of professional competence. The detail work involved in preparing a catalogue for a $5,000 mailing may be greater than that required for a $50,000 newspaper campaign, yet an ad agency working for 15 per cent gets ten times as much for the latter job. A good part of direct mail is consequently prepared by printing shops and advertisers themselves. Businessmen who would not presume to lay out a magazine campaign or write a radio commercial have no qualms about preparing mail advertising.

- It is the most personal or at least pseudopersonal of advertising media. Innumerable machines and techniques have been developed to preserve the illusion of intimacy; the facsimile signature is merely the most widely used, and most transparent, of these devices.

- Mail advertising is more heavily encrusted with superstition and legend than all other advertising put together. The urge to generalize from the specific is given free rein and nearly everybody has a pet theory.

While it is true that individual firms have developed great skill in specific areas of mail selling (magazines, for example, know just how many letters they must mail to increase their circulation any given amount), the direct-mail field as a whole remains a wilderness. Even the total-volume figures are only rough estimates derived from the volume of mail handled by the Post Office Department. The Direct Mail Advertising Association (D.M.A.A.) considers 85 per cent of all third-class mail, 35 per cent of the postcards, and 10 per cent of first-class and air mail to be direct-mail advertising. It ascribes an average unit cost to each class of mail to arrive at a total dollar volume. No one, however, has tried to break down the resultant aggregate and there is consequently ample room for speculation as to what industries spend how much for what direct-mail purpose.

## What's in a Name?

There are three elements in any business mailing: the proposition, its presentation, and the list of persons to whom it is sent. While all three must be right to ensure success, it is the list that perhaps most often causes trouble to advertisers and bewilderment to the general public. At least two out of every three people in the United States are on somebody's list and most are on several. Businessmen, particularly, fall into a multiplicity of categories, and often find themselves on a good many inappropriate lists besides. These lists are of three types:

House lists are the lists that nearly all firms compile of their actual and prospective customers. They are derived largely from salesmen's referrals and actual business transactions. Being exclusive lists of prime prospects, they form the solid base for most mail operations. Any businessman who has been approached by a salesman either at home or office is probably inscribed on that company's mailing list.

Compiled lists are sold by a few large firms and a multitude of small ones that make a business of sorting out, according to distinguishing characteristics, the millions of names to be found in directories, phone books, club lists, etc. W. S. Ponton of New York, one of the largest list houses, handles 12,000 lists with some 40 million names that sell for an average price of $15 a thousand or 1.5 cents apiece. For those who may have a need for such lists, Ponton offers eighty-two egg-albumen-and-yolk manufacturers ($5.50), 888 human-hair dealers ($17.50), fifteen dried-apple-pomace manufacturers ($5), 1,732,238 people worth over $5,000 ($16.50 per thousand), 12,262 millionaires ($40 per thousand), etc. Ponton's best-seller, however, is a composite list of some 300,000 executives who earn over $10,000. This one list is sold in its entirety some thirty or forty times a year.

R. L. Polk & Company of Detroit, the largest direct-mail house of all, compiles a mammoth catalogue of all automobile registrations in the U.S. It breaks down car owners geographically, and in every other conceivable way. As a result of this monumental work, Polk shares with Chicago's R. H. Donnelley the exclusive ownership of the principal lists used by the automobile, tire, oil, and related industries—all big direct-mail users. But since Polk spends about $3 million a year just keeping its car-ownership data current, its quasi-monopoly is one that nobody has cared to challenge.

Mail-order response lists are used primarily by firms that engage in mail-order selling. They contain the names of people who have previously responded to mail ads and are therefore considered likely prospects to do so again. Unlike compiled lists, these names are usually rented or swapped, rarely sold.

They form the basis for a lively commerce, provide rental income (as high as $100,000 a year) for some four thousand firms that accumulate them in the normal course of business.

A publication like the *Wall Street Journal,* for example, may want to try a list of people who replied to a business-school advertisement on the theory that such people are interested in further self-improvement; or a list of people who bought night-driving glasses because such people are wealthy enough to own cars, have previously bought by mail, and are presumably innately cautious. Such lists are available and can be most easily obtained through one of the twelve members of the National Council of Mailing List Brokers. Assume that one of the brokers negotiates a test rental of two thousand names for the *W.S.J.* from the Alexander Hamilton Institute (a correspondence school whose inquiry list is highly popular) and a like number from the Miles Kimball Co. of Oshkosh, Wisconsin (one of the biggest mail-order firms). The rental price for these lists is $15 per thousand names. The broker gets 20 per cent of this, and for its money the *W.S.J.* gets the one-time use of the names. The *W.S.J.* now sends empty envelopes to the letter houses that handle the Hamilton Institute and Miles Kimball mailings and there the envelopes are addressed. They are then returned to the *W.S.J.,* which checks the names against its subscriber lists, inserts the printed matter, and sends them out. Each batch of reply forms has been coded (i.e., return to Dept. X15 or JL5, etc.), and when the returns come in the *W.S.J.* decides whether either list "pulled" sufficiently well to warrant further mailings. If it did, the balance of the list or some part thereof is then rented in the same manner.

The way the *Wall Street Journal* handles rented lists, however, is highly exceptional. Characteristically, list renters never get an opportunity to cull the lists they rent or "clean" them in any way, and this accounts for most of the perplexity that besets recipients of inappropriate business mail. Who, for example, has not received a bid to subscribe to a magazine he already gets, or an offer of some product for which he has no possible use? Recently a fourteen-year-old boy received a letter describing an unguent guaranteed to fortify flagging virility. Such things happen because the addressed envelopes are usually returned to a renter's letter house and he never sees them. Even if he does he is honor-bound not to copy them down. Indeed, most list owners bury dummy names and addresses in their lists to guard against this temptation. The penalty for pirating names from rented lists for reuse: blackballing by all reputable brokers.

Even if the names are made available, however, it is extremely costly to cross-check them. One magazine recently arranged to do so and found that culling lists adds more than a penny to the cost of a nickel letter. It decided that enclosing a "please excuse" card was the most satisfactory and economic solution to the problem of multiple solicitations.

A more troublesome list problem—and one that can affect all mail advertisers—is the "nixie" or undeliverable letter. Americans are a restless people and their constant moving about makes any list of addresses quickly obsolete. Up to 5 per cent "nixies" are generally expected, up to 10 per cent tolerated. When the proportion rises beyond that, however, the list buyer tends to squawk. Which is why a good list of businessmen is expensive. It is a highly perishable commodity; only 53 per cent of U.S. executives stay put from one year to the next.

Mail-order selling may have its peculiar list difficulties but it is the one form of advertising that can be accurately controlled and analyzed for effectiveness. A mailing goes out and the returns come back. The percentage of response and even the selling cost per dollar of sales can be readily computed. Such computations can be eminently gratifying and mail order is consequently being used to sell a growing variety of products. . . .

### 16 Shots for $1

The economics of mail selling and advertising are not so simple as might be expected. There are over thirty cost factors in the simplest mailing and these can be adjusted and juggled in infinite ways. The D.M.A.A. estimates that a third-class-mail audience costs $70 per thousand or 7 cents per individual on the average. This includes only printing, preparation, and postage, however, and not the initial creative expenses, which can be considerable.

Now an audience that costs about 7 cents per person is not a cheap audience, particularly once it starts getting large. Even a postcard sent to every buyer of the *Saturday Evening Post* would cost six times as much as a full-page, four-color ad in the magazine itself. Newspapers provide audience for as little as a cent per thousand; radio for $1.50. The basic justification for using direct mail is that it reaches not just any audience but one composed largely of prospects. Thus although the audience cost is high, the cost *per prospect* can, and should be, low.

Here again the mail-order part of direct mail has an advantage, for the response measures audience value to some extent. But even in mail order there are no fixed criteria. A national magazine may send out millions of mail pieces and be pleased with a new-subscription response of less than 5 per cent, while a mail-order firm selling an inexpensive product often needs a 20 to 25 per cent return to break even. A magazine can sometimes spend more than the subscription price to get new subscribers because it knows the cost of *renewing* subscriptions will be low and because it derives a substantial part of its revenue from advertising. Each mail-order business has its idiosyncrasies, and the only generalization that can be made is that the higher the dollar value of each unit of sale, the lower the percentage of response that can be tolerated.

Unlike mail order, however, mail advertising does not solicit a cash response and its effectiveness is, consequently, more difficult to assess. Direct-mail enthusiasts cite the results of readership tests, but since such tests usually rely on coupon returns and free offers, the proportion of those responding who are free-loaders is a matter for conjecture. In any event readership is not, of itself, any index of audience composition, and proof that direct mail is read leaves unanswered the underlying question of whether it is read by the right people.

Probably the biggest single user of the mails for selling is the baby-chick industry. There are some 8,500 baby-chick dealers in the United States and many of them conduct their business entirely by mail.  One dealer in Missouri, for example, sends out 20 million pieces of direct mail a year.  Of the 1.75 billion chicks sold last year, about 600 million were shipped by mail and most were so advertised.  For chick sales are a delicate, multi-million-dollar business requiring precise timing and advance selling.  Only newly hatched chicks can be sent through the mails, and unless orders are on hand to permit delivery within sixty hours after hatching, the chicks must often be destroyed.

Another big group of mail-order and direct-mail users are competing advertising media.  Some magazines devote as much as 90 per cent of their promotion budgets to direct mail, and send out tens of millions of letters annually.  Radio and television broadcasters spend less over-all but more per piece.  Large networks like CBS and NBC may pay $2 or more for elaborate brochures and books to send to their small, sophisticated audience of ad agencies and sponsors.

The same is true of pharmaceutical firms like Abbott Laboratories.  To command the attention of the mail-saturated doctor audience, they vie in the preparation of expensive, confidence-inspiring brochures lavishly illustrated in four-color lithography.

There are other industries that spend impressive sums on direct mail—the auto makers, tire companies, nurserymen, etc.—but the medium is most effectively used and enthusiastically endorsed by those firms that have a narrow, well-defined market. . . .

With direct mail's growth . . . has come a realization of its immaturity.  Criticism is directed about equally toward the areas of competence and creativeness, i.e., the mechanical operations of printing, list use, control, etc.; and the copy itself.  In the competence area mailing lists probably cause the most trouble.  The tendency of lists to become obsolete before they are put to use evokes from disenchanted list purchasers and renters such comments as: "I don't believe we ever had a proper list."  "The damned things weren't accurate 2 per cent of the time."  "The firms were not operating—or had not been operating under the titles given for *five years*."

Reputable list houses like Ponton and Polk guarantee deliverability as high as 98 per cent on the names they sell, but they make no similar pledge as to quality. That there is a need for better list analysis is clear, if only it were an attempt by list brokers to ascertain whether foundation manufacturers are of the concrete or elastic variety. How much research would be economically feasible is itself a subject for study, but since the average name now costs 1.5 cents and the total cost of each mailed piece is about 7 cents, spending somewhat more per name for better names and mailing fewer total pieces would seem to make economic sense.

The other mechanical elements of the direct-mail process are similarly susceptible of improvement. Business-machine firms like A. B. Dick have developed some highly efficient and ingenious reproductive equipment, but the clattering, makeshift machines in use at many letter shops represent something less than the ideal of automatism. Advertisers, too, need to reconsider their direct-mail responsibilities. A survey recently conducted by the Tension Envelope Corp. showed that one-third of the companies studied took from two to ten weeks to respond to the inquiries they had solicited; that in their replies 40 per cent failed to tell interested prospects how or where to buy.

There is perhaps an even greater need for improvement in the quality of direct-mail copy. The great bulk of business mail is depressingly pedestrian. Too often its preparation is left to an underpaid, inexperienced member of the advertising department or farmed out to a printer who has a makeshift "creative department." The result, as Paul Bringe of Milwaukee Dustless Brush says, is there are "too many letters that assume the reader is a twelve-year-old moron and some that look as though the writer is."

Because its preparation is so haphazard, unordered, and unremunerative, direct mail is a neglected field; few business schools offer direct-mail courses, and almost no young men prepare for direct-mail careers. Of those in the business, one expert says, "There are too many comma hounds, type lovers, and technicians concerned only with minutiae. It's the message that's

important." Fresh ideas and imaginative talents are badly
needed. . . .

A way should certainly be found for the specialized talents
of the advertising profession to be utilized more widely and
effectively. The agencies' reluctance to get involved for 15 per
cent is only part of the problem; many firms flatly refuse to pay
even that. Actually the commission basis is not appropriate for
direct mail; the noncreative, detail, and supervisory work involved bears no fixed relation to the total outlay. The few agencies that specialize in direct-mail advertising—Dickie-Raymond
in Boston, Claude Grizzard in Atlanta, Jay Maish in Marion,
Ohio, and a few others—charge fees based on the hours actually
worked. The big agencies like J. Walter Thompson and Mc-
Cann-Erickson that do direct mail advertising for their clients
for the standard 15 per cent do so chiefly as an accommodation
and make little money on this end of their business.

The aversion of ad agencies, however, is not so pronounced
as it once was. More and more they are coming to realize that
direct mail is an integral part of any well-rounded promotional
effort and are taking it on. Some are undoubtedly motivated by
the instinct of self-preservation for there are countless small
agencies happy to take the direct-mail crumbs. Indeed, many of
them scattered across the country have banded together into
"networks" to provide out-of-city coverage for their clients. For
direct mail can be the toe in the advertiser's door. During the
thirties Lou R. Maxon built up his big Detroit agency (G. E.,
Heinz, Gillette, etc.) and became one of the highest-income men
in the country in just this way.

The services of an agency are not indispensable, however.
Very small enterprises cannot afford them and big corporations
usually have their own facilities. Indeed, many agencies know
less about direct mail than their big clients. But if outside professional assistance is not desired or available the internal equivalent in creative talent is probably essential to long-range success
in direct mail. Occasionally, of course, the ability to write effective copy—and it need not necessarily be *good* copy in the liter-
ary sense—is a management attribute. Elliott White Springs of
Springs Mills certainly needs no high-priced copywriters and

Frank E. Davis, the Gloucester fisherman who spent part of his declining years basking in Florida, owed his mailed-seafood success largely to his flair for writing tangy, appetizing copy.

### The Postman Goeth

Thus there are few rules or formulas for success in either mail-order selling or the promotion by mail of that intangible commodity, good will. The smallest businessman can afford it and the biggest corporation cannot do without it. It is the most flexible, versatile, and under certain conditions, effective of all advertising media. It is also the most fragmented: there are more than 36,000 printing shops in the United States and nearly all consider themselves direct-mail experts. It is an anomalous medium; while there are millions of users and practitioners of the art, they have no focal point of interest. The largest trade association is the D.M.A.A. and it has a scant two thousand members, a measly $94,000 budget.

But even if this crude weapon were to be burnished and sharpened, even if it were to become highly mechanized (list compiling, addressing, and inserting are still largely hand operations), even if research and the best creative talent were to be brought to bear, direct mail would still only be one sales tool. It could not, any more than any other medium, substitute for a good product or service, nor could it replace, except in a limited way, that slightly rusty mainspring of the distribution system, the human salesman.

John Howie Wright, one of the early pioneers in the direct-mail field and the publisher of a trade journal called *Postage and the Mailbag,* once said, "Anything that can be sold, can be sold by mail." People in the direct-mail business still quote him, but what the aphorism does not say is how much of anything can be sold by mail or to how many people. The postman delivers his sales message all right, but it is a low-pressure delivery. It may command the customer's undivided attention for a moment but if he doubts or questions or needs further persuasion there is no one to answer him. The postman has already departed on the swift completion of his appointed rounds.

# III. SOCIAL AND ECONOMIC EFFECTS

## EDITOR'S INTRODUCTION

To be for or against advertising in twentieth century America is akin to being for or against rain. The one is as much a part of our economic, social, and political climate as the other and advertising, like the rain, is here to stay. The whole American atmosphere of claims and counterclaims, pretensions and counter-pretensions is imbued with it and were it to disappear many would be left helpless and dismayed, forced to learn a new way of life. Economically its disappearance would remove the props from under our national structure; without widespread distribution production for profit could not continue.

To say that advertising is permanent and necessary, however, is not to say that advertising as we know it today is good. Certainly it has not always been, nor has it ever been, as bad as its more strident critics maintain. Mostly, if results are the criterion, it has been what the customers wanted, and frequently it has accomplished good that the advertiser himself neither anticipated nor intended. None of the social gains to which advertising so often points with pride were conceived in pure altruism, but their beneficial effects are frequently beyond dispute. Advertising was called upon to sell soap. Its primary purpose was to make money, not to make the nation cleaner. It did both. Advertising was called upon to sell automobiles at a profit. It did, but it also put the nation on wheels and gave it the kind of life the automobile makes possible. Advertising was called upon to market the chance discovery of a Labrador fur trader named Clarence Birdseye, not to change the dietary habits of America. It did both.

Results have not always been so happy, for advertising has frequently peddled merchandise that lacks the inherent virtues of soap, automobiles, and frozen food. One such was the patent medicines it sold with such zeal towards the end of the last century and in so doing brought down the wrath of the righteous upon its head.  The timing of this first major assault on American advertising is revealing, for most historians date it from a momentous day in 1901 when Samuel Sidney McClure "discovered" corruption and seized upon it as a mass circulation builder for his *McClure's Magazine*.  Corruption, of course, had flourished in the United States for decades before McClure, and has enjoyed periodic revivals since, but the United States— inured to it by the Grant administration, the Tweed Ring, and such business leaders as Jim Fisk and Jay Gould—had been too busy expanding to care.  There was pie for everyone in those booming days and the man who allowed ethics or conscience to come between him and his slice had small regard for his wife and children.  Only when the nation's resources suddenly appeared to have limits, when equality of opportunity to plunder seemed to disappear almost overnight, did moral indignation raise its lowered head and start looking around for a reason.  This change came almost precisely at the turn of the century, and S. S. McClure was ready with a staff of talented and resourceful writers to expose the villain.  It was corruption.

These writers bore names that are still respected and they found and attacked corruption everywhere.  First came Ida M. Tarbell's *History of the Standard Oil Company*, written with the naïve cooperation of the company itself, which showed that Standard Oil had been created through methods that included fraud, violence, bribery of railroad and government officials, and the destruction of competition by any and all means necessary.  Run serially in *McClure's* it created a sensation that led eventually to the dissolution of the corporation, and it was quickly followed by Ray Stannard Baker's exposé of the railroads and by Lincoln Steffens' lurid picture of collusion between business and political bosses in *The Shame of the Cities* and *The Struggle for Self-Government*.  Urged on by President Theodore Roosevelt, happily brandishing his big stick at "malefactors of great wealth," other publications mounted the bandwagon.  *Everybody's Magazine* ran Thomas W. Lawton's *Frenzied Finance*, an attack on investment syndicates and life insurance companies; Charles Edward Russell exposed the collusion between meat packers and railroads in *The Greatest Trust in the World*; Upton Sinclair described the filth and horror of packing houses in *The Jungle*. When *Cosmopolitan* published David Graham Phillips' *The Treason of the Senate*, showing that United States senators were elected by legislatures at the bidding of special interests, Roosevelt found the dirt flying too close to home and reached back to John Bunyan for an epithet to describe the writers he had once encouraged. He came up with "muckrakers," from the laborer in *Pilgrim's Progress* who held a muckrake in his hand and "could look no way but downwards." The name stuck, but circulations continued to soar and advertising—feeding the mouth that would bite it—clamored to buy space in the crusading magazines.

The inevitable attack on advertising itself first struck its most vulnerable point—patent medicine ads. Nostrums of dubious value and content had been advertised and attacked since colonial times with little effect on the national conscience or the national health, but excessive claims and dangerous or habit-forming ingredients had lately brought them under fire from the Department of Agriculture itself. Backed and briefed by Dr. H. W. Wiley, chief of the department, *Collier's* and *The Ladies' Home Journal* took up the cudgels for legislation that would drive the worst patent medicines off the market and end fraudulent advertising by them all. Their success, marked by passage of the Food and Drug Act of 1906, was a greater milestone in the history of advertising than of medicine. Cancer cures and wart removers had not been the only offenders, and loss of their profitable advertising presaged a similar loss in other suspect fields. Fraudulent financial advertising had bilked thousands of millions—$500 million in New England alone in a single decade—and scarcely a medium in the country had raised so much as an eyebrow. The Chicago *Tribune*, the New York *Times*, and the Cleveland *News and Leader* were among the refreshing exceptions and, following the hue and cry over patent medicine advertising, hundreds of others began to clean up their columns. Through their Advertising Federation of America newspapers drew up a code of ethical advertising, adopted "Truth in Advertising" as their slogan, and initiated efforts to have a model statute against false and fraudulent advertising adopted by the various legislatures. This statute, drawn by lawyers retained by *Printers' Ink*, first became law in Ohio in 1913 and within a few years had been adopted by thirty-seven states. Advertising clubs—through vigilance committees that later united into the Better Business Bureau—saw to it that violators of the code were prosecuted, and by the outbreak of World War I advertising had become so respectable that many of its old-time practitioners felt they had taken the cloth.

It was a passing phase. During World War I advertising sold Liberty Bonds, helped conserve foodstuffs ("Food Will Win the War"), and presented the Red Cross to the American people as "The Greatest Mother in the World." It placed itself unreservedly at the disposal of the government and it emerged from the conflict heavy with honors and high in the public's esteem. Three years later, along with the rest of the country, it was back on the primrose path and contributing its full share of inanity to "The Era of Wonderful Nonsense."

Looking back from the vantage of thirty years it is difficult to blame advertising for more than contributory negligence in the excesses of the decade that ended with the Wall Street debacle of 1929 and fathered the depression of the thirties. The twenties, as Frederick Lewis Allen wrote in *The Big Change*, saw the canonization of the salesman as the brightest hope of America. Bruce Barton (see "Advertising: Its Contribution to the American Way of Life," below) wrote a book to prove that Christ had been a combination salesman and advertising man of extraordinary talent. In *The Man Nobody Knows* he described Christ as a business executive, told how He founded modern business, and actually quoted from the Bible the alleged advertisements He had used in founding it. The book was a best seller and for the advertising man this was the best of all possible worlds. He could sell anything. He sold women on cigarettes ("Blow Some My Way") and he sold men on health ("An Old Man at 40—Young at 41!"). He made halitosis more fearsome than leprosy (see "How I Sold Listerine" by Gerard B. Lambert in Section I, above), and he made "The Skin You Love to Touch" more precious than rubies. He discovered B.O. and pyorrhea and he cured them both and he got Marie the Queen of Rumania to endorse his mattresses. He sold people everything they wanted and many things they didn't, and when the crash came in '29 they turned upon him with one accord to blame him for not teaching them thrift.

During the thirties only Herbert Hoover and the banks received more abuse than advertising. Its voice had been the voice of business and industry that had lured people into debt with bright promises and gaudy pictures of a false Utopia. It was the cause of lost jobs, breadlines, foreclosures, and want. It had promised the moon, had delivered dust, and should be destroyed. It almost was.

This was a far different attack from that of the early years of the century. Then false and fraudulent advertising had been the legitimate target. Now the entire economic system that advertising represented was under fire and the blows came from two directions—from disillusioned customers and from government. The latter, save for strengthening the Food and Drug Act of 1906 with the Federal Food, Drug, and Cosmetic Act of 1938 and imposing long-needed restraints on financial advertising with the Securities Act of 1933, did little beyond making threatening gestures. The customers were made of sterner stuff. In 1932 F. J. Schlink and Arthur Kallet, president and secretary respectively of Consumers' Research, Inc., published *100,000,000 Guinea Pigs.* Consumers' Research, outgrowth of an earlier Consumers' Club, was formed in 1929 to protect consumers against misleading advertising and the book by its top brass was a vitriolic attack on all advertising, with special emphasis on that for food and drugs. Many of its facts were outdated or suspect and few were typical but its success—sparked by a huge advertising appropriation—was so phenomenal that it became the first of a long series of books and articles hewing to the same line and demanding remedial legislation at all levels of government. Much of what they said was true, much was exaggerated, but they said what the public wanted to hear and the public heard it from all sides. It heard, and it obviously believed, for it took advertising four years of herculean and admittedly successful effort in the na-

tional interest in World War II to recapture the ground it lost
in the thirties.  During those years it took the blame for many
sins it never committed.  During the war it took the credit for
many achievements it never achieved.

Advertising emerged from World War II, as it had from
World War I, with banners flying and the world at its feet.
A tremendous war-built production facility, a tremendous war-
built reserve of wealth, and a tremendous war-starved market
presented it with the greatest opportunity for service and profit
that salesmen have ever had.  Advertising has embraced the
opportunity with the shrillest sales pitch in its strident history
and it has done much to turn what looked like a seller's market
into a seller's dream.  In an age of mediocrity it has made the
mediocre seem good and its success in selling practically anything to almost everybody has tempted it into fields where its
history and historic purpose would seem to make its motives
suspect.  Since the war it has sold political candidates to the
public like so many packs of chewing gum and, in the opinion
of many, to the same type of people.  Whether in this and
similar activities it is simply embellishing the mistakes of the
past or avoiding them with a new sense of responsibility and
the first faint stirrings of maturity is the underlying theme of
the section that follows.  Some of the writers represented, such
as Professor David M. Potter in "Advertising: The Institution
of Abundance," hope that it will grace and ornament the position of power to which a notoriously fickle public has once more
raised it.  Others, like James F. Kelly, Bruce Barton, and the
editors of *Printers' Ink,* believe it already has.  Gilbert Seldes, in
"The Immunity of Advertising," is inclined to wait and see.
The reader may well wish to do the same.

## ADVERTISING: THE INSTITUTION OF ABUNDANCE [1]

For millions of people throughout the world, during the
past three centuries, America has symbolized plenty.  This pro-

[1] From article based upon a Walgreen Foundation lecture at the University of
Chicago by David M. Potter, William Robertson Coe Professor of American History
at Yale and a member of the editorial board of the *Yale Review*. *Yale Review*.
43, no 1:49-70. Autumn 1953. Copyright 1953 by Yale University Press. Reprinted
by permission.

fusion of wealth, this abundance of goods, has borne a significance that far transcends the field of economics.  American
democracy, in the broad sense, was made possible to begin with
by a condition of economic surplus, and the constant incidence
of this abundance has differentiated American democracy from
the democracy of other, less richly-endowed countries.

Abundance, then, must be reckoned a major force in our
history.  But one may question whether any force can be regarded as possessing major historic importance unless it has
developed its own characteristic institution.  Democracy, for
instance, produces the institution of popular government—the
whole complex of parties, elections, representative bodies, con-
stitutions, and the like.  Religion manifests itself in the church,
with a canon law, a clergy, and a whole ecclesiastical system.
Science and learning find institutional embodiment in universities with all their libraries, laboratories, faculties, and other
apparatus of scholarship. . . . If we seek an institution that
was brought into being by abundance, without previous existence in any form, and, moreover, an institution which is peculiarly identified with American abundance rather than abundance throughout Western civilization, we will find it, I believe,
in modern American advertising.

Advertising as such is by no means a neglected subject.  The
excesses of advertising and of advertising men have been a
favorite theme for a full quorum of modern satirists, cynics,
and Jeremiahs.  From the patent medicine exposés in the early
years of the century to the latest version of *The Hucksters*, advertising men have incurred fairly constant attack—their unscrupulous natures and their stomach ulcers being equally
celebrated.  Since advertising lends itself both to esthetic criticism and to moral criticism, and since humanity is ever ready
with views in each of these areas, the flow of opinion has been
copious.

But advertising as an institution has suffered almost total
neglect.  One might read fairly widely in the literature which
treats of public opinion, popular culture, and the mass media
in the United States without ever learning that advertising now
compares with such long-standing institutions as the school and

the church in the magnitude of its social influence. It dominates the media, it has vast power in the shaping of popular standards, and it is really one of the very limited group of institutions which exercise social control. Yet analysts of society have largely ignored it. Historians soldom do more than glance at it in their studies of social history, and when they do they usually focus attention upon some picturesque or titillating aspect, such as the way in which advertising has reflected or encouraged a new frankness about such previously tabooed subjects as ladies' underwear. Histories of American periodicals and even of the mass media deal with advertising as if it were a side issue. Students of the radio and of the mass-circulation magazines frequently condemn advertising for its conspicuous role as if it were a major interloper in a separate, preexisting, self-contained, esthetic world of actors, musicians, authors, and scriptwriters; they hardly recognize that advertising created modern American radio and television, transformed the modern newspaper, evoked the modern slick periodical, and remains the vital essence of each of them at the present time. Marconi may have invented the wireless and Henry Luce may have invented the newsmagazine, but it is advertising that has made both wireless and newsmagazine what they are in America today. It is as impossible to understand a modern popular writer without understanding advertising as it would be to understand a medieval troubadour without understanding the cult of chivalry, or a nineteenth-century revivalist without understanding evangelical religion. . . .

A century ago, advertising was a very minor form of economic activity, involving relatively small sums of money, occupying a very modest position in the newspapers and magazines of the day, and playing only a negligible part in the distribution of goods or the formation of consumer habits. It was practiced principally by retail distributors who offered items without the mention of brands. Producers, who regarded the distributors as their market and who had as yet no concept of trying to reach the ultimate consumer, did not advertise at all, and did not attempt to signalize their products by a distinctive name or label. Advertisements themselves were, for the most part, short, prosaic notices like the want ads of today. Their tone was didactic rather than hortatory or inspirational, and their content was heavily factual.

Publishers usually assumed that advertisments ought to be of this nature, and to protect the position of the small advertiser, some of them refused to accept notices using any type larger than agate [Five and one half points—about one-fourteenth of an inch]. But, to apply *The New Yorker's* phrase historically, there has always been an ad man, and some of the ad men of the mid-century began to use great numbers of agate-sized letters, arranging them in the shape of large letters, just as the members of a college band are sometimes arranged in formation to spell out the initials of the alma mater. Publishers also correctly assumed that any considerable number of small, compact advertisements would lend a deadly monotony to the printed page, and some of them accordingly limited rather narrowly the amount of advertising that they would accept. In 1874, for instance, *The Youth's Companion* restricted the quantity of its advertising. As late as the seventies, when the Howe Sewing Machine Company offered $18,000 for the back cover of *Harper's* [for one year] it was somewhat astonished to meet with a polite but firm refusal.

But those days are gone forever, and no other phenomenon of eighty years ago is now more remote. By 1880 advertising had increased threefold since the Civil War period. By 1900 it stood at $95 million a year, which marked a tenfold increase over the amount in 1865. By 1919 it exceeded half a billion dollars, and by 1929, it reached $1.12 billion. After 1929 it declined because ot the Depression, but by 1951 it had again surpassed all previous levels and stood at $6.548 billion a year.

This immense financial growth reflects a number of vast and far-reaching changes. To begin with, the physical appearance of advertising underwent a complete transformation. The small box-insert ad gave way increasingly to larger spreads, and at last the full-page advertisement became the dominant form. . . . In the sixties and seventies the average advertisement in the Boston

*Evening Transcript* and the New York *Tribune* was about four column-inches; . . . by 1918 it was four times this size. In magazines, advertisers in the eighties used half-page spaces two and a half times as often as they used full pages; by 1920 they did so only one third as often. Before 1890 full-page entries constituted only a fifth of the advertising in magazines; but by 1920 they account for nearly half, and today the proportion must easily exceed half. . . .

Along with these changes in form went significant changes in the economic interests which advertised. For the first time, producers began to perceive the possibilities in general advertising. At an earlier time they had addressed advertising by mail or on other limited bases to the distributors whom they hoped to induce to handle their goods, but they had left it to the distributor to deal with the ultimate consumer. They had apparently never conceived of the possibility of manufacturing their product under a distinctive brand name, of using general advertising to create a consumer demand for their brand, and thus of exerting a pressure upon the distributor to keep their products in stock. But in the 1880's four pioneer producers began regularly to advertise their brands on a large scale. Significantly, perhaps, three of these were soaps: Sapolio, Pears', and Ivory; the fourth was Royal Baking Powder. All of them achieved a large growth which was indisputably the result of advertising, and by doing so they demonstrated a truth which other producers were quick to grasp. As early as 1905 *Printers' Ink* [the advertising and marketing trade journal] proclaimed this new gospel when it declared:

> This is a golden age in trademarks—a time when almost any maker of a worthy product can lay down the lines of a demand that will not only grow with years beyond anything that has ever been known before, but will become, in some degree, a monopoly. . . . Everywhere . . . there are opportunities to take the lead in advertising—to replace dozens of mongrel, unknown, unacknowledged makes of a fabric, a dress essential, a food, with a standard trademarked brand, backed by the national advertising that in itself has come to be a guarantee of worth with the public.

As producers recognized the possibilities of this golden age, their advertising grew until it has become primary: almost all so-called national advertising in magazines and over large networks is advertising by producers—while advertising by distributors, mostly in newspapers and over local broadcasting stations, has become secondary. The historian of the N. W. Ayer and Son Advertising Agency reports that

in the seventies and eighties, those who advertised through the Ayer firm were largely retailers and others who sold directly to the public. By 1890, most of these had ceased to use the Ayer agency, and its principal work was the advertising of manufacturers who sold through dealers and retailers but preferred to get control of their ultimate market.

Concurrently, the nature of the appeal which advertising employs was transformed. Producers were no longer trying merely to use advertising as a coupling device between existing market demand and their own supply; rather they were trying to create a demand. Since the function of advertising had become one of exerting influence rather than of providing information, the older factual, prosy notice which focused upon the specifications of the commodity now gave way to a more lyrical type of appeal which focused instead upon the desires of the consumer. This change was foreshadowed as early as 1903 by Professor Walter Dill Scott, in an article on "The Psychology of Advertising," which formulated the basic law of the subject so clearly that he deserves to be regarded as the Archimedes, if not the Nostradamus, of the advertising world:

How many advertisers [he asked] describe a piano so vividly that the reader can hear it? How many food products are so described that the reader can taste the food? How many describe an undergarment so that the reader can feel the pleasant contact with his body? Many advertisers seem never to have thought of this, and make no attempt at such a description.

That was in 1903. Today many advertisers seem to have thought of nothing else, and certainly all of them understand that advertising operates more to create wants in the minds of people than to capitalize on wants that are already active.

Inevitably a question arises: Why did this immense growth of advertising take place? To this query each of us might offer responses of his own, but perhaps the most carefully-considered answer, at least in terms of economics, is provided by Neil H. Borden in his extremely thorough study of *The Economic Effects of Advertising* (1942). Professor Borden explains this growth partly in terms of the widening economic gap between producers. and consumers, and the consequently increased need for a medium of communication, and he attributes the growth of large-scale national advertising, with its color, large spreads, and other expensive features, to the growth of big corporations able to pay for such publicity. But in addition to these explanations he adds another very essential one: "The quest for product differentiation became intensified as the industrial system became more mature, and as manufacturers had capacity to produce far beyond existing demand."

In other words, advertising is not badly needed in an economy of scarcity, because total demand is usually equal to or in excess of total supply, and every producer can normally sell as much as he produces. It is when potential supply outstrips demand— that is, when abundance prevails—that advertising begins to ful- fill a really essential economic function. In this situation the producer knows that the limitation upon his operations and upon his growth no longer lies, as it lay historically, in his productive capacity, for he can always produce as much as the market will absorb; the limitation has shifted to the market, and it is selling capacity which controls his growth. Moreover, every other pro- ducer of the same kind of article is also in position to expand output indefinitely, and this means that the advertiser must distinguish his product, if not on essential grounds then on trivial ones, and that he must drive home this distinction by employing a brand-name and by keeping this name always before the public. In a situation of limited supply, the scarcity of his product will assure his place in the market, but in a situation of indefinitely expandable supply, his brand is his only means of assuring himself of such a place.

Let us consider this, however, not merely from the standpoint of the enterpriser, but in terms of society as a whole. At once the vital nature of the change will be apparent; the most critical point in the functioning of society shifts from production to consumption, and as it does so the culture must be reoriented to convert the producer's culture into a consumer's culture. In a society of scarcity, or even of moderate abundance, the productive capacity has barely sufficed to supply the goods which people already desire and which they regard as essential to an adequate standard of living. Hence the social imperative has fallen upon increases in production. But in a society of abundance, the productive capacity can supply new kinds of goods faster than society in the mass learns to crave these goods or to regard them as necessities. If this new capacity is to be used, the imperative must fall upon consumption, and the society must be adjusted to a new set of drives and values in which consumption is paramount. . . . Clearly it must be educated, and the only institution which we have for instilling new needs, for training people to act as consumers, for altering men's values and thus for hastening their adjustment to potential abundance, is advertising. That is why it seems to me valid to regard advertising as distinctively the institution of abundance.

If it is correct to regard advertising in this way, we must recognize at once that we are dealing with a force that is not merely economic. We are dealing . . . with one of the very limited group of institutions which can properly be called instruments of social control. These institutions guide the life of the individual by conceiving of him in a distinctive way, and encouraging him to conform as far as possible in the concept. . . . [And] one may add that the traditional institutions have tried to improve man and to develop in him qualities of social value, though, of course, these values have not always been broadly conceived. The church has sought to inculcate virtue and consideration of others—the Golden Rule; the schools have made it their business to stimulate ability and to impart skills; the free-enterprise system has constantly stressed the importance of hard work and the sinfulness of unproductive occupations. And at least two of these institutions, the church and the school, have been very self-conscious about their roles as guardians of the social values and have conducted themselves with a considerable degree of social responsibility.

In contrast with these, advertising has in its dynamics no motivation to seek the improvement of the individual or to impart qualities of social usefulness, unless conformity to material values may be so characterized. And though it wields an immense social influence comparable to the influence of religion and learning, it has no social goals and no social responsibility for what it does with its influence. . . . If one can justifiably say that advertising has joined the charmed circle of institutions which fix the values and standards of society, and that it has done this without being linked to any of the socially-defined objectives which usually guide such institutions in the use of their power, then it becomes necessary to consider with especial care the extent and nature of its influence—how far it extends and in what way it makes itself felt.

To do this, it may be well to begin with the budget, for the activity of all major institutions—great churches, great governments, great universities—can be measured by what they spend, and though such measurements are no substitute for qualitative evaluation, they are significant. In political history, the importance of the power of the purse is proverbial. I have already said that the amount spent for advertising in the United States in 1951 was $6.548 billion. Perhaps this may be a little more meaningful if I add that the amount is equivalent to $199 per year for every separate family in the United States. Compare this with what the nation paid for primary and secondary public education in 1949, which amounted to a total expenditure of $5.010 billion. This means that, for every family, we paid $152. Our national outlay for the education of citizens, therefore, amounted to substantially less than our expenditure for the education of consumers. . . . In 1949-1950 the operating expenses of Yale University were $15 million; in 1948 the expenses for newspaper advertising only of two major distilleries, Schenley and National Distillers, were more than half of this amount. . . .

With expenditures of this order of magnitude, advertising clearly thrusts with immense impact upon the mass media, and through them upon the public. The obvious and direct impact is, of course, through the quantity of space it occupies in the newspapers and magazines, and the amount of time it occupies in radio and television broadcasts. Either in space or in time, the totals are impressive, and if advertising had no influence upon the information in newspapers, the stories in magazines, and the programs in radio and television, it would still be a force worthy of major consideration because of the influence of the advertising matter itself. But it does have a profound influence upon the media, and for students of American opinion and American life, it is important that this influence should be understood.

To appreciate this influence, let us consider the position of most magazines a century ago, as contrasted with today. At that time the only financial support which a magazine could expect was from its readers. This meant that if a person did not care to read, the magazine had no means of appealing to him and no objective in doing so. If editors worried about circulation, it was because they needed more revenue from subscriptions, and if they had enough subscriptions to support them on a modest scale of operations, they could safely proceed on a basis of keeping their standards high and their circulation limited. They did not worry very much about advertising, for the reason that there was not much advertising to worry about. At the time of the Civil War, for instance, it is estimated that the total income from advertising received by all newspapers and periodicals averaged about 25 cents per capita yearly for the population at that time.

Today, of course, these conditions have ceased to apply. Newspapers and magazines no longer look to their subscribers as the major source of revenue. As long ago as 1935, the revenue of all newspapers in the country was $760 million, of which $500 million came from advertising and $260 million from subscriptions. At the same time, the magazines of the United States enjoyed . . . $144 million from subscriptions and $186 million from advertising. That is, approximately two out of every three newspaper dollars came from advertising, and more than one out of every two magazine dollars came from the same source. The subscriber had been reduced to a sad position: where at one time periodicals had fished for subscribers, they now fished for advertisers, and used subscribers as bait. Since that time, newspaper advertising has increased more than threefold, to the total of $2 billion [in 1951] and magazine advertising has risen to $562 million from which we may infer that the subscriber is now, more than ever before, a secondary figure. If I may express the same point in a different way, the situation is this: In 1935, American families paid an average of $6.60 a year to receive newspapers, but advertisers paid an average of $12.70 to have newspapers sent to each family, and in 1951, advertising was paying $56 a year to have newspapers delivered to each family. Clearly that was far more than the household itself could possibly be expected to pay. Similarly with magazines: while subscribers in 1935 were paying $3.60 a year to receive them, advertisers were paying $4.70 to have them sent, and by 1951, American advertising had increased enough to pay $14 per family per year as its stake in the magazines on the living-room table of the American home. In many cases, as with magazines with large advertising sections, the real situation is that the advertiser buys the magazine for the "purchaser," and what the purchaser pays as the "price" of the magazine is really only a kind of qualifying fee to prove [usually to the Audit Bureau of Circulations] that he is a *bona fide* potential consumer, and not a mere deadhead on whom this handsome advertising spread would be wasted.

If this were merely a matter of some magazines being published for consumers and other magazines being published for readers, with the public retaining a choice between the two, the result would not have been quite so sweeping, but the effect of this change has been to threaten with extinction the magazine that is published first and foremost for its readers.

The threat operates in this way: the magazine with large advertising revenue can afford to pay its contributors more and therefore it can secure better contributors than the magazine which enjoys very little revenue of this kind. In a sense, the advertiser is prepared to buy better authors for the reader than the reader is prepared to buy for himself. But this means at once that any magazine which wishes to secure or retain the best writers must get advertising. But to get advertising, it must also get mass circulation. To get mass circulation, it must publish material with a mass appeal. Also, it must keep its subscription costs low, which in turn makes it more dependent than ever upon advertising revenue. At this point, a fixed cycle is virtually inescapable: millions of readers are essential to secure a large revenue from advertising, advertising is essential to enable the magazine to sell at a price that will secure millions of readers—therefore the contents of the magazine must be addressed to the millions. Thus the best writers, those who have proved able to write for the most discriminating readers, are put to work writing for consumers who may not be readers at all.

But it is even more significant to realize that other media are far more completely part of the institutional apparatus of advertising than are periodicals. Magazines and newspapers are still paid for in part by the consumer. But radio and television programs are paid for almost wholly by advertisers. In 1951 it was estimated that there were 100 million radios in the United States, and radio advertising was estimated at $690 million. That is, advertisers were annually spending $6.90 to provide each set with programs, while the programs received by the 15 million television sets were being subsidized at the rate of $32 a set.

What this means, in functional terms, it seems to me, is that the newspaper feature, the magazine article, the radio program, do not attain the dignity of being ends in themselves; they are rather means to an end: that end, of course, is to catch the reader's attention so that he will then read the advertisement or hear the commercial, and to hold his interest until these essential messages have been delivered. The program or the article becomes a kind of an advertisement in itself—becomes the "pitch," in the telling language of the circus barker. Its function is to induce people to accept the "commercial," just as the "commercial's" function is to induce them to accept the product.

A year or two ago, an English critic complained of American periodical writing that it "fixes the attention but does not engage the mind." If this is true, it is not because of any intrinsic vacuity on the part of American writers, but because the most important financial supporters of such writing are paying for it to do exactly what is alleged. To fix the attention, but not to engage the mind, is a precise statement of the advertiser's formula.

In saying this, I do not mean at all to suggest that advertisers are personally hostile to thoughtful writing or that they consciously desire to encourage writing which has a low intellectual content. On the contrary, it should be recognized that some of the advertising associations have shown themselves soberly aware of the power they yield and acutely desirous of using it for the public good. But it is the nature of advertising that it must aim for a mass appeal, and it is the nature of the mass media that they must present any item—an idea, or a fact, or a point of view—in such a way that it will attract the maximum number of readers. To do this, of course, they must suppress any controversial or esoteric aspects of the item, and must express it in terms of the least common denominator. But these terms are usually emotional ones rather than rational ones, for the emotional impulses of a large group of people are much more uniform throughout the group than are the mental processes of various individuals in the same group. Walter Lippmann expressed this idea very precisely in his *The Phantom Public*. He was speaking of political action, but his words nevertheless apply to all communication which involves masses of people.

> Since the general opinions of large numbers of persons [he said] are almost certain to be a vague and confusing medley, action cannot be taken until these opinions have been factored down, canalized, compressed, and made uniform. The making of one general will out of a multitude of general wishes . . . consists essentially in the use of symbols which assemble emotions after they have been detached from their ideas. . . . The process, therefore, by which general opinions are brought to cooperation consists in an intensification of feeling and a degradation of significance.

Mr. Donald Slesinger [lecturer on analytic psychology at New York University] . . . made a very similar observation in a context which included other matters besides politics.

Since common experience is essential to communication [he said] the greater the number to be simultaneously reached, the simpler the communication must be.

These factors of simplification, of intensifying the feeling while degrading the significance, and of fixing the attention of the mass audience, are all related to one basic condition of the media, namely, that they are not concerned with finding an audience to hear their message, but rather with finding a message to hold their audience. The prime requisite of the message is that it must not diminish the audience either by antagonizing or leaving out anyone. Moreover, since the actual personnel and tastes of a vast, amorphous, and "invisible" audience cannot possibly be known, the result is in effect to set up an axiom that the message must not say anything that, in the opinion of a cautious proprietor, might *possibly* offend or leave out some of those who might *possibly* form part of the audience. For such an axiom there are several implicit corollaries of far-reaching importance. First, a message must not deal with subjects of special or out-of-the-way interest, since such subjects by definition have no appeal for the majority of the audience. Second, it must not deal with any subject at a high level of maturity, since many people are immature, chronologically or otherwise, and a mature level is one which, by definition, leaves such people out. Third, it must not deal with matters which are controversial, or even unpleasant or distressing, since such matters may, by definition, antagonize or offend some members of the audience.

If I may examine each of these corollaries briefly, we are confronted first with the fact that many perfectly inoffensive and noncontroversial subjects are excluded from the media simply because these subjects appeal only to a limited number of people. Being directed to the millions, the media must necessarily avoid consideration of subjects which interest only the thousands or the hundreds. This implies a danger to freedom of expression, but not the precise danger against which the guardians of our liberties are usually warning us. They fear that large publishers and advertisers, wielding automatic power, will ruthlessly suppress minority ideas. The dynamics of the mass market, however, would seem to indicate that freedom of expression has less to fear from the control which these advertisers exercise than from the control which these advertisers permit the mass market to exercise. In the mass media we have little evidence of censorship in the sense of deliberate, planned suppression imposed by moral edict, but much evidence of censorship in the sense of operative suppression of a great range of subjects—a suppression imposed by public indifference or, more precisely, by the belief of those who control the media, that the public would be indifferent. . . .

Closely related to the exclusion of special subjects is the avoidance of advanced or mature treatment of the subjects which are accepted. Paul F. Lazarsfeld [chairman of the department of sociology at Columbia University] has investigated this aspect of the matter, as it manifests itself in connection with radio, and has stated his conclusions very pointedly. He speaks of the appearance of a new type of "radio consumer" in many cultural areas.

Radio [he said, writing in 1941] has helped to bring to the attention of the American people the important events in Europe and thus has contributed to the generally increased interest in news. However, it has been shown by special studies that this new type of news consumer created by radio has a more hazy knowledge and a less acute interest in those events than the traditional and smaller groups of people with long-established news interests. A similar audience has been developed in the field of serious music. There is no doubt that the broadcasting of good music over hundreds of stations in the country has enlarged the number of those who like it. Still, a more detailed study of their tastes and attitudes has shown that the musical world of these new music lovers is different, if not inferior, to that of the musical elite of past decades and as judged by classical standards.

In a democracy no one should disparage the value of any activity which serves to raise the level of popular taste, but it is still legitimate to count the cost of such a gain. Particularly in connection with news broadcasting and in connection with popular articles on public affairs, it seems to me that we can easily

see the application of Walter Lippmann's formula, "the intensi-
fication of feeling and the degradation of significance."

Finally, there is the avoidance of the controversial or distressing. This manifests itself not only in connection with obvious
matters such as labor unionization, racial relations, or the like,
but more fundamentally in the creation of a stereotype of society
from which all questions of social significance are carefully
screened out. . . . In a sense—a negative sense—the desire to
offend no one involves an attitude of what may be called tolerance. As David Riesman tellingly remarks in *The Lonely Crowd:
A Study of the Changing American Character,* the writer or
broadcaster, addressing himself to the amorphous audience, does
not know how the virus of indignation may be received, and he
must therefore "be preoccupied with the antibodies of tolerance."
But clearly, this tolerance is, as the phrase implies, one of mental
asepsis, rather than one of mental nourishment. It deals with
ideas not by weighing them but by diluting them. Tolerance
once implied that the advocates of an idea might be heard without
prejudice and judged on their merits, but this toleration merely
implies that since society will refrain from exercising power to
judge them, it will relieve itself of responsibility to hear them.
It involves not impartiality of judgment, but simply default of
judgment.

In the realm of politics, of course, antagonistic points of
view do continue to receive a hearing, and the continued presence
of vigorously partisan editorials and radio addresses by men in
political life may seem to disprove all that I have just been saying,
but the significant fact is that the political sector is the only
one where the indulgence, or even the recognition, of vigorously-
maintained viewpoints is permitted. Many social questions, many
of the profound problems of American life, lie beyond the pale.

In this discussion of the importance of advertising, the
purpose has been to explore its effects upon the noneconomic
phases of our culture. For . . . the most important effects of
this powerful institution are not upon the economics of our
distributive system; they are upon the values of our society. If
the economic effect is to make the purchaser like what he buys,

the social effect is in a parallel but broader sense, to make the individual like what he gets—to enforce already existing attitudes, to diminish the range and variety of choices, and, in terms of abundance, to exalt the materialistic virtues of consumption.

Certainly it marks a profound social change that this new institution for shaping human standards should be directed not, as are the school and the church, to the inculcation of beliefs or attitudes that are held to be of social value, but rather to the stimulation or even the exploitation of materialistic drives and emulative anxieties, and then to the validation, the sanctioning, and the standardization of these drives and anxieties as accepted criteria of social value. Such a transformation, brought about by the need to stimulate desire for the goods which an abundant economy has to offer, and which a scarcity economy would never have produced, offers strong justification for the view that advertising should be recognized as an important social influence and as our newest major institution—an institution peculiarly identified with one of the most pervasive forces in American life, the force of economic abundance.

## THE CASE FOR ADVERTISING: WHAT IT DOES FOR THE PRODUCER, THE CONSUMER, THE COUNTRY [2]

Advertising is communication—mass produced, a brain child of our mechanized civilization. And although in mechanization we may have lost a few grains of individuality, we have gained a great deal more in individual well-being.

We know these truths. They are self-evident. And yet we seldom sit down and evaluate them properly. Since [World War II] we have risen to new heights of mechanical skill in our factories. We have harnessed great new chemical discoveries to the betterment of health and home, we have developed new methods of physical distribution of goods that both improve the delivered quality of the goods and reduce the cost of distribution. We have developed new major media like television. As we reevaluate advertising in the light of these many changes, is

    [2] From "What Advertising Is . . . What It Has Done . . . What It Can Do Now," a special report by the editors of *Printers' Ink*, the weekly magazine of advertising and marketing. *Printers' Ink.* 243:43-5+. May 15, 1953. Copyright 1953 by Printers' Ink Publishing Co., Inc. Reprinted by permission.

advertising still important to our way of life? Are its basic values the same? Can it perform the same miracles today?

Our answer, of course, is Yes to all three questions—but why?

We believe that the basics of advertising are very much the same as they were ten years ago, twenty years ago, thirty years ago. What has changed is the means of putting the same basic principles into action. The basic fact about advertising never changes: It is the most economical way of bridging the gap between the man with an idea and the man who can benefit by buying it.

Why this is so is explained, we believe, by the following twenty-four basic accomplishments of advertising:

1. Advertising makes possible better merchandise at lower prices.

This is its great service to the consumer. And by making it possible to deliver the goods at less cost, advertising makes it possible for the consumer to spread his purchasing power over more merchandise, thus creating still greater demands for other advertised products.

This is a mass-production era; and . . . mass production puts within the reach of the average American consumer all manner of household, office and factory conveniences. It makes possible such taken-for-granted things as light bulbs and such new wonders as home freezers. It turns out the new, life-saving, wonder drugs at a price we can afford.

But this would all be just an engineer's dream if it were not for advertising. Mass production is of no value without some means of telling people about it, some means of making people want to pay for and use it. . . . The miracle of America lies not only in the production but also in the absorption of what we produce. . . .

2. Advertising helps cut the cost of distribution.

It makes it possible for the manufacturer to contact more distributors, dealers, consumers—and more production managers, purchasing agents, plant foremen—in more places more quickly and to secure quicker action as a result of that contact than any other method of communication he can use.

Because advertising does cost money—and spectacular sums for some of the most effective types—the economic theorists sometimes lose sight of its economy. The value of a force like advertising cannot be judged on the basis of its cost, but rather in its cost-result ratio. . . .

3. Advertising pre-sells known brands.

Advertising is not only a means of telling large numbers of people about the merchandise that is to be had, but also the means of presenting that merchandise in a favorable light. It creates consumer acceptance in the mass at phenomenally low cost. In the pre-selling process through advertising there is no cost of salesmen; there is no cost of heavy inventories; there is no necessity to carry the merchandise to the buyers in order to convince them to buy. . . .

4. Advertising makes markets.

It has the power to create desire to own where no desire existed before. By presenting new ideas in a favorable light, advertising broadens horizons for the people that are reached by it. . . .

In doing this, advertising breeds dissatisfaction, but it is dissatisfaction of a good kind—the kind that says: Old ways of doing things are no longer good enough for me. I want something better. And here it is. So off with the old, and on wth the new, like the guy says in this ad. . . .

5. Advertising is the vehicle through which our industrial know-how is spread and augmented in war and in peace.

The most dramatic evidences of this came to light during World War II, when advertising in industrial publications played a very essential informative role. Suppliers used advertising to warn of shortages. Manufacturers used it to suggest substitutes for critical materials. Machine-tool suppliers used it to teach customers how to make available tools last longer. Industries found new uses for advertising in training quickly the vast new armies of production workers. . . .

And now—however less dramatic the present cold-war activities of industry may be—industrial advertising is performing the vital task of channeling know-how into the plants where it is needed in order to maintain the efficiency of our big and little industries.

6. Advertising helps set up the channels of physical distribution and keep them streamlined.

The normal flow of merchandise from manufacturer to distributor to retailer is guided by advertising all the way. Advertising tells the tradesmen the facts about the goods, helps them decide which items will sell best in their trading areas, shows them how to get the most value out of the consumer advertising placed behind national brands. . . .

7. Advertising speeds the introduction of new products that are needed.

This applies both to the manufacturer who is just cutting his eyeteeth as an advertiser and to the advertiser of an established line who is adding to it. Advertising quickens the acceptance of new items and creates acceptance of what is new at least cost. . . . One of the saving graces of our economic system is that the small advertiser can be as big an advertising toad in his small puddle as the largest national advertiser. This gives the small man a chance to compete on his home grounds—and to expand market by market once he gets his feet on the ground at home. . . .

8. Advertising safeguards the position of established products for which there is still a need.

With the market constantly bombarded by new promoters selling new products and new versions of old products, the advertiser must keep everlastingly at it to safeguard his market position. The fact that his merchandise still fulfills a need is not enough. He has to keep reminding people of the benefits that the product continues to offer or others will reap the harvest. . . .

9. Advertising enables the manufacturer of a product that is becoming obsolescent to switch to a new product.

No amount of advertising or anything else short of the cartel system or economic dictatorship by the state can safeguard the position of products for which there is no longer a need. But when obsolescence sets in, the advertiser with an established trademark is in a position to switch more quickly and more surely to a new product that does answer a need. . . .

10. Advertising is a competitive weapon for both the newcomer and the established concern.

It's as democratic as the Bill of Rights to have open competition for the consumer's dollar. And advertising helps keep competition open—out where people know who's making what, how much the price is, where it is for sale, why the manufacturer believes his product offers a bigger benefit than his competitor's.

The newcomer has as good an opportunity as the established concern to hawk his wares. The result is a free competitive market set in a glass house; the public gets a full view of what the choice is in products, trademarks, and prices. . . .

11. Advertising protects against destructive price competition.

Advertising in general tends to reduce prices. But there is one specific situation in which it does not: that is when price wars and competition based only on price (with quality and stability of future production disregarded by the price cutter) tend to destroy a market.

At such a time, the safeguard of a strong consumer franchise helps the advertiser weather the period of destructive price competition. By holding the price line, telling the public why and continuing to stress quality at a fair price, the manufacturer can win out. . . .

12. Advertising helps stabilize a business.

By its very nature, advertising looks to the future as well as the present. It builds market acceptance in advance—and leads to stable operations. The advertiser is able to invest part of the proceeds of his most profitable business years in building up a head of consumer desire that can be tapped in later years when his market may be depressed. . . .

Advertising is of great help to many companies in eliminating seasonal slumps [and seasonal unemployment]. Off season promotions have resulted in the creation of what amounts to new marketing seasons in many fields.

13. Advertising smokes out new prospects.

It is the means of finding out who will buy—and often enough customers turn up among people that the manufacturer might never have thought of as prospects. Market research can determine where most of the sales potential for a product lies, but it can't locate all the unusual sources of sales. . . .

14. Advertising keeps them sold.

Advertising reassures the new owner that he has made a wise purchase. . . . The best advertisement is a satisfied customer; and it takes advertising that reaches consumers *after* as well as before they buy to fortify that satisfaction. Advertising *after* the sale engenders word-of-mouth advertising.

15. Advertising is a key sales tool for the manufacturer's salesman.

The salesman who calls on dealers or industrial purchasing agents has a valuable identity when the line he sells is nationally advertised. The buyer already knows something about the salesman's company and his product.

In addition, the fact that the product he sells is advertised is of real value—something extra to offer the buyer in addition to a good product for resale. Because of the advertising, the salesman has not only a good product but also consumer acceptance for sale. . . .

16. Advertising covers marginal sales territories, releases salesmen for selective selling.

. . . Retail volume is becoming concentrated to an ever greater extent in fewer marketing areas, fewer retail outlets. The time of salesmen has to be concentrated where the big retail potential is located.

This leaves the marginal territories and outlets out in the cold—unless advertising is used to contact them direct at less cost.

This function of advertising applies both to the marginal trade contacts and to marginal consumers. Mail-order advertising replaces direct sales contact entirely in thin markets. . . .

17. Advertising reaches the prospects who won't see a salesman.

Many doors are closed to salesmen. There are buyers who refuse entry to the representatives of merchandise or companies they have never heard about. But advertising gets into these offices, establishes name recognition, opens the door to sales to buyers who won't see a salesman.

In the consumer field, there are the people who shy away from talking to a salesman . . . [who] shop the ads in the privacy of their own homes—and order either by mail or by telephone. Advertising reaches the prospects [wholesale or retail] who won't see a salesman. . . .

18. Advertising helps procure the best in materials and manpower.

Competition for the top-dog positions in any market calls for competitive enterprise in all departments of the business; it is not only a matter of competitive advertising and selling. As company presidents well know, success also lies in securing the very best materials and manpower at fair prices. And in this sphere of competition for the ingredients and the people that are needed, advertising plays another very important part.

Companies that are known are the ones that producers of new materials contact first. And the inventors and idea men of all kinds do the same thing. The result is that the better known a company is, the more likely that it will get first crack at all the new developments—and will continue to stay ahead of the field in use of new and better materials and inventions.

Companies that are known are also the ones that high-caliber personnel think of first when they are seeking advancement. So the company that is a well-known advertiser has the advantage of attracting the most alert, ambitious and skillful employees. . . .

19.  Advertising establishes friendly relations with the public.

The public-relations aspects of advertising are taken a great deal more seriously today than they were ten years ago; and more companies are using advertising to establish friendly relations with all the people they deal with: employees, stockholders, suppliers, customers. The objective of this type of advertising differs widely from the advertising that is aimed squarely at selling goods. But in the long run, by creating a friendly atmosphere and respect for company policies, good public-relations advertising contributes to greater business efficiency in all departments—including sales. . . .

20.  Advertising increases the capital value of a business.

Advertising is a real investment in corporate assets—a fact that is well recognized by the financial fraternity. Companies that advertise consistently find it much easier than non-advertisers to borrow money at low rates for business expansion, plant improvements, the development of new products and new markets.

The fact that a trademark is advertised proves its existence invested with companies that exercise sound product and public-relations advertising campaigns. They know that good product advertising assures a continued market, and that good public-relations advertising [frequently called "institutional advertising"] helps stabilize operations.

21.  Advertising protects against infringers.

The fact that a trade-mark is advertised proves its existence and value as far as the law is concerned. One of the most helpful pieces of evidence in any court case in support of a trademark is the proof that the mark has been widely and properly advertised—that it is, therefore, well known in its field.

22. Advertising is a public servant—used in the public interest.

Another recent development is the use of advertising by business groups and individuals to further the public welfare. The . . . contributions of the Advertising Council in behalf of the Red Cross and similar worthy causes are just one shining example. Another is the campaign to stamp out forest fires. Another is the informative ads used to help direct rescue operations in several flood and other disaster areas. Another is the . . . successful Get Out the Vote campaign. . . .

And in the controversial area of legislation and politics are the free expressions of opinion in advertisements about legislation and the policies of political candidates of all parties. These—both the ones you agree with and those you don't like—help maintain the freedom of expression that is part of our democratic heritage.

23. Advertising helps combat harmful propaganda.

Both overseas and at home, advertising is a very real weapon in the war of ideas that has boiled down now to capitalism versus communism. It deserves a large share of the credit for the new appreciation by folks here at home of the virtues of our economic system. . . . By the same token much has been done to explain to Americans the evils of communism—a job of utmost importance as a defensive measure against the ideological inroads of the Kremlin's salesmen.

24. Advertising foots most of the bill for our mass media.

The financing of media that stems from advertising is done for selfish reasons, of course. The advertisers share the bill so that they can reach a broad audience at low cost. But the end result is a great benefit to the public: most of the mass communication media that play so large a part in all our lives.

Without advertising they could not exist. . . . Our free press and entertainment world is to a large extent financed by advertising.

These 24 things that advertising does are its fundamentals.

## ADVERTISING TECHNIQUES AND THE MORAL LAW [3]

Use of certain high-pressure advertising techniques has arisen from the need, in a super-productive industrialist order, such as that of contemporary America, to have the stream of goods flowing from its factories actually purchased and consumed in a regular, reliable market. There must be a constant turnover of what is produced and what is destroyed in use. The steadily increasing volume and velocity of mass-production must be matched by similarly expanding sales and consumption. Otherwise, there will be a breakdown of the industrial machine, a weakening of the whole economy, general unemployment and the flooding of our warehouses with commodities.

To make sure that these misfortunes do not occur, all the areas of our society have become manned by great numbers of salesmen, very much like shock-troops, who are actually engaged in the business of distributing commodities, guaranteeing their purchase, and establishing a bridge between those who produce goods and those who are destined to use them. Every mass-producer is constantly alert, through his agents, for mass-consumers. And it has become an accepted American idea that, if there be no existing mass-consumers for a particular product, it is the privilege of the manufacturer to use all his energies and talents to create them. Ordinarily, the mass-producer will delegate this responsibility of insuring his market to an advertising man, a man who is specially equipped to guarantee the eventual distribution of his goods or the sale of his services.

Textbooks used to describe the advertising man as "one who is paid to disseminate information about a commodity or a serv-

[3] From article by Thomas P. Coffey, special projects editor for The World Publishing Company of Cleveland and New York. Mr. Coffey has taught philosophy at Fordham University, New York, and St. Peter's College, Jersey City; has contributed articles to *Saturday Review* and *The Reporter*; and is the author of *A Popular History of Heresies. Catholic World.* 186:174-9. December 1957. Reprinted by permission.

ice." But, as business enterprise widened in range and increased in momentum with the years, the advertiser came to acquire the status of a careful student of human behavior, one who seeks to determine the motivations of human conduct, a manipulator of the public mind, and an arbiter of human values. No longer the huckster that early American society despised, the advertising man is now a top-flight representative of the business order. He has been crowned with respectability and his activities have taken on the intensity of a crusading religion.

Recently, in response to special business pressures, the "ad man" was turned into a "depth man." He now associates with psychiatrists, motivational analysts, psychologists, social scientists; and all these men enjoy a certain equality in their efforts to use intricate patterns of argumentation and mass-psychoanalytical techniques, techniques to "activate" the market and to "step-up" consumer reaction.

Not content merely to ogle, stimulate, and inveigle the public, from without, into purchases, the ad man is now concerned with controlling, from within, the entire process of human thinking in respect to desire for commodities and the actual decision to pay for them. Even in cases where there is no real demand for a particular product, advertising men set out "to persuade" the public to consume in order that society will meet the needs of the productive process and cooperate in what they call the dynamics of an ever expanding economic system.

It is important, from the moral point of view, to note some of the actual techniques that are used in the process of persuasion.

First, advertisers are taking increasing advantage of the many logical fallacies possible in limited human thinking. An unscrupulous advertiser will burrow into all sorts of fallacious reasoning processes in an attempt to persuade the inattentive potential buyer. A particular cigarette will, for instance, be majestically described by him as containing no more than one fourth of one per cent nicotine: a figure that is quite correct and actually found to be true by independent laboratories. Yet such a nicotine content is, as the same laboratories further demonstrate, much higher than that of most other cigarettes on the market and, more important, still insufficiently low to protect health: an implication which the average buyer cannot be expected to draw. Such argumentation on the part of the advertiser amounts to a suppression of information to which the buyer has every right. . . .

Many other goods are sold under misleading descriptions. Clothing, for instance, is alleged to be shrink-proof or color fast, at least by reasonable interpretation of the instructions given for washing and drying; but it is shown, in laboratory test, that the material in the clothing could never have been such as was implied.

Advertisers of patented food additives, deficiency correctors, vitamin preparations, and custom made cure-alls are also frequently shown by the Food and Drug Administration to have misrepresented their products under such tags as "contains twice as many," "works many times faster," or "your money will be cheerfully refunded." And certain premiums, discounts, "free trials" likewise profit from lack of public knowledge about some matter essentially related to the decision to purchase.

All these misrepresentations, startling as they are found to be when viewed outside the big type and color plates of the usual printed advertisements or similar means of emphasis on radio and television, seem almost to be accepted as the normal thing in the processes of trade today. They are, it is said, even defensible in courts of law on the basis of the principle: "Let the buyer beware." Yet this principle, however legitimate it was at one time, cannot be regarded as morally or legally valid today. For underneath the great barrage of false information about products with which the average citizen can never expect to be familiar in advance of purchase, there is very little opportunity for the buyer to acquaint himself with the real nature of the things he buys, or to protect his rights to a fair exchange. He has no ready standard of reference by which he can determine the quality of the goods in question. And only through costly trial and error will he ever be able to distinguish between the reliable and the untrustworthy manufacturer. He must, in the final analysis, place a great degree of confidence in the truthfulness and honesty of the merchandiser and the advertising people who represent him.

Such a situation involves many injustices not only to the individual buyer and to society but also to other, conscientious, manufacturers. But the most tragic result of such misrepresentations is the pollution of the channels of communication between man and man. Announcements on radio and television, or notices in the newspapers and magazines are, it has been shown, the source of almost all knowledge about practical affairs. When the code of ethics which regulates such communication has been corrupted, the very springs of human judgment are vitiated, and life itself contaminated wth cynicism and the accelerated rhythm to nothingness characteristic of the modern city. . . .

The first and most important thing for our society is its general moral reconstruction. And this over-all task might begin with at least a minimum of legislative action in regard to specific moral problems, such as those that arise from advertising malpractice. Even educational campaigns, like that recently initiated by the Food and Drug Administration cannot, for all their value, efficiently combat those manufacturers whose principal ambition seems to be to exploit an uninformed public. Literature, discussion, and lectures—however helpful these things may be— will never really replace practical and concrete regulation of the processes of advertising through laws: laws which look not only to the safety of a product and the degree of its actual usefulness to prospective buyers but also to the quality and especially the veracity of the advertising concerning it.

It will, of course, be objected by manufacturers that such legislation would contravene established legal rights to freedom of speech and of press; and it may happen in a particular instance that there will be unfortunate results from restrictions on advertising. But without any legislation, how will our society protect the fundamental rights of the buyer to honesty and to integrity on the part of the manufacturer, or curtail the bold-faced instances of injustice that occur when there is no restraint exercised by public authority over unscrupulous and piratic advertisers?

Massive sales campaigns must be met wth more than mere suggestions for massive sales resistance, or boycott of manufacturers who make use of untruthful advertising, or only educational efforts. There must also be a constant review by the state of advertising procedures; a general policing of advertising practices and claims; and the enforcement of punitive measures against those who misrepresent their product or who try to deceive the public. What the actual nature of the necessary laws will be is a matter for elected representatives, with the help of their legal practitioners, to determine; but that they are necessary is a matter of increasing conviction to every intelligent citizen.

Aside from the actual misrepresentation of products, the persuasive techniques of modern advertising also make use of appeals to subconscious needs, desires, and drives. As the *Wall Street Journal* once put it: "The businessman's hunt for sales boosters has led him into a strange wilderness: the subconscious mind." Recent surveys show that more than two thirds of America's hundred largest advertisers have geared their campaigns to the established findings of the depth interview, to the advice and practical philosophy of psychiatrists, and even to unproved assumptions of mind-probers. [See "Motivation Research," in Section I, above.]

There are special motivating factors beneath the depths of consciousness on which admen like particularly to dwell: the drive to conformity, the obsession for taste pleasures, and the yearning for security. High pressure campaigns regularly return to these weaknesses and vulnerabilities of man in a frantic attempt to bypass the conscious guard of the public. And it is conservatively estimated that the sale of billions of dollars' worth of products depended last year upon successful manipulation of guilt feelings, fears, hostilities and anxieties, inner tensions and loneliness. Living like parasites on the secret miseries, doubts, and weaknesses of man, "people-persuaders" are constantly at work on the mind and soul: now seeking to implement their knowledge of the psyche, now in search of new ways to regiment man's thinking and decisions in regard to economic life.

Mr. Vance Packard, author of *The Hidden Persuaders,* has described many of the sources of specific advertisements that incorporate the depth approach to the potential buyer. He shows, for instance, how the psychologist-advertisers encouraged housewives to buy family food on the basis of nonrational and impulsive factors rather than as a result of logical planning. He describes how man's deepest sexual sensitivities and yearnings were delved into and exploited for commercial profit. He further points out how the "psychological obsolescence" of products was "stepped up" by admen who encouraged stylishness, competition, and wastefulness with regard to products already in use; an attitude of cheerfulness rather than of truthfulness came to be the mark of economic reports and forecasts; and every product seemed to acquire a "built-in overtone" that had some relation to depth needs and infantile hangovers.

To play in this way on man's psychic weaknesses and unconscious vulnerabilities raises a number of serious moral questions.

A tendency to narcissism, a strange and excessive love of self with roots deeper than reason can probe, is known to lurk in the impulsive drives and subconscious needs in man's make-up. In view of fundamental laws of Christian charity, laws which every enterpriser must take into strict account in assessing his responsibilities to the community, is there any justification for encouraging the growth and continual satisfaction of these narcissist leanings? Does respect for man's spiritual nature permit the advertiser to cajole a person, to wheedle and intimidate him, to tempt him, viciously and covertly, so that every nonrational and selfish instinct may be turned to economic gain?

Not a single philosophical or theological principle of traditional Western thought will condone this exploitation of the human personality which, in reality, is worse than exploitation and amounts to an attempt to seduce man's soul. Exploitation there has always been; but this debasing of human society to a series of mere "technical relations," rather than "essential relations"—as Martin Buber [Israeli theologian] distinguished them—and this reduction of human beings to the order of manipulatable things marks a new and a frightening stage in the disintegration of Western culture.

Further, the steady barrage of advertising information is geared, in large degree, to establishing the value of man's life on the number and the quality of his possessions. Symbols of status are everywhere proclaimed; and it is generally held today that what a man has tells us the sort of person he is. Even professed Christians have taken very little trouble to scrutinize the nature of such beliefs, so opposed to everything Christ taught in the Gospel texts.

Religion itself is sometimes invoked to support the principles of this thoroughgoing materialism. This, of course, is only a sign that Christianity is becoming increasingly nominal and that the Philistinism, already widespread in regard to modes of living, manners, and esthetic expression, is beginning to trespass on the inmost cloisters of thought, ritual, and creed. A devastatingly cynical approach to all human values, personal and social, religious and humanistic, is evident in this attempted deification of unimpeded enterprise. And it does not require a vivid imagination to see that, unless things change radically, the infallible law of supply and demand will overwhelm us.

A third morally questionable technique of persuasion in modern advertising stems from its associating "distinctive" and "highly appealing" personalities [see "Elsa Maxwell Loves Mazola," in Section I, above] with products that are by themselves essentially undistinctive. Such projection has been seen by advertisers as necessary because of the growing standardization of the ingredients in most products of a type and the fear by enterprisers that their products defied "reasonable" discrimination. If, marketers argued, people cannot discriminate reasonably, they should be helped to discriminate unreasonably, through things which are projected into a product from purchasers' own subconscious minds. Here advertising ceases to be a discussion of a product's merits and advantages. It has become a multiplier of symbols of commodities, a reflector of images in the subconscious of the buyer, a means strictly outside a good for its distinction from many competing brands almost the same in content.

The public naturally bears the expense for this form of fictitious conviction—an expense which has no corresponding value in the item purchased, and which, therefore, constitutes a breach of commutative justice. For even though the advertisers retort that customers are "more pleased" and "more happy" with exchanges made in this way, they cannot deny that no buyer would really be so if he clearly understood the nature of the transaction. Only the absence of logic and the use of psychic manipulation can explain the difference between one price and another.

A Christian ethic cannot countenance any advertising technique which deprives the buyer of the right to clear and correct information about the item under consideration for purchase. Neither can it justify the use of any "persuasion" which seriously violates personal liberty of choice and impedes discrimination. Where such malpractices exist, they are not more, in effect, than sins against commutative justice. And even though they should come to support the economy of the entire world, they deserve to be denounced.

## ADVERTISING: ITS CONTRIBUTION TO THE AMERICAN WAY OF LIFE [4]

One day when I was young in advertising I slipped a piece of paper into my typewriter and wrote an advertisement for a life insurance company. It was addressed to young husbands and fathers. One of the coupons received in reply came from a traveler in Rio de Janeiro, whose home was in New Jersey. He was thirty-eight years old, married, and the father of three children. He wanted information on a policy that, in case of his death, would guarantee his family an income of $3,000 a year.

On the man's return to New Jersey, the policy was written and the first payment made. A few days later he went to his dentist to have a wisdom tooth extracted. Somehow the cavity became infected, the infection spread and he died.

[4] By Bruce Barton, a founder and now chairman of the board of the Batten, Barton, Durstine & Osborn advertising agency. Reader's Digest. 66:103-7. April 1955. Reprinted by permission.

That incident made a deep impression on me. Many times in the intervening years I have been reminded that somewhere in New Jersey there are a mother and three children, now grown up, who, without the slightest suspicion of my existence, have had their whole lives changed by the fact that one day I put together some words that were printed in a magazine, and read in a faraway country by their husband and father, who was influenced to do what I suggested.

It is a terrific power we wield, we men and women in advertising; it needs to be handled carefully, truthfully, sometimes even prayerfully. It is one of the most potent of all the forces that, for better or worse, can influence and change human lives.

Roy Durstine [the Durstine of Batten, Barton, Durstine & Osborn] once made this sage comment: "Advertising came into the world when man became too impatient to wait for Mrs. Jones to tell Mrs. Smith that Brown's pickles were good." That's an interesting way of pointing out that advertising, as a technique, is simply mass selling. But in its wide influence on our American way of life, advertising is much more than that. It is a creative force that has generated new jobs, new ideas, has expanded our economy and helped to give us the highest standard of living in the world.

Take jobs. In 1900 almost nobody was building automobiles. Now we have a ten-billion-dollar, 772,000-worker industry which depends on additional thousands of workers in steel, rubber, glass, petroleum and allied fields.

Advertising did not invent the products or services which called forth those jobs, nor inspire the pioneering courage that built factories and machinery to produce them. What advertising did was to stimulate ambition and desire—the craving to possess, which is the strongest incentive to produce. To satisfy this craving the little factory was impelled to turn itself into a growing factory; and then, by the pressure of mass demand, into many factories. Mass production made possible mass economies, reflected in declining prices, until the product that began as the luxury of the rich became the possession of every family that was willing to work.

This happy result, if it could have been achieved at all without advertising, would have taken many years longer. The patent on the sewing machine was granted to young Elias Howe in 1846, but most of his mature years were passed in disappointment and poverty because no one bought his machine—advertising was too limited to spread the good news of its arrival. A whole generation of housewives, whose work could have been made lighter and pleasanter, died without ever having heard that such a wonderful home-helper had been born.

There is no such waste of time and life in the present-day world. The mechanical refrigerator, dishwasher, home freezer and dozens of other utilities and comforts were made known almost instantly to America's millions of women and became a welcome part of their lives—at prices that dropped lower and lower—as more factories were built and equipped.

With the coming of the washing machine, the vacuum cleaner and other household utilities, I prepared an advertising campaign for the women's magazines. The illustration of each advertisement was different—a tired woman bending over a wash-tub, scrubbing the floor, or performing some other distasteful duty. The copy was brief and unchanged throughout the series; it read:

Any woman who is doing any household task that a little electric motor can do is working for three cents an hour. Human life is too precious to be sold at a price of three cents an hour.

This and similar campaigns were widely effective. The wholesale emancipation of women from the drudgery of kitchen, laundry and cellar is one of the dramatic phenomena of our times, carrying with it vast enrichment of the intellectual, social, religious and political life of the nation. Advertising didn't inaugurate it, but it speeded it up. . . .

Thirty-two years ago Earnest Elmo Calkins, one of the leaders to whom advertising owes a great debt, pointed out that "few have noticed the remarkable effects of advertising upon those who use it. It lays the advertiser under the necessity of living up to his advertising."

One of my early experiences was inaugurating a campaign of institutional advertising in which my advertisements set forth the public-service ideals of the corporation's management. One day a disgruntled dealer stormed into the president's office, threw down on the desk a magazine containing one of the ads, and exclaimed: "I see that you claim to be a very high-minded organization. I just want to tell you from my experience that you are nothing of the kind!"

The president sent for me, and said: "Bruce, maybe we are pitching our campaign a little too high!"

I protested violently. "It's my business to walk out in front with a big banner," I argued. "It's your business not to call me back, but to bring the business up to me." He agreed, and bit by bit the big business shaped up according to the picture we had painted for it.

The important part played by advertising in standardizing prices is rarely remembered now.

Fifty years ago [Mr. Calkins pointed out] the prices in stores were not marked intelligibly to the customer. The selling price was whatever the salesman could get. The higher the price, the better the salesman. The secret price was an injustice to most customers. Only good bargainers could beat the salesman at his own game.

Along came advertising. Some merchant, feeling around for a message, a story that would give him the individuality at which all advertising aims, abolished the secret price and announced: "All goods plainly marked." A new era in selling had begun which was to continue until goods could be returned if unsatisfactory, money cheerfully refunded; until the customer's continued satisfaction was placed higher than the profits on any sale. It is only within the memory of men now living that it has been believed that both parties to a bargain could be satisfied.

Advertising is of the very essence of democracy. An election goes on every minute of the business day across the counters of hundreds of thousands of stores and shops where the customers state their preferences and determine which manufacturer and which product shall be the leader today, and which shall lead tomorrow. In this fair but fierce competition for public preference every manufacturer must strive through continuous research to improve his product. Incidentally, what little ad-

vertising there is under totalitarianism is rigidly controlled, and
understandably so.   It is dangerous to let a captive people choose
freely their food, their clothing, their tools or their homes;
such freedom can too easily expand to the ultimate goal of
choosing their leaders and their way of life.

Advertising has its follies, and its faults.   To quote Mr.
Calkins again:

> Advertising was once looked upon with justifiable suspicion.   Patent-
> medicine people and out-and-out swindlers owed their existence to it.
> Publishers began to see that they were fouling their own nests in ac-
> cepting business that destroyed the confidence that is the lifeblood of
> business.   Edward Bok, editor of the *Ladies' Home Journal*, launched
> a crusade that stirred the patent-medicine world to its depth.   The
> magazines cleaned house.   They were followed by the newspapers.

Too many printed advertisements still make exaggerated
claims.   Too many still insult the sensitive intelligence and offend good taste.   Too many radio and TV commercials are too
long and too loud.   But the business is young, less than one
hundred years old.   It turns out some 30 million publication
advertisements every year, something like 115 million radio and
TV commercials.   Under the pressure of such mass production
there is bound to be a percentage of error and poor taste.

But during an examination of more than a million advertisements of all types, the Federal Trade Commission labeled
less than 3 per cent as possibly misleading.   If advertising
sometimes encourages men and women to live beyond their
means, so sometimes does matrimony.   If advertising is too often
tedious, garrulous and redundant, so is the United States Senate.

The American people like advertising, want it, depend on
it for information and, if it were abolished, the demand for its
return would be overwhelming.   For eleven days in the fall of
1953, most of the newspapers of New York City were out of
business because of a strike.   The effect on the business and
social life of the city was cataclysmic.   Department store sales
dropped as much as 25 per cent.   Job applications fell; the sale
of used cars sagged.   Even funeral attendance dropped because
no death notices could be run.   On the day the strike ended,
a survey organization asked people: "What did you miss most

in not having your paper?" Forty-two per cent answered, "The advertisements."

Clients know too that advertising brings a bonus in better morale of employees who take pride in working for a well-known and widely respected company and do a better job because of it. Today's national advertiser asks the agency not, "How little can you get along with?" but, "How much can we profitably spend?" . . .

Every three seconds of the business day a baby is born in America; each month we add to the consuming public a city the size of Omaha. And pacing this population growth is an ever-higher standard of living throughout the country. Our economy is based on huge production, financed by tremendous consumer purchases, propelled by more advertising than is done by all the rest of the world together. It sustains a system that has made us the leaders of the free world: The American Way of Life.

## QUESTIONS AND ANSWERS ABOUT ADVERTISING [5]

How much is spent for advertising in the United States?

Is is estimated that in 1958, for the third straight year, over $10 billion was invested in all forms of advertising in this country. Some seventy firms spent more than $10 million and over three hundred companies more than $1 million each. But a major part of the investment was made by the many smaller advertisers—retail stores, specialty shops, realtors, auto dealers, the rest of the 4 million business enterprises, and even by individuals. . . .

Doesn't advertising add to the cost of the goods advertised?

In most cases, no. In some cases, yes. Obviously all marketing expense (including advertising) must be included in the sales price. But to sell without advertising almost always costs

[5] From a booklet published by the Advertising Federation of America. 250 West 57th Street. New York 19. 1959. p2-7.

more than to sell with the aid of advertising. Moreover, advertising, by increasing the sales of the product, often enables the manufacturer to lower the unit cost of production and thus to sell the articles more cheaply. In the long run, advertising usually helps to lower the sales price. . . .

What about the claim sometimes made, "We save by doing no advertising and pass the saving along to you"?

It usually isn't true. . . . If the seller doesn't advertise, he has to use some less efficient, more costly method of telling about and selling his goods. Usually, the claim covers up an attempt to sell lower quality goods at a higher profit to the seller than he can get on advertised goods.

Can advertising be believed and trusted?

Yes. According to the experience of the Federal Trade Commission, only a very small per cent of advertising is fraudulent or even misleading. Our best estimate is that less than 1 per cent of advertising is fraudulent and a smaller per cent deliberately misleading. The firm which wants to stay in business knows that it can do so only on a reputation for honest dealing. And the fly-by-night operator is under watch from all sides.

Do advertisers and media owners try to keep advertising above reproach?

Yes, because they realize that the offender hurts all the others. The various media associations (newspapers, magazines, radio, outdoor, etc.) are constantly tightening their restrictive codes on the advertising they will accept. Advertising Clubs and the national advertising associations keep raising the standards higher and work closely with the Better Business Bureau, the Federal Trade Commission, the Food and Drug Administration [and the Post Office Department] toward that end.

Why shouldn't advertising be restricted to a simple statement of facts about the goods without appeals to the emotions?

Because we humans do not act (do not buy) simply on
statements of facts. Our desires and emotions must be aroused.
And that calls for romance, art, colorful language, attractive
claims, catchy slogans. Advantages and benefits from buying
must be presented attractively. Even the purchasing agent or the
engineer who in theory buys from a mere listing of the facts
about the goods for sale is susceptible to emotional appeals.
So long as it is consistent with truth and does not mislead, it is
proper (and quite necessary) for advertising to appeal to the
emotions.

Doesn't some advertising overstep the bounds of good taste?

Occasionally, yes. This is due in part to intent or careless-
ness on the part of some advertiser. But advertising leaders
are constantly trying to raise the standards in this regard and
the offenders are under constant fire from advertising people.
The trend is steadily upward.

Does advertising give any benefits to the public besides
stimulating the sale of goods?

Yes indeed: For example, broadcasting gets all its income
from advertising; newspapers and magazines get over half their
income from advertising. Without advertising, broadcasting
would have to be supported by some form of government subsidy
or a tax on sets; our 1,700 daily and 9,000 weekly newspapers
and our thousands of magazines would have to charge much
more than they now do for subscriptions or individual copies.
In other words, advertising helps make possible our great system of mass information at a minimum of cost to the public.

Advertising also helps much in public service. For instance,
during the war, other nations usually had to force the public by
law to the efforts necessary for victory. In the United States,
under the leadership of the War Advertising Council, our advertisers and advertising media informed the public about what

needed to be done and persuaded them to do these things voluntarily. Without cost to the government, they conducted more than one hundred national advertising campaigns—on fats, paper and steel salvage, bond selling, blood banks, nurse recruiting, victory gardens, etc., etc. Similar public services by advertising go on all the time led by the Advertising Council and by Advertising Clubs. Every general public cause, such as Community Chest, Red Cross, etc., is given a large amount of advertising support. . . .

Do big advertisers control the editorial contents of newspapers and magazines because they spend so much for space in these publications?

No. Any experienced public relations man knows better than to ask for special consideration of a story about an advertiser—he knows that is the poor way to get what he wants. The editorial departments of newspapers and magazines are separate from the advertising departments and very jealously guard their freedom from influence by the advertisers. Editorial independence is higher in the United States than in many countries where there is much less advertising.

Moreover, the publisher knows that if he permits the advertisers to control the policies of his publication, he will soon lose the confidence of his readers. As they stop buying the publication, the advertisers will no longer want to advertise in it.

What would happen if all advertising were discontinued?

Radio and television broadcasts would all stop since there would be no income for them. Newspapers, magazines and business papers would have to cut down in size and raise their prices.

Within a short time, retail sales would begin to drop and sales clerks be laid off. People would have no way of knowing about new products or sources of new products. Soon production would slow down and a creeping paralysis of business would follow. There would be little incentive to improve old products or make better ones since there would be no effective way of creating a demand for the new.  Our economy is built around aggressive selling and advertising and would go to pieces without them. . . .

*slow down*

Do advertisers try to help the consumer buy to best advantage or are they interested only in selling their goods?

In earlier years the general rule was just to sell and let the buyer beware.  In more recent years and increasing steadily is the trend to make advertising more factual and informative and to help the public buy more intelligently.  Advertisers realize more and more that they grow and prosper as they serve better the needs and wants of their customers.

 Whom does advertising benefit?

Three groups particularly:

A.  You as a consumer.  Think of the time and trouble you would have in shopping if there were no advertising and no well-known brands.  You would not know where to go for particular products; you would not know the qualities of goods; you would not know what prices were right; you would not know about new or improved articles.  You would have to rely on hearsay, on the advice of sales clerks, and on your own testing.

B.  The businessman.  Advertising cuts his selling cost and saves the time of his sales people.  It speeds up his turnover and increases his sales.  It helps him in both his buying and selling.  Without advertising we could not have our present business economy.

C.  All of us who work for a living.  Advertising is a sparkplug of our economy.  It helps make mass distribution possible; that in turn calls for mass production.  Mass production and distribution together employ most of us.  And they generate the prosperity on which all of us depend.

## OUTDOOR ADVERTISING: A DEBATE [6]

### 1. What Is America For?

It was my unhappy lot to sit at a green-felt conference table while my colleagues of the Senate Public Works Committee voted down my bill to provide Federal assistance in the control of signboards along the 41,000 miles of our new Interstate Highway System. . . .

The greatest advertising bonanza in history has thus come to the men who dominate the signboard industry. The publishers of a newspaper or magazine, as well as the operators of TV and radio stations, must risk heavy investments to give their media some value to advertisers. They must buy tons of costly paper, purchase or lease huge printing presses, erect elaborate studios and transmitting equipment, hire editors and photographers and entertainers, and finally often distribute their product from door to door or through the mails. No such burden falls on what is euphemistically known as the "outdoor advertising industry." It will have its media ready-made, after the American motoring public spends $33 billion to construct a vast network of roads linking every major metropolitan area in the land.

Furthermore, the signboard proprietors hold enslaved a captive audience. I need not read the displays in the Washington *Post* or Pendleton *East-Oregonian*. But the motorist must look at the signboards along U.S. 30 or else prepare to meet his Maker. Indeed, among the relatively modest expenses of the billboard industry lurks the pay of skilled road engineers, who craftily locate the sprawling twenty-four sheets where the driver's eye cannot possibly shun these signs as he wheels his sedan around a curve or over the crest of a hill. They are purposely situated to be within his normal sweep of vision.

[6] From "What Is America For?" by Richard L. Neuberger, Democratic senator from Oregon, author, and magazine writer, and "What's the Shouting About?" by Harley B. Markham, president of the Markham Advertising Company and board chairman of the Outdoor Advertising Association of America. *Saturday Review*. 40:10-12+. November 9, 1957. Copyright 1957 by Saturday Review, Inc. Reprinted by permission.

The threadbare case for outdoor advertising is exposed bv the flimsy arguments advanced in support of allowing our road-sides to be defaced for private profit. In testimony before the Senate Public Works Committee these arguments fitted into three principal categories:

1. States' rights
2. Highway safety
3. Free enterprise

My wife and I know how hollow and hypocritical is the trite shibboleth of "states' rights" with respect to this particular issue. As members of the Oregon State Legislature, we tried to secure anti-billboard legislation at the state level. There we were told that such matters were more properly the concern of cities, counties, and local zoning authorities. We also were advised, of course, that keeping highways free of billboards by law would be a first step in "Sovietizing" America. Although the signboard operators raised the cry of "states' rights" to defeat my bill in the United States Senate, there is no record of the industry ever having supported effective regulation or control in any of the forty-eight states. [Senator Neuberger's bill died in committee in 1957. Congress subsequently enacted legislation giving states a bonus of one half of one per cent of the cost of the highway in return for regulation of advertising on their portions of the Interstate Highway System. Many have done so.—Ed.]

Then, in its presentation before our committee, the outdoor advertising colossus claimed that its gaudy picket-fence of signs would keep motorists from falling asleep at the wheel. The insult implicit in this claim is that the senses of the average American have been so deadened by raucous sales messages that he needs the stimulus of whiskey, gasoline, and soft-drink ads in order to break the monotony of rivers, fields, and groves of evergreen or alder trees! Two main roads connect the teeming Washington and Baltimore citadels of population—U.S. 1 and the Washington-Baltimore Freeway. U.S. 1 is a verdant bill-board jungle. Signs sprout along it like undergrowth in the

Matto Grosso.  The Freeway has been protected—thus far—
from mutilation.  It is my understanding that the Freeway, in
addition to affording an infinitely more pleasant pilgrimage between the two cities, actually is safer than its sign-plastered
sister route.  Certainly, no statistics uphold the thesis of the
companies that the billboards flanking U.S. 1 are a safe contrast
to the dangerous monotony of the Freeway.

The free-enterprise argument of the signboard companies
implies that they have an inherent right under our Constitution
to plaster with signs any road built with public funds.  If this
is an inalienable American privilege, why should not other
advertisers set up their material at the Government Printing
Office or hang posters from Federal courthouses?  And what
of the right of Conrad Hilton to install a guest wing at the
Pentagon Building?

One of the most effective claims of the outdoor advertisers
was that rigid control of signs would work a grim hardship on
small business along the roads—motels, hotels, garages, restaurants.  Ex-Senator Scott Lucas, one of the leading spokesmen
for the advertisers, even referred ominously to an adverse impact on the entire U.S. economy because of the $25 billion spent
by families touring our highways.  This, of course, implies that
people traveling a sign-free road will not buy fuel for their
cars, food for their stomachs, or seek shelter at night!  I have
always thought the warning voiced by Mr. Lucas was exactly
contrary to facts.  For example, there are three places in the
world where tourist expenditures comprise a major source of
income—Switzerland, Hawaii, and Alaska.  All these realms
are virtually free of billboards.  Indeed, such protection of the
alpine and tropical countrysides actually may stimulate the flow
of wayfarers' dollars, pounds, or francs.

One of our most authoritative witnesses was Bertram D.
Tallamy, appointed by President Eisenhower to . . . have charge
of the great new interstate road program.  In his home state of
New York, Mr. Tallamy supervised the 432-mile Thruway from
New York City to Buffalo.  Signs on the Thruway are restricted
to neat, standardized panels which indicate the distance to a

general "Service Area" or the fact that a gas station and coffee shop are one mile away. These signs are in precisely the same pattern as those which herald distance, speed limits, directions, or curves. Actual commercial or brand advertising, as such, is forbidden. Two or three times I asked Mr. Tallamy if roadside business had suffered as a result of these controls on signs and billboards. He always answered in the negative.

Depite so categorical a reply from a famous highway engineer with actual experience in this domain, the outdoor advertising companies insisted that restrictions on billboards would seal the fate of small entrepreneurs pumping gas, serving food, or patting down beds beside the roads. Yet, if our highways are made more attractive to the eye, will not a larger number of nomads set out upon them with their families—and will not these people need all the commodities and services offered along the way?

With one breath the outdoor advertisers try to hide behind the backs of small locally-owned roadside facilities by mourning that these places will suffer in patronage if signs are controlled. But with their next gasp the advertising firms insist that the ugly signs are not those erected in the interest of the mighty national brand-name corporations but, rather, the on-the-premises signs heralding restaurants, motels, etc.

Regardless of the equity of this claim, it is academic. The new interstate highways are, by law, to be breached by only limited-access conduits of travel for reasons of safety. Motels and filling stations cannot hem in the interstate roads because such direct intrusion would be illegal. These accommodations will be clustered principally around the interchanges—near the widely-scattered clover-leaf turnoffs. My bill, for cooperative Federal-state regulation of signs, would allow a limited number of signs at the interchanges but—to all practical purposes—not in the open countryside.

Such concessions have never budged the big outdoor advertisers. Their appetite for plastering our nation's roadsides is insatiable. What if Mount Hood is shut off or a thicket of lush cedars barricaded? Who cares? The so-called self-policing imposed by the industry is largely confined to areas where signs do not have a high media value, anyway. The tiger vows not to eat carrots!

Said ex-Senator Lucas: "This country was built on economics, not beauty." Perhaps this explains why, only 150 years after Lewis and Clark were first to span what is now our nation, we have made such awesome depredations upon so many of our natural resources. . . .

Is that what we want in America?

## 2. WHAT'S THE SHOUTING ABOUT?

The current attack on "billboards" is intensely emotional in origin, and is being waged with complete disregard of facts, logic, and economics. Satirical cartoons and poems, biting editorials, clarion senatorial orations, and other militant speeches make lively reading and listening. They have all but drowned out the voices of outdoor advertising men and advertisers as they ask: "Where are these 'billboard canyons' you say blot out your views of mountains, fields and rivers?"

The truth is that they don't exist. Actually, standardized outdoor advertising—call them "billboards" if you will—is a socially conscious, legitimate, and useful business which makes substantial contributions to the economic and social welfare of our country.

For generations outdoor advertising has been a medium of proved effectiveness, an integral part of a growing America. Standardized outdoor advertising displays have a colorful heritage as part of Americana. As a popular art form they have won recognition by museums and other art authorities throughout the country. They are just as much a part of the American scene as baseball or the neighborhood drugstore—and they have just as much right to exist. Most important of all, they have helped build many great names of American industry: Coca-Cola, General Motors, Wrigley, Standard Oil, Ford, and many others.

Standardized outdoor advertising is represented by the Outdoor Advertising Association of America, Inc., which had its origin more than sixty-five years ago. There are 776 member companies in the Association, doing business in more than 15,000 communities. Their annual volume is about $200 million, which is more than 90 per cent of the total volume of standardized outdoor advertising. These member companies operate standardized poster panels and painted bulletins on land which they own or lease for the purpose, as distinguished from miscellaneous signs.

This distinction is important. Nine times out of ten, when our critics charge that "billboards deface the countryside," we have found that they are not talking about our standardized displays at all, but about other kinds of signs for which our industry is in no way responsible.

Like all good citizens and good neighbors, we recognize and accept our public and social responsibilities. Our policies are in the public interest. Our Association members voluntarily pledge adherence to a strict code of practices imposing high ethical standards upon our industry. For instance, this code says: *"We share the public interest in natural scenic beauty, parks and historical monuments. We do not erect our advertising displays in such areas."*

That is plain enough and it means just what it says. We want to keep America beautiful, too. Here are other provisions of our self-imposed code to insure operations in the public interest: *"We believe in and support zoning based on sound community planning."*

Many communities have adopted zoning standards and restrictions for such purposes to distinguish between business and commercial areas and those which are residential in character. We agree that reasonable restrictions affecting business and commercial practices are desirable in any well-planned community. We, therefore, pledge full support of sound zoning, and are willing to be treated under zoning just like any other business. *"We place outdoor advertising displays only upon property we own or lease for that purpose."*

Critics who would legislate us out of business either don't know or ignore the issue of proper and lawful land use—the fact that private property rights are involved because our dis-

plays are always located on private land owned or leased by us—
never on highway rights of way.  And these same critics who
scream that "billboards" are despoiling scenic beauty also con-
veniently ignore the fact that more than 85 per cent of all standardized outdoor displays are in strictly urban areas zoned for
business.

*"We locate our structures with discretion and good taste
with respect to frequency and concentration."*

Again playing fast and loose with the facts, some critics
would have the public believe that "billboards" are placed indiscriminately along virtually every inch of highway, thus creating so-called "billboard canyons" or "ribbon slums."  Nothing
could be further from the truth.  As businessmen we are deeply
interested in the orderly growth of the communities where we
operate.  We recognize the need for discretion and good taste
in developing business and industrial areas.  Accordingly, we
locate outdoor displays in a manner which will promote the
business interests of the community, and at the same time preserve attractive features.

The term "ribbon slums" has been used to describe heavy
concentrations of business and the signs of varied size and shape
advertising them.  They are for the most part "on premise" signs
advertising goods and services available on the premises.  They
may not be pleasing to some people, but from another viewpoint
they represent one way of doing business in a highly competitive
area.  Thus, "ribbon slums" exist because the people in the area
permit them.  If a remedy is needed or desired, it lies in proper
zoning at the local level. . . .

We are proud of our record.  It is shocking to have mis-
informed or malicious critics slander us with the charge that
outdoor advertising displays create a traffic safety hazard and are
a factor in causing accidents.  But we are glad to note, however,
that even some of the most reckless and irresponsible of critics
are dropping that line, because when challenged they have been
unable to muster a single fact to support the charge, not from
insurance companies, traffic authorities, or anybody else.  On
the contrary, a scientific test conducted at Iowa State College

said in part: "Numerous signs in the driver's field of vision in no way influenced efficiency at the wheel adversely, and in fact seemed beneficial by about 10 per cent."

Much of the argument against outdoor advertising is on esthetic grounds: "Outdoor advertising is ugly, a highway blight, marring beautiful scenery." We admit that it's not easy to win an argument solely on esthetics. That's because art and esthetics are subjective; opinions, not facts, and not always informed opinions at that. It's all a matter of personal viewpoint and taste. The picture that hangs proudly in the Louvre as a great work of art is just a blob of paint to some people.

As for our poster panels and painted bulletins—well, we try to make them as attractive as we can. They are simple and functional. A few years ago we retained Raymond Loewy, the noted industrial designer, to develop a new standard panel. More than half of the panels being rebuilt each year are now Loewy designed.

Prize-winning artists such as Howard Scott, Raymond Savinac, and Norman Rockwell illustrate our advertising copy. Their work is judged annually in national competition by leading art authorities. Outdoor advertising art has been praised for its simplicity of design, directness and symbolism.

These are some of the facts about our business, as distinguished from fancy. We don't pretend to be perfect. Like any other business, we have our problems and we make mistakes. But on the whole we think we have a pretty good record. We ask for no special treatment. All we ask is the same fair treatment accorded any other legitimate business. We regard our outdoor advertising structures as business installations, just as much so as the garage or store. . . .

With respect to all the punitive legislation proposed against us, we'd like to make one point clear. We have no intention or desire of exploiting the Interstate Highway System in rural areas. In keeping with the policies set forth in our code, the only place we want to be, or have any right to be, is in business or industrial areas or where business is appropriate. We are a business. We create business. We belong with business.

Americans are a fair-minded people. We have every confidence that when they have the facts—all the facts—they will join us in demanding: What's all the shouting about?

## IN DEFENSE OF MADISON AVENUE [7]

Like Hollywood, Wall Street and Broadway, Madison Avenue is known by the companies it keeps. Like them also, Madison Avenue has been dreamed about, written about, lied about—and become a label. It is, *last* of all, a narrow thoroughfare running from Twenty-third Street to the Harlem River on the east side of Manhattan and peopled during the daylight hours by messenger boys, chic office girls, and level-eyed executives with undented hats and shiny shoes. *First* of all, it is the accepted capital of a community of 45,000 advertising people (about 25,000 of them in New York City alone) who have been entrusted by hard-headed big and little business men with the spending of an estimated $10 billion . . . [annually]. By popular consent, it is the voice, image and brandmark of our own free enterprise. Or by not-so-popular consent.

Madison Avenue these days is under sharp indictment. Advertising is America's pagan religion, the Account Executive for Indictments says, and it forces a fantastically false way of life through expert use of its own Golden Rule: "We have something to sell and we can make you buy it." Tantalized and tempted by dream-world pictures dangled before them, the victims of Madison Avenue have an itchy urge to buy now and pay later. They mortgage their futures in installment buying.

Beware the amoral power now loose in the land (the indictment goes on). Look out for the euphoric products that may lead you down the primrose path to puffy overweight and cancer. Bert Piel, Harry Piel and Snooky Lanson are paid by the smile, and no questions asked.

It is shocking (the indictment goes on *and* on) that nobody seems to care whether an advertising campaign is good or bad

[7] Article by James F. Kelly, vice president of Compton Advertising (agency), Inc. of New York, frequent contributor to magazines, and book reviewer for the New York *Times Book Review* and *Saturday Review*. New York *Times Magazine*. p 15+. December 23, 1956. Reprinted by permission.

for the country. It is all a numbers game, with virtuoso agency men playing the public like a piano. Headlines with a benefit twist, short copy and shorter ideas designed to fit the reader's attention span, illustrations that people can identify themselves with—the tired old one-two-three pitch for the mass audience.

And here's that bright new medium, television, operating in exactly the same way. On behalf of a television client, an agency will prepare hard-sell commercials and frame them in an elaborate show supplied full-blown by one of the super-specialist television package companies. And success or failure depends upon how many people saw the show (reported by hocus-pocus ratings), not upon how many enjoyed it. The same success or failure applies to politics as well as products. Madison Avenue sells ideologies and candidates just as it sells soap, in quantity and by advertised brands. All right.

Fuzzy thinking, stoutly replies Madison Avenue. In the first place, the American consumer is a beneficiary, not a victim, of our so-called commercialism. He is better housed, dressed, fed, entertained and catered to than anybody living anywhere else in the world. Solely because of mass production and multiple distribution, his standard of living is higher. If he has the dollars to installment-buy a car or TV set, he is supposed to have the sense of what to buy and how much. Credit is a privilege, not an opiate—a vote of confidence in a land of plenty with an abundant future. Don't forget that the extreme opposite of credit is barter. That even General Motors expands by borrowing. That everybody who owns an insurance policy is buying future security on the installment plan. And that every business house, including banks, steel companies and utilities, is at least partly made of glass.

A second line of defense is to imagine what it would be like to live without Madison Avenue. A knowing merchant from Gallipolis, Ohio, thinks he could live without it very readily. Instead of paying for gimmicked-up advertisements with eyepatches, white horses, and thin but sexy models trying to look like housewives, let's just save the $10 billion and lower prices all the way along the line. The way he figures it, 15 per cent of that staggering sum goes to advertising agencies to sell things the public never missed and doesn't want now.

It is true that no other force besides advertising pushes the philosophy of obsolescence so hard or spreads the frontiers of human requirements so far. It wins acceptance for new products before their time and sets the wheels of technology in motion. But what is wrong with that? Without Madison Avenue, mass production would stop in its tracks. Unit costs of consumer goods would shoot up through the ceiling and out the roof. A ranking officer of the Ted Bates agency (founded in 1941 and billing an estimated $100 million annually among just sixteen clients) declared that the American standard of living as we recognize it would go out of existence without the forced distribution of advertising.

He believes that the staggering billions of dollars spent for advertising in America actually cost the consumer little or nothing when one considers the low unit costs made possible by mass production. "Advertising sells superiority, after superiority has come into its own," this adman firmly stated. "You can't sell it if the product hasn't got it."

Advertising must be on the scene to create a consumer unrest that will make a monopolistic manufacturer improve his product and lower his price. Otherwise, the kitchen mixer which could weigh six pounds and sell for $16 would continue to weigh 150 pounds and sell for $128.50. Q.E.D. Free countries can expand their economies through advertising; controlled countries cannot.

Without advertising, our entire mass communications network would turn into a non-network: a real body blow for the 626 magazines of general circulation, 1,700 daily newspapers, 9,000 weekly newspapers, 2,947 radio stations and 465 television stations with over 38 million television homes. Newspapers would become four- or six-page handbills on cheap paper, without illustrations. Our popular magazines and trade and professional publications would be eliminated.

American business requires a maximum audience, and it is up to Madison Avenue to deliver. If the system didn't work, the shrewd, cold-blooded management men who are paid to give their investors the best of it would find another system. The fact is that never in the economic history of civilization have so many (160 million) depended upon so few (45,000) and entrusted them with so much money ($10 billion).

The few, of course, get their rewards, but they are just enough by ordinary corporate standards: an average of 7 per cent profit received on net income, or 1 per cent on gross billing.

For this modest percentage Madison Avenue, to phrase its key defense with a flourish, serves as alarm clock for America's sleeping desires. It quarterbacks our way of life, operates as custodian of our enthusiasms, and keeps those dollars in stream-lined circulation. It accepts the heavy responsibility for who we are and for the shape of our collective personality in the world at large.

Putting America's urge for self-improvement back to back with the equally strong urge to do-it-yourself, Madison Avenue has breathed new life into the ninety-seven-pound weakling and the girl whose friends wouldn't tell her. It shows mother how to get the kids to eat their cereal (Snap! Crackle! Pop!), and it shows grandfather how to set up a little extra security for himself and grandmother during the greater number of retirement years they can now look forward to together. It builds the showcase, fills it with alluringly styled and priced products, and shills for the sale.

Human nature is the force we are dealing with. The publisher of *Printers' Ink* has observed that advertising holds a mirror in front of basic human needs—and then adds the wish-fulfillment images. But the wish-fulfillment images will change, and possibly improve, only as human nature allows it. Soap opera will give way to singing opera when the audience is ready.

Advertising is not a hungry predator on the prowl nor is it a fey branch of show business; it is an integral part of society and should be judged as such. It is naïve to be surprised that depend-able techniques, used to sell goods and services, are used to sell *desire* for goods, services—and the desirability of one particular candidate over another. This is a free economy, isn't it?, with the freedom of the individual to choose a way of life and the amenities that go with it.

Maybe the men of Madison Avenue think of these great Moral Questions or maybe they don't, but they get pretty tired of snapping into the same old conditioned responses when a person from some other avenue lowers his head and begins to raise cocktail-party questions. Sometimes, too, they may try the jocular evasion gambit and identify themselves as foot doctors or piano players in houses of ill repute. But cocktail queries can have a lemon twist of truth that draws out the serious adman, if he can concentrate under the circumstances.

*Is advertising a profession, a business, or a game of wits in which anybody can join if he has any?* A consensus on Madison Avenue gives it the business label. One prominent agency president put it this way:

> A good advertising agency today is a collection of trained specialists with performance standards not exceeded in any profession. Guesswork moves out when knowledge of product, market and sales moves in. No client can be served in present competitive conditions by an agency which tries to fly by the seat of its pants or use intuition in place of informed judgment. When you are paying $50,000 for three minutes of commercial time on a half-hour show, it had better be good.

*Advertising accounts and advertising people seem to be bounced around from agency to agency all the time. Is this what causes the tensions, ulcers and drinking after work?* When an agency loses an important account, it is a spectacular performance held (in a manner of speaking) in Macy's window and duly celebrated by the communications media directly affected. Most of the wholesale firings, however, occur in smallish tent-show agencies.

As for tensions and ulcers, they certainly exist. Especially among peripheral copywriters, art directors and account executives who would be doing something loftier "if it weren't for the money." These are the colorful ones whose goings-on are most celebrated in fiction and in fact. It is of course possible that some of the admen one sees having a martini or two at the Biltmore Men's Bar may *not* be tense or insecure. They are really eating peanuts, not tranquilizer pills. And they are drinking with clients.

*Why do they dress and talk like that?* Not many of them do. The men of Madison Avenue most aware of the flair of the clothes they wear are usually new Princetons and Yales starting out in the mailroom, or smart operators who believe that there is an official dress for the road to success. As for the colorful jargon by which advertising men are alleged to address one another, dismiss it as a word game started by bright satiric minds and caricatured by dull ones who never quite caught the joke (but know hepness when they hear it). Madison Avenue-ese is used with the same frequency in direct communication as Elizabethan verse.

So, the defense of Advertising Row and its inhabitants can be summed up quickly: *it* functions and *they* do. The plot is orderly, with a climax at the point of sale. After all, we made you what you are today, says Madison Avenue modestly to critics and friends—but don't get too satisfied! Let's just skim *this* idea on the pond and see whether it reaches the other side.

## THE IMMUNITY OF ADVERTISING [8]

I should like to convoke a meeting of copywriters, heads of advertising agencies, sponsors, manufacturers, and crackpots (intellectuals). To this group of the elite (between 75,000 and 3 million individuals) I would like to recite a portion of a current television commercial for a cigarette. The commercial runs for approximately ninety seconds. Part of this time is taken up by the statement that a United States patent had been granted to the filter tip used by this cigarette. I would also repeat verbatim the three words used at the end of a commercial for hair spray: "no prescription needed." Having covered this data I would then ask the convoked multitude to write an essay on these two commercials. I think we might hold this meeting in the Mississippi Basin and that the prizes for the best essays should be permanent exile to Labrador or Madagascar, two spots on the

[8] From article by Gilbert Seldes, author of *The 7 Lively Arts*, television critic of the *Saturday Review*, and director of the Annenberg School of Communications at the University of Pennsylvania. *Tide* (the magazine for advertising executives, now incorporated with *Printers' Ink*). 32:17-20. February 14, 1958. Copyright 1958 Executive Publications, Inc. Reprinted by permission.

earth which so far as I know are not subjected to the vagaries of American advertising.

In spite of being an intellectual who has never met a payroll, but who has been on several nice ones, I know that this meeting will never take place. I therefore suggest the following questions to be answered by the readers of this magazine for somewhat smaller prizes:

1. Is there any filter now in use which is *not* protected by a patent?

2. Is there any hair spray for which a doctor's prescription *is* required?

There is a third question I would like to ask but it involves mathematics and as I grew up in the literary-sociological age and not the post-Sputnik-all-out-for-science age I am on shaky ground. I make the rough calculation that a ninety-second commercial on a nationally sponsored program costs $X$ dollars—let us say for convenience, $50,000. At that rate, the statements made about the patent and the prescription would cost roughly $1,000 each. Question: Are they worth it? I am aware of the fact that every word uttered on a television or radio commercial, every word printed in a newspaper or magazine or painted on a billboard, is carefully examined by philosophers, anthropologists, sociologists, psychologists and, when they get out from under the academic disciplines, practical business men. I still put it to all of these people that they might use their time more advantageously. They might for instance have a small boy puff at a cigarette, rubbing his stomach in a circular motion saying "Mmm, mmm," or a bald-headed man rubbing his pate and saying "Man, oh man, it's a *man's* spray."

You would never think it from the breakneck speed at which commercials are delivered that the sponsor had time to spare, but even if he did, I suggest that the plus, the clincher-effect which these statements have—which can only be effective for halfwits— is actually a serious minus. Both of these statements come at the end of the commercials, they are the last words left in the minds of the viewers, and each of them sets up a train of thought *away* from the commodity advertised. A dozen lush (and always

hyphenated) adjectives and the ramming belligerent voice of the
announcer may strike me as unnecessary, but at least they pertain
to the subject in hand. These irrelevancies do not. . . .

I know how tedious specific examples are to a reader who is
eager for the theory, the generalized abstractions behind them, but
I risk one more ad—for a cigarette again and as it happens the
brand I have smoked until now. I have had little reason to
believe that its filter is any more effective than the others, but I
like the taste. Now I am informed that it has an incalculable
number of filter traps, which is still all right with me. Then the
pitch: "no other filter delivers less nicotine and tar . . ." I
heard this with surprise, I repeated it (and wrote it down) with
dismay, and I look at it here on the page with profound disbelief.
That statement, to be at all effective, requires mental gymnastics.
You have to recall the object of all filters which is to stop the
intake of nicotine and tars. Then you have to argue with yourself
to the effect that nothing is perfect so some of these noxious
substances do get through and you want the filter which stops
more of them than any other. Finally, reversing yourself to the
negative, you say, "he means that no other filter *allows* less to
go through" which is an awkward way of saying that no other
filter stops as much. And you are still left with the word
"delivers" which is a positive word, a word with the most
affirmative suggestions ("that boy delivers the goods"). Either
I or the creator of that statement knows nothing of the art of
persuasion—and I think I do know something.

These are a few of the verbal oddities I have picked. I have
another batch—pictorial ones and several in which the concept
is totally strange. I put these others aside because the examples
cited are enough to back up the single point I want to make here:
that advertising is one of the great influential forces of our time
and it is singularly immune to criticism, especially to public
criticism.

I suggest that this is bad for advertising without suggesting
a cure. No doubt there are anxious meetings in board rooms
when an agency loses an account, but what advertising needs is
the same sort of regular continuous criticism that books and

plays and movies and radio and television get—and that newspapers, magazines, and preachers do not get. All of these are
among our cultural institutions and should not only accept, but
eagerly ask for criticism and the place for it is precisely in the
mass media. But the mass media which live on advertising will
not even discuss the esthetics, let alone the intelligence or the
morality, of the ads they run and the copywriter goes on scribbling
formulas on his slate, not knowing whether he has written
$e = mc^n$ or $2 + 2 = 7$. If the explosion goes off as scheduled,
he knows that he hasn't been totally wrong—if it is a bomb, he
blames the product and moves to another agency.

Without guidance, the public is apathetic. In the past ten
years I can recall only one instance of public remonstrance
against an advertisement and this was, as I remember, sparked by
the newspapers. Somebody trying to sell TV sets began a series
with an ad openly inciting children to rebellion against parents
who deprived them of their natural right to life, liberty, and
the pursuit of programs. This was too much and a long loud
rumble of protest was heard—the remainder of the series never
appeared. There have been some less flagrant abuses of the public
which have passed unrebuked, but the instigation to riot of little
children continues in a hidden persuaderish way and the abuse
of the adult mind also goes on—and nobody says a word.

The reason for this is that while we all know how essential
advertising is to our economy, we are not aware of its significance in our culture. We make one compartment into which
we put education (and a few highly suspicious intellectual
activities) and we make others for politics, entertainment, advertising, newspapers and magazines—as if these weren't the most
potent cultural influences we undergo every day of our lives.

The consequence of all this is that advertising is chiefly
subjected to the criticism of its enemies, of those who would
like to see it disappear from the face of the earth as a preliminary step to the dissolution of the capitalist system. This
kind of criticism, seldom informed and always intemperate, the
advertiser easily laughs off—and begins to think that he really
deserves the immunity he enjoys. In some instances he does

so well by us that he is entitled to a little smugness. But the general principle still prevails: *No institution affecting the public welfare should be immune to public criticism.*

We are, at this moment, witnessing a kind of public criticism. The proponents of subliminal advertising, as a matter of ethics and/or publicity, have let us in on their secret. [See "Subliminal Projection—The Phantom of the Soap Opera," in Section I, above.] Sermons, letters to the papers, and editorials followed. I don't suppose that more than 5 per cent of all the adults in the United States are aware of subliminal projection and half of that number, I make a guess, don't give a damn about it. But if public awareness of all advertising had become a constant part of our lives, we should have known long ago that a good part of all advertising is in the technical sense subliminal. We should by now be a critical public.

Obviously this is what the advertiser doesn't want. He thinks that if the public begins to be skeptical of advertising, the foundations of our economy will totter. Not for the first time he is confusing the welfare of the nation with his own balance sheet.

For the fact is that while advertising has tended to become ingrown and extravagant, the commodities advertised have to a high degree improved themselves. The consumer may not always be a skeptic, but if the handle of a plastic-sponge mop breaks off after two days' use, he doesn't buy that kind any more—and the simple fact is that, by and large, the American consumer is satisfied with the goods he buys. Setting apart the frauds and near-frauds which need to be dealt with by the FTC [Federal Trade Commission], the consumer may be led to the commodity by silly or offensive advertising, but he usually feels he has gotten his money's worth. So let us take heart: a little more intelligence and even probity in advertising will not wreck the American system.

And, on the other hand, a public as critical of advertising as it is of the commodities advertised, would be of vast assistance to the copywriter, the layout division, the campaign-planners. They now get together in brainstorming sessions, a process ideal for their purpose, since it prevents thinking.

They do not subject themselves to fundamental brainwork applied from the outside. They run one kind of ad in one community, another in another, and this is supposed to prove something—but the something it proves isn't essential. The best of them will tell you that, in the end, they don't know exactly what makes their work effective. They are not being criticized from the outside and their self-examination is always directed to results, not to the process by which the results are obtained. . . .

I suggest that there may, just possibly, be defects in contemporary advertising. I suggest further in the competitive situation, familiarly known as a rat-race, of advertising these and other defects will continue because the whole business of advertising is not subject to constant critical examination outside of the professional journals like this one devoted to the techniques of the trade.

# BIBLIOGRAPHY

An asterisk (*) preceding a reference indicates that the article or a part of it has been reprinted in this book.

## BOOKS AND PAMPHLETS

Adams, J. R. Sparks off my anvil. 181p. Harper & Bros. New York. '58.

*Advertising Federation of America. Questions and answers about advertising. 8p. The Federation. 250 W. 57th St. New York 19. '59.

Allen, F. L. Big change. 308p. Harper & Bros. New York. '52.

American Association of Advertising Agencies. Advertising business—its career opportunities. 16p. The Association. 420 Lexington Ave. New York 17. '56.

American Marketing Association. Frontiers of marketing thought and science. 336p. The Association. 27 E. Monroe St. Chicago. '58.

*Association of National Advertisers. Outdoor Advertising Committee. Essentials of outdoor advertising. 128p. The Association. '52. Distributed by Outdoor Advertising, Inc. 360 Lexington Ave. New York 17.

Association of National Advertisers and Point-of-Purchase Advertising Institute. Advertising at the point-of-purchase. 240p. Mc-Graw-Hill Book Co. New York. '57.

Audit Bureau of Circulations. Story of the Audit Bureau of Circulations. 38p. The Bureau. 123 N. Wacker Drive. Chicago. '54.

Barger, Harold. Distribution's place in the American economy since 1869. 224p. Princeton University Press. Princeton, N.J. '55.

Barnouw, Erik. Mass communication: television, radio, film, press. 288p. Rinehart & Co. New York. '56.

Barton, Bruce. Man nobody knows. 267p. Bobbs-Merrill Co. Indianapolis, Ind. '24.

Barton, Roger. Advertising agency operations and management. 384p. McGraw-Hill Book Co. New York. '55.

Beard, Miriam. History of the business man. Macmillan Co. New York. '35.

Bernays, E. L. and others. Engineering of consent. 246p. University of Oklahoma Press. Norman. '55.

Bogert, C. G. Cases on the law of sales. 770p. Foundation Press. 268 Flatbush Avenue Extension. Brooklyn 1, N.Y. '56.

Borden, Neil. Economic effects of advertising. 988p. Richard D. Irwin. Chicago. '42.

Borden, Neil and others. National advertising in newspapers. 486p. Harvard University Press. Cambridge, Mass. '46.

Brennan, Ed. Advertising media. 410p. McGraw-Hill Book Co. New York. '51.

Brewster, A. J. and others. Introduction to advertising. 480p. McGraw-Hill Book Co. New York. '54.

Bridge, H. P. Practical advertising. 848p. Rinehart & Co. New York. '49.

Brown, L. O. and others. Advertising media. 395p. Ronald Press. New York. '57.

Burt, F. A. American advertising agencies. 282p. Harper & Bros. New York. '40.

Burton, P. W. and others. Advertising copywriting. 521p. Prentice-Hall. New York. '49.

Calkins, E. E. "And hearing not. . . ." 387p. Charles Scribner's Sons. New York. '46.

Chamber of Commerce of the United States. Advertising, the magic key. (Information bulletin no33) 8p. The Chamber. Washington 6, D.C. '54.

Chase, Stuart. Power of words. 308p. Harcourt, Brace & Co. New York. '54.

Cherington, P. T. Consumer looks at advertising. 196p. Harper & Bros. New York. '28.

Cheskin, Louis. How to predict what people will buy. 241p. Liveright Publishing Co. New York. '57.

Cheskin, Louis. Why people buy: motivation research and its successful application. 319p. Liveright Publishing Co. New York. '59.

Chester, Giraud and Garrison, G. R. Television and radio, an introduction. 652p. Appleton-Century-Crofts. New York. '56.

Clark, Blake. Advertising smoke screen. 238p. Harper & Bros. New York. '44.

Corbin, Arnold. Premium use and supply. 32p. Premium Advertising Association of America. 608 Fifth Ave. New York. '55.

Cox, Reavis. Economics of installment buying. 525p. Ronald Press. New York. '48.

Crow, Carl. Great American customer. 252p. Harper & Bros. New York. '43.

Dewhurst, J. F. and others. America's needs and resources: a new survey. 1148p. Twentieth Century Fund. 330 W. 42d St. New York. '55.

Direct Mail Advertising Association. Story of direct advertising. 34p. The Association. 3 E. 57th St. New York 22. '59.

Dreiser, Theodore. Genius: the life story of an agency man. 736p. World Publishing Co. Cleveland, Ohio. '46.
    Originally published in 1915.

Duvall, E. J. Take it from here. 121p. Frederick J. Drake & Co. Chicago. '57.

Edwards, Frank. My first 10,000,000 sponsors. 185p. Ballantine Books. New York. '56.

Eskew, G. L. Guinea pigs and bugbears. 269p. Research Press. Dayton, Ohio. '38.

Fellows, H. E. Advertising stopped at ten o'clock this morning. 11p. National Association of Broadcasters. 1771 N St. N.W. Washington 6, D.C. n.d.

Fellows, H. E. I can get it for you retail. 15p. National Association of Broadcasters. 1771 N St. N.W. Washington 6, D.C. '52.

Foreman, D. L. Ad man ad-libs on TV. 173p. Hastings House. New York. '57.

Fortune, Editors of. Adventures in small business. 273p. McGraw-Hill Book Co. New York. '57.

Fortune, Editors of. Amazing advertising business. 178p. Simon and Schuster. New York. '57.

Freeman, W. M. Big name. 230p. Printers' Ink Books. 100 Garfield Ave. New London, Conn. '57.

Frey, A. W. and Davis, K. R. Advertising industry. 424p. Association of National Advertisers. 250 W. 57th St. New York. '58.

Galbraith, J. K. Affluent society. 368p. Houghton Mifflin Co. Boston. '58.

Galbraith, J. K. American capitalism. 208p. Houghton Mifflin Co. Boston. '56.

Geller, M. A. Advertising at the crossroads: federal regulation vs. voluntary controls. 535p. Ronald Press. New York. '52.

Gilbert, Eugene. Advertising and marketing to young people. 378p. Printers' Ink Books. 100 Garfield Ave. New London, Conn. '57.

Gill, L. E. Advertising and psychology. 192p. Rinehart & Co. New York. '54.

Goodman, Walter. Clowns of commerce. 278p. Sagamore Press. New York. '57.

Graham, Irvin. Advertising agency practice. 303p. Harper & Bros. New York. '52.

Grosbeck, Kenneth. Invitation to advertising: how to get the most out of it. 392p. Simon and Schuster. New York. '51.

Heidingsfield, M. S. and Blankenship, A. B. Marketing. 270p. Barnes & Noble. New York. '57.

Henderson, Hubert. Supply and demand. 142p. University of Chicago Press. Chicago. '58.

Hepner, H. W. Modern advertising. 740p. McGraw-Hill Book Co. New York. '56.

Hill, J. W. Corporate public relations. 189p. Harper & Bros. New York. '58.

Hollander, S. C. History of labels. 47p. Allen Hollander Co. New York. '56.

Hotchkiss, G. B. Advertising copy. 469p. Harper & Bros. New York. '49.

Hotchkiss, G .B. Outline of advertising. 605p. Macmillan Co. New York. '50.

*Hower, R. M. History of an advertising agency (N. W. Ayer & Son, Inc.) 647p. Harvard University Press. Cambridge, Mass. '49.

Hutchins, M. S. Cooperative advertising. 235p. Ronald Press. New York. '53.

Institute for Research. Advertising as a career. 24p. The Institute. 537 S. Dearborn St. Chicago 5. '52.

Jones, Duane (as told to Mark Larkin). Ads, women, and boxtops. 128p. Printers' Ink Books. 100 Garfield Ave. New London, Conn. '55.

Kelley, Stanley, Jr. Professional public relations and political power. 247p. Johns Hopkins Press. Baltimore. '56.

Kenner, H. J. Fight for truth in advertising. 298p. Round Table Press. New York. '36.

Kirkpatrick, C. A. Advertising: mass communication in marketing. 638p. Houghton-Mifflin Co. Boston. '59.

Klass, Bertrand. Evaluating the effectiveness of advertising; a problem in orientation. 18p. Stanford Research Institute. Menlo Park, Calif. '55.

Kleppner, Otto. Advertising procedure. 775p. Prentice-Hall. New York. '50.

Lackey, J. B., Jr. Transportation advertising, 1940-48. 303p. Harvard University. Graduate School of Business Administration. Boston. '50.

Lambert, G. B. All out of step. 316p. Doubleday & Co. New York. '56.

Lasker, A. P. Lasker story. 86p. Advertising Publications. 200 E. Illinois St. Chicago 11. '53.

Lee, A. M. Daily newspaper in America. 792p. Macmillan Co. New York. '37.

Lund, J. V. Newspaper advertising. 459p. Prentice-Hall. New York. '47.

McMahan, H. W. Television commercial. 200p. Hastings House. New York. '57.

Martineau, Pierre. Motivation in advertising. 210p. McGraw-Hill Book Co. New York. '57.

Marx, H. L. Jr., ed. Television and radio in American life. (Reference Shelf. v25, no2) 198p. H. W. Wilson Co. New York. '53.

Mason, Lowell. Language of dissent. 314p. World Publishing Co. Cleveland,    Ohio. '59.

Matthews, J. B. and Shallcross, R. E. Partners in plunder. 444p. Covici, Friede. New York. '35.

*Mayer, Martin. Madison Avenue, U.S.A. 332p. Harper & Bros. New York. '58.

Mayer, Martin. Wall Street: men and money. 274p. Harper & Bros. New York. '55.

Mayfield, F. M. Department store story 269p. Fairchild Publications. New York. '49.

Mead, E. S. Big ball of wax. 246p. Simon and Schuster. New York. '54.

Minnick, W. C. Art of persuasion. 295p. Houghton-Mifflin Co. Boston. '57.

Moore, Robin. Pitchman. 352p. Coward-McCann. New York. '56.

Morgan, J. N. Consumer economics. 440p. Prentice-Hall. New York. '55.

Mott, F. L. History of American magazines. 4v. Harvard University Press. Cambridge, Mass. '57.

Murphy, E. J. Movement West: the impact of advertising upon the development of the West and the years ahead. 178p. Sage Books. Denver, Colo. '58.

Newman, J. W. Motivation research and marketing management. Harvard University. Graduate School of Business Administration. Division of Research. Boston. '57.

Opdycke, J. B. Mark my words. 687p. Harper & Bros. New York. '49.

Outdoor Advertising Association of America. Federal control of outdoor advertising (Senate and House debate on Federal Aid Highway Act of 1958). 93p. The Association. 24 W. Erie St. Chicago. '58.

Packard, Vance. Hidden persuaders. 275p. David McKay Co. New York. '57.

Packard, Vance. Status seekers. 376p. David McKay Co. New York. '59.

Palmer, R. L. and Alpher, I. M. 40,000,000 guinea pig children. 249p. Vanguard Press. New York. '37.

Pease, O. A. Responsibilities of American advertising; private control and public influence, 1920-1940. 232p. Yale University Press. New Haven, Conn. '58.

Platten, J. H., Jr. Opportunities in market research. 112p. Vocational Guidance Manuals. 1011 E. Tremont Ave. New York 60. '51.

Potter, D. M. People of plenty. 219p. University of Chicago Press. Chicago. '54.

Presbrey, F. S. History and development of advertising. 651p. Doubleday & Co. New York. '29.

Riesman, David and others. Lonely crowd. 386p. Yale University Press. New Haven, Conn. '50.

Roberts, E. B. Television writing and selling. 515p. The Writer. 8 Arlington Street. Boston 16. '57.

Rowell, G. P. Forty years an advertising agent. 517p. Printers' Ink Books. 100 Garfield Ave. New London, Conn. '06.

Rowland, C. M. Advertising in modern retailing. 268p. Harper & Bros. New York. '54.

Rowse, E. J. and Nolan, C. A. Fundamentals of advertising. 442p. South-Western Publishing Co. Cincinnati, Ohio. '57.

Sampson, Henry. History of advertising from the earliest times. 584p. Chatto & Windus. London. 1874.

Sandage, C. H. Radio advertising for retailers. 280p. Harvard University Press. Cambridge, Mass. '45.

Sandage, C. H. and Fryburger, Vernon. Advertising, theory and practice. 701p. Richard D. Irwin. Homewood, Ill. '58.

Sarazan, B. M. Delusions in advertising. Progress Press. Washington, D.C. '47.

Sargent, W. W. Battle for the mind. 236p. Doubleday & Co. New York. '57.

Schechter, F. I. Historical foundation of the law relating to trademarks. 211p. Columbia University Press. New York. '25.

Schlink, F. J. Eat, drink and be wary. 322p. Covici, Friede. New York. '35.

Schlink, F. J. and Kellet, Arthur. 100,000,000 guinea pigs. 312p. Vanguard Press. New York. '33.

Schwimmer, Walter. What have you done for me lately? 256p. Citadel Press. New York. '57.

Scott, J. D. Advertising: principles and problems. 803p. Prentice-Hall. New York. '57.

Seelye, A. L. ed. Marketing in transition. 337p. Harper & Bros. New York. '58.

*Shannon, M. A. One hundred years of premium promotions—1851-1951. 12p. Premium Advertising Association of America. 527 Lexington Ave. New York 17. '51.

Simon, M. J. Law for advertising and marketing. 645p. W. W. Norton & Co. New York. '56.

Spectorsky, A. C. Exurbanites. 278p. J. B. Lippincott Co. Philadelphia. '55.

Spring, Samuel. Risks and rights. 385p. W. W. Norton & Co. New York. '56.

Steinberg, Charles. Mass communicators. 470p. Harper & Bros. New York. '58.

Sumner, G. L. How I learned the secrets of success in advertising. 246p. Prentice-Hall. New York. '52.

Turner, E. S. Shocking history of advertising. 351p. E. P. Dutton & Co. New York. '54.

Wagner, C. H. Story of signs. 123p. The author. Cunningham St. Hopkinton, Woodville Section, Mass. '54.

Wakeman, Frederic. Hucksters. 307p. Rinehart & Co. New York. '46.

Wallance, Don. Shaping America's products. 193p. Reinhold Publishing Corp. New York. '56.

Waller, J. C. Radio, the fifth estate. 482p. Houghton-Mifflin Co. Boston. '50.

Whittier, C. L. Creative advertising. 585p. Henry Holt & Co. New York. '55.

Wilson, Sloan. Man in the gray flannel suit. 304p. Simon and Schuster. New York. '55.

Wiseman, Mark. Anatomy of advertising. 404p. Harper & Bros. New York. '45.

Wolff, J. L. What makes women buy. 320p. McGraw-Hill Book Co. New York. '58.

Wolseley, R. E. Magazine world. 427p. Prentice-Hall. New York. '51.

Wood, J. P. Magazines in the United States. 386p. Ronald Press. New York. '56.

Wood, J. P. Story of advertising. 512p. Ronald Press. New York. '58.

Young, J. W. Advertising agency compensation in relation to the total cost of advertising. 186p. University of Chicago Press. Chicago. '33.

## PERIODICALS

Advertising Age. 29:1+. Mr. 10, '58. Ad is express warranty to buyer; Ohio high court rules in Toni case.

Advertising Agency Magazine. 51:14-19. My. 23, '58. Subliminal advertising.

American Heritage. 5, no3:6-9+. Spring '54. Advertising and publishing in colonial America. H. H. Boyce.

American Heritage. 5, no4:10-13. Summer '54. Advertising in America. H. H. Boyce.

American Mercury. 82:134-5. My. '56. What kind of talk is this? David Holland.

American Mercury. 83:5-10. S. '56. Selling Presidents like soap. J. J. Seldin.

American Mercury. 86:89-96. Ja. '58. Watch out for ad rackets. H. L. Oleck.

American Speech. 31:13-20. F. '56. Some pun among the hucksters. E. K. Sheldon.

Annals of the American Academy of Political and Social Science. 250:105-12. Mr. '47. Molding public opinion through advertising. Drew Dudley.

Annals of the American Academy of Political and Social Science. 250:121-9. Mr. '47. Measurement of public opinion. E. C. Wilson.

Atlantic Monthly. 200:55-9. S. '57. Growing power of admen. Vance
    Packard.
    *Reply.* 201:71-3. Ja. '58. F. M. Cone. *Rejoinder.* 201:28. F. '58.
Broadcasting. 54:35-42. Mr. 3, '58. Private life of advertisers and
    agencies; Frey report.
Business Topics (Michigan). 7:5-12. Winter '59. Role of the adver-
    tising agency: is it changing? V. D. Reed.
Business Week. p43-4+. O. 25, '52. Publisher's conscience and cop
    (ABC).
Business Week. p 132-4+. My. 21, '55. Getting away from the peaks
    and valleys.
Business Week. p 136-8+. O. 8, '55. Making U.S. customers abroad.
    *Discussion.* p8. O. 29, '55.
Business Week. p30-1. S. 21, '57. Ads you'll never see; invisible com-
    mercials.
Business Week. p53-4+. Ap. 19, '58. Now the sponsors call the tune.
*Catholic World. 186:174-9. D. '57. Advertising techniques and the
    moral law. T. P. Coffey.
Commonweal. 67:230-2. N. 29, '57. Madison Avenue witchcraft. E.
    Van Den Haag.
Commonweal. 69:310-12. D. 19, '58. Enter the man's man. J. P. Sisk.
Consumer Bulletin. 42:12-14. F. '59. Fact and fancy in mail order ads.
Consumer Reports. 23:161-3. Mr. '58. Gray flannel couch.
Coronet. 41:143-4. D. '56. Amazing lady who ran away with a com-
    pany: Betty Crocker. Norman Carlisle.
Fortune. 42:77-83+. S. '50. Is anybody listening?
Fortune. 42:113-17+. N. '50. Language of business.
Fortune. 43:114-15+. Ap. '51. Why professors are suspicious of
    business. Bernard De Voto.
    *Discussion.* 43:99-100+. Je. '51.
Fortune. 44:118-19+. S. '51. Newspaper business: the death of a
    formula.
Fortune. 46:98-101+. S. '52. Language of advertising. W. H. Whyte,
    Jr.
*Fortune. 47:134-7+. F. '53. Postman rings for sales.
*Fortune. 53:144-7+. Je. '56. Motivation research. Perrin Stryker.
Fortune. 54:93-4+. Ag. '56. What makes women buy? Gilbert Burck.
*Fortune. 54:107-10+. S. '56. Amazing advertising business. Daniel
    Seligman.
*Fortune. 54:123+. S. '56. How I sold Listerine. G. B. Lambert.
Fortune. 54:142-3+. O. '56. Advertising: the battle of 15 per cent.
    Spencer Klaw.
    *Reply.* 55:20+. Ja. '57. E. D. Winius.
Fortune. 54:123-6+. D. '56. How much for advertising? Daniel
    Seligman.
*Fortune. 54:124+. D. '56. Dog-food account. Spencer Klaw.
Fortune. 54:125+. D. '56. Edsel account.

Fortune. 57:123-4+. My. '58. Mr. Ragsdale's eventful shopping trip. Robert Sheehan.

Fortune. 58:78-81+. D. '58. TV: the light that failed. R. A. Smith.

Harper's Magazine. 202:85-91. F. '51. Is there too much advertising? Otto Kleppner.
  Discussion. 202:30 Ap.; 202:23. My. '51.

Harper's Magazine. 203:95-8. N. '51. Crusade resumed (The Easy Chair). Bernard De Voto.

Harper's Magazine. 204:56-63. Ja. '52. Unseemly economics of opulence. J. K. Galbraith.

Harper's Magazine. 210:51-6. My. '55. Ogilvy, the ineffable ad man. Thomas Whiteside.

Harper's Magazine. 215:40-5. S. '57. Is the bloom off Madison Avenue? John McCarthy.
  Reply. 215:8+. D '57. I. W. Rubel.

Harper's Magazine. 215:52-7. O. '57. Great coupon bonanza. Peter Margulies.

Harper's Magazine. 216:25-31. F. '58. What is advertising good for? Martin Mayer.

Journal of Accountancy. 96:464-9. O. '53. Auditing program of Audit Bureau of Circulations. J. K. Lasser.

Media/scope. 1:33-40. Jl.-Ag. '57. Firm foundation for media evaluation; the functions of the ABC. A. T. Wolcott.

Media/scope. 1:40. Jl.-Ag. '57. About the Audit Bureau of Circulations.

Nation. 176:143-5. F. 14, '53. Freud and the hucksters. Ralph Goodman.

Nation. 180:136-7. F. 12, '55. So round, so firm. J. J. Seldin.

Nation. 180:442-3. My. 21, '55. Selling the id. J. J. Seldin.

*Nation. 182:295-7. Ap. 14, '56. Elsa Maxwell loves Mazola. Walter Goodman.

Nation. 182:523-6. Je. 23, '56. Madison Avenue jungle. David Cort.

Nation. 183:217-19. S. 15, '56. Together in a sea of soap. David Cort.

*New York Times Magazine. p 15+. D. 23, '56. In defense of Madison Avenue. J. F. Kelly.

New York Times Magazine. p22+. Ja. 12, '58. Most hidden hidden persuasion; Subliminal Projection Company, Inc. Gay Talese.

New York Times Magazine. p 14-15+. Mr. 16, '58. Salvo in the billboard battle. Robert Moses.

New York Times Magazine. p 10+. My. 11, '58. Resurvey of hidden persuaders. Vance Packard.

Newsweek. 48:48. Jl. 23, '56. Exposing paradise in Florida.

Newsweek. 53:66-8. My. 18, '59. TV ratings, the men behind them.

*Newsweek. 54:61-2. Ag. 3, '59. Male animus.

*Printers' Ink. 243:43-5+. My. 15, '53. What advertising is . . . what it has done . . . what it can do now.

*Public Relations Journal. 14:6-8. Mr. '58. Phantom of the soap opera. W. H. Kalis.

Reader's Digest. 58:17-21. Mr. '51. Advertising abuses and the Digest. R. G. Clough.

*Reader's Digest. 66:103-7. Ap. '55. Advertising: its contribution to the American way of life. Bruce Barton.

Reader's Digest. 67:54-6. S. '55. How to read the amazing bargain ads. A. Q. Maisel.

Reader's Digest. 70:105-7. Je. '57. How to beat the homework racket. R. L. Smith.

Reader's Digest. 71:118-21. N. '57. Ad and the id. Vance Packard.

Reader's Digest. 72:49-52. My. '58. Let's keep billboards off our new highways. Holman Harvey.

Reporter. 9:27-31. O. 13, '53. Adman's nightmare: is the prune a witch? Robert Graham.

Reporter. 15:34. D. 27, '56. Miltown place; or life with sponsors. Marya Mannes.

Reporter. 16:47-8. My. 2, '57. Onward and upward with the admen. J. K. Galbraith.

Saturday Review. 39:9-11. Mr. 31, '56. Annihilation of privacy. Ashley Montagu.

Saturday Review. 40:19. O. 5, '57. How powerful are the persuaders? Elmo Roper.

*Saturday Review. 40:10-12+. N. 9, '57. Outdoor advertising: a debate. R. L. Neuberger; H. B. Markham.

Saturday Review. 42:34-40. Ap. 18, '59. SR's seventh annual advertising awards. W. D. Patterson.

*Tide. 32:17-20. F. 14, '58. Immunity of advertising. Gilbert Seldes.

Tide. 32:75-7. Mr. 14, '58. Frey report. J. O. Young.

Tide. 32:36-44. My. 9, '58. Agency man's agency.

Time. 54:89-92+. S. 19, '49. Billion dollar baby.
    Same condensed. Reader's Digest. 55:47-50. D. '49. Goddess of plenty.

Time. 66:86. O. 31, '55. Betty grows up; Betty Crocker.

U.S. News & World Report. 42:72-80. Ja. 4, '57. We can sell $600 billion of output; interview. S. B. Resor.

Vital Speeches of the Day. 22:601-3. Jl. 15, '56. Promotion's answer to a 9 billion dollar problem. J. S. Williams.

*Yale Review. 43, no 1:49-70. Autumn '53. Advertising: the institution of abundance. D. M. Potter.